Linking Europe

Transport Policies and Politics in the European Union

John F. L. Ross

Westport, Connecticut
London

Library of Congress Cataloging-in-Publication Data

Ross, John F. L.
    Linking Europe : transport policies and politics in the European
Union / John F. L. Ross.
        p.   cm.
    Includes bibliographical references (p.   ) and index.
    ISBN 0–275–95248–7 (alk. paper)
        1. Transportation and state—European Union countries.   2. Europe—
Economic integration.   I. Title.
    HE242.A2R67   1998
    388'.096—dc21   97–21850

British Library Cataloguing in Publication Data is available.

Library of Congress Catalog Card Number: 97–21850
ISBN: 0–275–95248–7

First published in 1998

Praeger Publishers, 88 Post Road West, Westport, CT 06881
An imprint of Greenwood Publishing Group, Inc.

Printed in the United States of America

The paper used in this book complies with the
Permanent Paper Standard issued by the National
Information Standards Organization (Z39.48–1984).

10 9 8 7 6 5 4 3 2 1

Copyright Acknowledgment

The author and publisher gratefully acknowledge the European Communities for granting
permission to reprint Figures 4.1, 4.2, 7.1, 7.2, and 7.3. These illustrations are from the following European Communities publications: *The Trans-European Networks—The Group of Personal Representatives of the Heads of State or Government*, pp. 102 and 105 (Catalogue No. CM–
85–94–777–EN); *The Trans-European Networks—Towards a Master Plan for the Road Network
and Road Traffic*, p. 94 (Catalogue No. C3–76–92–617–EN–C); *The Trans-European Network*,
p. 29 (Catalogue No. C3–85–94–842–EN–C); and *Europe 2000 + —Cooperation for European
Territorial Development*, p. 70 (Catalogue No. CX–86–94–117–EN–C).

To Rebecca,
For Patience

Contents

Tables and Figures

TABLES

FIGURES

Preface

This book aims to provide a broad sectoral analysis of European transport issues, and especially of their evolving policy and political context, on the cusp of the 21st century. After decades of relative neglect, transport has enjoyed a remarkable resurgence of interest on the European scene since the Single European Act (SEA) of the mid-1980s. As the Maastricht Treaty's "weighty" issues such as monetary union (EMU) have encountered significant obstacles, transport cooperation has, in increasingly vivid if less visible contrast, forged ahead along numerous fronts. Indeed, in the 1990s transport has emerged—figuratively as well as literally—as a genuine policy of movement, and as one of the few issue-areas capable of facilitating as well as hindering European integration.

Renewed attention to transport questions has come at multiple levels. Institutionally, the European Community and its successor body, the European Union, have rediscovered the strategic value of the Common Transport Policy (CTP), and have pushed hard for industry liberalization together with new harmonization initiatives to link national infrastructures, aimed at no less than a pan-European transport system. As such, transport has moved up the EU's own scale of priorities, eliciting policy attention at the highest levels, not least at recent European summits. The January 1995 appointment of Neil Kinnock, longtime British Labour leader, as European Transport Commissioner is indicative of the growing political significance of the Transport Directorate-General (DG VII), once a relative backwater in the Brussels hierarchy.

In turn, these policy initiatives reflect the ongoing, bottom-up transformation of Europe's transport industries. Mergers, cooperative agreements, and multimodal initiatives have proliferated as industry scrambles to maximize the comparative advantages, and to minimize the competitive risks, of an integrated European market within an increasingly global economy. These cross-pressures have produced changes in the transport environment almost unthinkable as little as a decade ago. And yet, it re-

mains an unfinished revolution. Full liberalization of transport services remains years away; uneven modal prioritization continues to encourage inefficiency and waste; congestion and transport-related pollution grow
worse by the year; transport infrastructures still divide European states as
much as unite them. Indeed all the attention is question-begging as well as
problem-solving, especially as it has produced a multitude of policy prescriptions many regard as inherently inconsistent or even contradictory.
The decade elapsed since the SEA thus provides a healthy perspective by
which to measure the extent of progress so far, and to highlight those issues
requiring further attention.

Underpinning this research effort is a strong conviction that transport
is an unusually fertile, though often overlooked, subject in the firmament
of European studies, and an underappreciated factor in integration
processes. In contrast to more recent issues on the European agenda such
as environmental or regional policy, transport figured prominently in the
original Treaty of Rome. Further, the field is "horizontally integrated"
with a wide array of related policy areas, its finger in nearly every EU pie.
Few policy areas better illustrate the tension between intergovernmentalist
and supranationalist approaches to integration, or provide a veritable mi-
crocosm of the EU's wider political struggles over time. Just as discussions
about European transport issues are inconceivable without consideration
of the EU's role, no analysis of the EU itself can ignore transport's wide
sweep: its role in European cultural and societal development; its ability to
facilitate the exchange of people, goods, and ideas; its power as a determinant of individual preferences and lifestyles; and its universalist themes. A
major aim will have been achieved if this study advances appreciation of
the pivotal importance of transport questions in the overall European enterprise.

Arguably, the extant EU-related literature has not fully grasped the
significance of transport's resurrection as a European and EU policy concern. Accordingly, a key motivation behind this work is the lack of a ser-
viceable, sufficiently broad political analysis of EU transport issues. Traditionally, transport has been a subject of economic analysis, micro as much
as macro, often highly technical in content, and usually focused on individual modal concerns. Such approaches attest to the complex, fragmented
nature of the industry and to the success of modal-based interests at defending their own turf; however, they unduly "compartmentalize" the field
and defy the realities of travel itself, which is not about rail vs. road vs. air
but is inevitably and inherently multi-modal.

Alternatively, many analysts and policymakers have argued over the
years that transport is *sui generis* and, by implication, resistant to comparative policy treatment. Whatever the case, the resulting impression of narrow parochialism and tedious technical detail scarcely does justice to its
much broader relevance, and hinders consideration of its relationship to

other policy areas and its impact on the overall integration process —political no less than economic—itself. Only recently have systematic attempts been made to transcend these limitations and to conceptualize more broadly about Europe's overall future needs; and more must be done if a truly coordinated, efficient pan-European transport system is not to remain as elusive as the Holy Grail.

There is also, admittedly, some desire to challenge the frame of mind that has led, among other things, to frequent descriptions of the field as "unglamorous"—themselves an odd counterpoint to the romantically intrepid connotations of the art of travel itself. A transport panel at a well attended professional meeting (the 1995 European Studies Conference at Charleston), attracting an audience varying between three and five, drove the point home further. While popularizing the field may be too ambitious (not to say dubious) an undertaking, a desire to liberate it from the charge of narrowness and philistinism arguably is not.

The book itself has three major sections, throughout offering intermodal comparisons and utilizing illustrative, EU-wide examples in a conscious effort to avoid the frequent tendency to restrict discussion to the largest states. Chapter 1 discusses general aspects of transport and its role in the overall European economy, the nature of the "transport crisis," and the special problems (economic, political, and social) facing the sector. Chapter 2 examines the historically uneven development of the Common Transport Policy, in which earlier neglect has been succeeded by a more recent flurry of activity. One key aim here is to emphasize the long-term, developmental nature of Europe's transport problems, and the political structures and pressures that have hindered their resolution.

Part II (Chapters 3-6) analyzes key issues relevant to policymaking in each of the four major modes, respectively rail, road, air, and shipping. These chapters examine, both separately and via cross-references, the relative speed of industry deregulation and depth of cooperation achieved at European level. The focus is on the special problems facing the different modal industries and the mooted institutional solutions for their future development.

The final section (Part III) examines these disparate transport questions as parts of a greater whole, namely the emerging pan-European transport system, and looks to the future. Chapter 7 examines recent European structural initiatives, particularly the trans-European networks projects, and assesses the progress and problems met thus far. It also discusses specific European infrastructure works (the Channel Tunnel; development in Greece; Swiss transport issues; and Scandinavian initiatives) in order to illustrate the numerous dilemmas arising in efforts to coordinate cross-border development and public-private funding. Finally, Chapter 8 synthesizes some of the major trends to date and examines the possibility of organizational changes to help cope with the transport conundrums facing 21st-century Europe.

Every effort has been made to keep the work as current as possible (updated to spring 1997), even in the painful realization of the speed at which new developments are likely to overtake the present. The cascading pace of international events can handicap research efforts even as it provides grist for the mill. One saving grace in this field is the value of attention to elements of continuity from the past that bear on present realities and future trends; Europe's transport dilemmas were not created yesterday, nor will they be solved tomorrow. Second, the past decade has highlighted key problem areas and established the basic policy guidelines, often in the form of general (framework) directives. Future progress will be measured in relation to this growing corpus of policy initiatives.

Finally, two brief stylistic notes. One relates to the endless proliferation of that bane of modern political economy, the acronym. As a means of accommodation, I generally spell out the proper noun or term on first use, thereafter (except in cases of long gaps) referring to its abbreviated form. But as even this system serves only that rare individual who reads from start to finish with cumulative retention, the reader is urged to make liberal use of the (purposely inclusive) list of abbreviations in the frontmatter.

Second, anyone writing about European integration faces the annoying problem, possibly unique in the social sciences, of uncertainty regarding the institutional point of reference. History, however, allows some method to the apparent madness, and my references here coincide with the accepted denotation of the period referred to, namely to the European Economic Community (EEC) from the 1950s to the early 1970s and the European Community (EC) up through the 1980s. The term European Union (EU), though by now universally in use, remains a post-Maastricht term of the 1990s, and one that allows continued use of the term "Community" in referring to its core (Pillar I) tasks.

Abbreviations

AA	American Airlines
ABB	Asea-Brown Boveri
AEA	Association of European Airlines
BA	British Airways
BAA	British Airports Authority
BAe	British Aerospace
BEC	Bulletin of the European Communities
BEU	Bulletin of the European Union
BR	British Rail
CAP	Common Agricultural Policy
CBA	cost-benefit analysis
CBI	Confederation of British Industry
CCEE	Countries of Central and Eastern Europe
CCR	Central Commission for Navigation of the Rhine
CEC	Commission of the European Communities
CER	Community of European Railways
CFSP	Common Foreign and Security Policy
COREPER	Committee of Permanent Representatives
COST	European Coordination of Scientific and Technical Research
CTP	Common Transport Policy
DASA	Daimler-Benz Aerospace
DB	Deutsches Bundesbahn
DIHT	German Industrial and Trade Association
DOT	Department of Transportation
EAGGF	European Agricultural Guidance and Guarantee Fund
EBRD	European Bank for Reconstruction and Development
ECAC	European Civil Aviation Conference
ECE	[United Nations] Economic Commission for Europe
ECJ	European Court of Justice
ECMT	European Conference of Ministers of Transport

ECSA	European Community Shipowners' Association
ECSC	European Coal and Steel Community
ecu	European Currency Unit
EEA	European Economic Area
E(E)C	European (Economic) Community
EFTA	European Free Trade Association
EIB	European Investment Bank
EIF	European Investment Fund
EMU	European Monetary Union
EP	European Parliament
EPU	European Political Union
ERDF	European Regional Development Fund
ERT	European Round Table of Industrialists
ESC	Economic and Social Committee
ESF	European Social Fund
ESPRIT	European Strategic Program for Research and Development in Information Technology
EU	European Union
Euratom	European Atomic Energy Community
EUREKA	European Research Coordination Agency
EUROS	European Registry of Shipping
FOC	Flag of Convenience
GATT	General Agreement on Tariffs and Trade
GDP	gross domestic product
HSR/T	high speed rail/train
IATA	International Air Transportation Association
ICAO	International Civil Aviation Organization
ICE	Intercity Express
ICJ	International Court of Justice
ICPR	International Commission for the Protection of the Rhine
ILO	International Labor Organization
IMF	International Monetary Fund
IMO	International Maritime Organization
IRF	International Road Federation
KLM	Royal Dutch Airways
MIF	Maritime Industries Forum
NCI	New Community Instrument
OECD	Organization for Economic Cooperation and Development
PBKAL	Paris-Brussels-Köln-Amsterdam-London
PFI	Private Finance Initiative
PPP	public-private partnership
QMV	qualified majority voting
SAS	Scandinavian Airlines System
SEA	Single European Act

SJ	Sveriges Järnvägen
SME	small and medium-sized enterprise
SNCB	la Société nationale des chemin de fer de belgique
SNCF	la Société nationale des chemin de fer de français
SOLAS	Safety of Life at Sea
TACA	Trans-Atlantic Conference Agreement
TAP	Portuguese National Airways
TAV	treno alta velocita
TEN	Trans-European Network
TERN	Trans-European Road Network
TGV	Train à grande vitesse
TMR	Training and Mobility of Researchers
TWA	Trans-World Airways
UGS	Union of Greek Shipowners
UIR	International Union of Railways
UNCTAD	United Nations Conference on Trade and Development
WTO	World Trade Organization

Part I

EUROPEAN TRANSPORT: PROGRESS AND PROBLEMS

◈ *Chapter One*

Perspectives on European Transport

For my part, I travel not to go anywhere, but to go.
I travel for travel's sake. The great affair is to move.
—R.L. STEVENSON
Travels with a Donkey in the Cévennes

INTRODUCTION

Transport, both as an industry and as a policy area, has played a curiously uneven role in postwar European integrative processes. In apparent reflection of the above dictum, European goods and people are more mobile than ever before, yet the transport industry which has facilitated this mobility is widely regarded as crisis-ridden. Common transport policymaking, initially considered pivotal to the single European market, has instead languished in obscurity for much of the past forty years. Transport links are, by nature, uniquely capable of eliminating barriers and promoting cross-border interaction, yet the sector long has been characterized by rigid state protectionism. And while transport policy has emerged as one of the few dynamic policy areas in post-Maastricht 1990s Europe, its origins date back to the Treaty of Rome itself. Transport questions pervade the European discourse even while policy progress has been fitful, perennially caught in the crosscurrents of high expectations and a bottom-heavy political and industry reality.

Such multiple contradictions indicate a sector characterized by sheer complexity: of the economic context within which it operates; of the policy context shaping its development; and of the political context likely to constrain the direction and pace of future change. There is uncertainty and confusion regarding the extent, and even the nature, of transport-related problems; and consensus on possible solutions continues to elude transport experts and policymakers, thus reflecting, at an intellectual level, the segmentation of Europe's transport systems and markets themselves. For these reasons, transport issues are certain to attract significant institutional attention, as well as political contention, in coming years.

The European transport debate has reached a critical stage in part because of the rapidly changing geopolitical and spatial dimension of the European Union (EU). Once confined to an economic grouping of but six neighboring, industrialized states in west-central continental Europe, the EEC/EC/EU has grown in all four directions. In the 1970s it expanded to the north and northwest, adding its first non-contiguous territories; in the 1980s it spread southward across the north shore of the Mediterranean basin from the Atlantic to the Balkans. The 1995 expansion added vast new territory to the north and east, extending across the Arctic Circle in Sweden and Finland and even bordering Russia.

EU territory now includes two island polities (Britain and Ireland); a third (Denmark) consisting of islands and a peninsula; and a fourth (Greece) with a distended archipelago and awkward, lengthy land connections with Europe, problems worsened by Yugoslavia's breakup into war. Mountain barriers, especially the "Alpine wall," separate north and south Europe psychologically and culturally as well as physically; the Pyrenees do much the same for the Iberian states. This expansion creates a threefold regional dimension with major transport implications: a populous, developed European core, where congestion is a serious problem and land-use issues take precedence; an unevenly populated, less developed southern periphery, where poor infrastructure hinders growth and encourages inefficiency; and now a sparsely populated, developed northern periphery, where distance and all-weather access is a major concern.

The daunting challenge of unifying these far-flung regions into a single market, much less into a political and economic union, has induced greater EU activism in transport issues, if only to prevent further decoupling of the periphery from the center. Policy has evolved along three main fronts: *harmonization* initiatives to standardize members' technical, social, and fiscal policies; *liberalization,* using the discipline of market forces to breathe life into inefficient, debt-burdened transport industries; and most recently, *structural policies,* via commitments to developing cross-border European transport infrastructure and efforts to devise nontraditional means of paying for it.

To these concerns will soon be added the vast needs of the countries of Central and Eastern Europe (CCEE), which EU leaders have pledged to incorporate, eventually, into the EU fold. Membership negotiations are now on the cards for an array of states from the Baltic (Estonia) to the Balkans (Slovenia) and Cyprus. The efficiency of transport systems will play an absolutely critical role in determining whether future expansions succeed in truly incorporating these new states, or whether they will become burdensome territorial appendages. Will the current litany of transport-related problems, including uneven usage patterns, pollution, and operator indebtedness outstrip the policy responses to them (so far dominated by industry liberalization and establishment of basic "Community rules" for operators), or will collective efforts succeed in forging the long-awaited but still unfulfilled Common Transport Policy? Much indeed hinges on developments prior to the next enlargement, a point recognized by the EU itself in targeting transport development as an integral component of programs (e.g. Phare) designed to prepare CCEE states for EU membership.

This chapter first discusses the roles of transport within the context of Europe's economic development. This is followed by an overview of transport's growing interlinkages with other policy areas, both in the literature and functionally. It then discusses the transport crisis facing Europe, and its economic, social, and especially its policy/political aspects, introducing a typology of levels at which transport policy is emerging as a political issue.

TRANSPORT'S MULTIPLE FUNCTIONS

A transport system's relative efficiency is a key growth and developmental determinant of the broader system of which it is part, be it the European Single Market or any other politico-economic entity. Indeed transport's role is so extensive and ubiquitous that it is often, paradoxically, overlooked as a separate factor in its own right. Kenneth Button speaks of transport's "lubricating" function for a working economic system, which is "itself an input into a larger political and economic process" (1994: 28, 31); Nijkamp and Vluegel (1995b: 6) liken transport to the "blood circulation in an economy," similarly implying that its importance is not sector-specific but is general and all-pervasive. It has direct implications for the range of human activity from individuals to large-scale enterprises; it enables both passenger and goods movement. The transport industry straddles the line between the secondary and tertiary economies, playing an intermediate role in economic theory (Kammerer 1990: 28) between the production of goods and services.

Transport is an undeniably important factor in European economic development, though its actual strategic role in the integration process is more often assumed than understood. Including own-account operations, it directly accounts for about 7–8 percent of European gross domestic [sic] product (Gwilliam 1983; CEC 1985; Molle 1990); counting its knock-on effects in other industries and sectors would increase its total market impact to around 15 percent (Button 1994: 28). It is equally significant as an employment generator, and (at a time of EMU-mandated budget cutbacks) an increasingly crucial source of politically sensitive manufacturing and service jobs (see Table 1.1). Salaried transport employment is often in the form of *Beamten* (civil service employees with job security), which presents its own problems in the face of attempted industry reform, while Europe's transport equipment industry is second in size only to the food sector (CEC 1993a). Lifetime employment assumptions even affect private transport companies, indicated by the wide political objections to Renault's decision to downsize at its Belgian plant in early 1997.

Including suppliers, the dominant auto sector accounts for around 10 percent of EC-wide employment, while in the larger European countries, auto manufacturing alone accounts for up to 8 percent of the industrial workforce, and at least as much again in associated (e.g., components) supply (Owen 1983: 47). More striking still is the transport sector's high "take" of overall public investment in the Community, accounting for up to 40 percent (Topmann 1994: 182). This figure testifies to the traditional importance of transport's social and distributional function, but also to the dire economic condition of European transport companies, many of which require heavy public subsidies just to stay afloat.

Along with deepening understanding of economic processes in market systems has come a growing acknowledgment of the system-wide impact of transport links. Where once regarded primarily as a means of getting from A to B, there is now wide appreciation of transport's numerous micro-economic effects, particularly as a factor of production and a determinant of firms' locational decisions, competitiveness, and growth prospects (Vickerman 1991: 39). It is often assumed that growing transport usage mirrors overall industrial expansion, as a "derived demand" (Button 1994: 37), that is shaped by wider industry needs. Yet historically, transport has been a direct stimulus as well as a recipient of that process; 18th century inland waterway systems and 19th century railways facilitated industrialization and even state-building processes. Few factors have determined pat-

Table 1.1
European Transport Employment (1991)

Mode	Jobs	Overall Percentage
Road	2,509,000	45.1
Rail	897,800	16.1
Aviation	349,600	6.3
Maritime	217,300	3.9
Inland Waterways	24,200	0.4
Related	1,569,900	28.2
TOTALS:	5,567,800	100.0

Source: CEC 1993a.

terns of European urban and industrial development more decisively than proximity to transport routes and facilities, whether in the form of sea- or river-ports, road-based trade routes, or rail junctions.

Willem Molle has demonstrated (1990: 349) that the growth of EC transport freight between 1970 and 1985 (around 3.5 percent) was approximately double that of overall industrial production (1.7 percent), mainly due to rapid growth of intra-Community trade due to the elimination of EC tariff barriers. World air transport in the 1980s averaged a full 6 percent annual growth rate (*Expanding Horizons* 1994). Thus clearly, the transport industry has its own dynamics apart from those hived off the broader economic system. Indeed Heinze and Kill (1994: 129–130) assert that the growth of both passenger and goods traffic in Europe has been "systematically and substantially underestimated," creating more rapid and severe capacity constraints on existing infrastructure than planners expected, rather as generals are criticized for planning for the previous war.

It is now well established that the expansion of transport capacity (e.g. supply) will unleash latent demand, both essential and non-essential (e.g. recreational excursions). Such has been the case, for example, with TGV rail development in France, and more recently with the Channel Tunnel, as new capacities and travel alternatives put downward pressure on fares. This factor, with its Parkinsonian and Downsian overtones,[1] has major implications for transport policymaking in Europe, given that the solutions hitherto adopted to cope with relentless traffic growth, namely periodic expansions of infrastructure capacity, is not only inadequate (being demand-driven and hence essentially passive in nature) but in itself contributes to other transport-related problems of overcrowding, pollution, and safety (Heinze and Kill 1994: 134). The growing attention to limiting traffic movement, as opposed to managing its growth, is a consequence of this phenomenon—especially since Single Market-led growth in cross-border travel has also contributed to pressures on individual domestic systems.

On the other hand, Vickerman (1991: 37) notes that the correlation between transport and the broader economy may be negative, in the sense that the absence of good transport links constrains growth, but that their existence is only one of many factors affecting the overall development of a given region. Dieter Biehl goes further, suggesting that it (infrastructure) has been "one of the main determinants of regional development," both nationally (as in Germany) and in the EC at large (1991: 9). Development is best enhanced when a region has multiple, rather than singular, access to efficient transport systems; both Bourgogne and Nord-Pas de Calais in France have shown dramatic growth since the 1980s because of proximity to major road and inland waterway routes that help feed France's growing high-speed rail network.

Shifts in Modal Emphasis

Though overall growth in intra-European motorized traffic has reflected the growing interdependency of EU economies, the relative impact on different modes has been far from even. In fact, a pronounced skewing in goods and passenger usage is evident; as Tables 1.2 and 1.3 indicate, the rail and maritime sectors have been in long-term decline, while the road and airlines sectors have greatly expanded as carriers of goods and, especially for the latter, passenger traffic. As discussed below, these major modal shifts in demand, and the powerful economic forces behind them, have fostered a growing sense of crisis in the overall transport industry, since the modes most in demand are also the most wasteful in terms of fuel use, pollution, and (especially for roads) land take.

The rail sector has actually suffered absolute declines, both in its capacity (its network shortening by around 4 percent in the 24 Organization for Economic Cooperation and Development (OECD) countries over the period 1970–1985; Button 1994: 30) and in its movement of freight tonnage; and while its carriage of passenger traffic has risen modestly, its market share has declined relative to other modes. As discussed in Chapter 3, rail's long-term decline has spurred recent national and EU efforts to promote high-speed train projects partly as a means of regenerating the overall sector.

Similarly, waterborne traffic, particularly via inland waterways, has continued to decline as a passenger carrier despite the sector's considerable natural advantages (low energy requirements, less noise, high safety levels); and here too, recent renewal efforts (e.g., mega-ferries) have been spurred by falling demand. The displacement of both (rail and waterborne) sectors has also been dramatic in policy terms because it has highlighted the sharp discrepancy between economic efficiency objectives and social considerations now dominating the transport debate in Europe. Especially the (relatively) ecologically friendly rail sector has been largely displaced by a much more fuel-intensive, polluting one (road), now accounting for 70 percent of freight transport and 80 percent of the passenger market (Tables 1.2 and 1.3).

Table 1.2
European Passenger Transport Use, 1970–1990 (in percent)

Year	Private Car	Bus/Coach	Rail	Air
1970	76.1	11.7	10.0	2.2
1980	77.8	10.6	8.0	3.5
1990	79.0	8.9	6.6	5.6

Source: CEC 1993a.

Table 1.3
European Freight Transport Use, 1970–1990 (in percent)

Year	Road	Rail	Inland waterway	Pipeline
1970	50.6	27.8	13.6	8.0
1980	60.6	20.2	9.8	6.3
1990	69.9	15.4	9.2	5.5

Source: CEC 1993a.

This shift reflects the numerous advantages of flexibility, speed over shorter distances, and overall network reach (in the freight sector), while the increasingly pervasive influence of the "car culture" in developed societies, and its attendant connotations of mobility, freedom, and independence, need hardly be elaborated upon. In the former command economies of eastern Europe, once heavily reliant on inefficient rail networks, a "landslide-type shift" from rail to road use is expected (Heinze and Kill 1994: 133); on one estimate, east-west road haulage from 1990 to 2010 will increase up to fourteenfold, and road passenger traffic as much as eighteenfold (Topmann 1994: 183; Blum 1991). According to Ifo, a research group, the total number of cars in Europe will likely rise from 168.5 m in 1994 to 205 m in 2005, reflecting much higher CCEE annual growth rates (4.3 percent versus just 1.6 percent in western Europe).

The air industry has seen the most epochal shifts in demand since the 1950s, due less to displacement from other modes than to the creation of genuinely new markets and indeed whole civil air industries built virtually from scratch since World War II. Though high-speed rail services provide, up to a point (estimated at between 300 and 500 km) genuine competition with the airlines, in general the airlines sector operates quite separately from that of the other modes, due to the global reach of long-haul jumbo jets and the much greater speeds attainable in the air.

It has also been closely associated with the tourism industry's rapid European postwar expansion, particularly with the Mediterranean region previously beyond the reach of most travelers for short holidays; and it has promoted rapid growth of the charter industry, with numerous knock-on effects in the hotel, restaurant, and other related service industries. In transport discussions dominated by road haulage and business travel, it is infrequently recognized that tourism has emerged as the world's largest industry in terms of employment, income and expenditures; it also accounts for the lion's share of world travel by volume.[2] Despite decades of rapid growth, the air sector shows no signs of slowing; passenger volumes will likely double between 1990 and 2000 (Heinze and Kill 1994: 135), and air liberalization could increase these figures further.

Transport and the Integration Literature

Transport's manufacturing and service role is magnified further by its significance for numerous other industries and economic sectors. Indeed, transport is a prime example of issue-linkage at the European level, with increasingly direct bearing on prioritization of other policy areas, and vice versa. The numerous horizontal associations attest to the broad sweep of transport concerns, and these interlinkages are reflected in the markedly divergent treatment of the subject in the European integration literature. An overview of commonly used texts on EU studies[3] reveals surprising variance, even among European experts, in assessing transport questions.

For example, John Pinder (1991) treats transport briefly as a background issue, bearing upon early EEC institutional development. In his often cited text, Derek Urwin (1995) similarly discusses it as a factor in building the European Coal and Steel Community (ECSC) in the early 1950s, plus a short discussion concluding a chapter on EC internal policies. Juliet Lodge's edited volume (first edition in 1989), despite extensive treatment of policy areas, has no separate discussion of transport, but combines it (briefly) with industrial policy. Dennis Swann (1995) considers transport along with agriculture and energy in the same chapter, while Archer and Butler's work (1992) on the EU through Maastricht discusses it, again briefly, in relation to social and environmental policies. Hackett (1990) includes only the briefest of mentions in another context (technology policy), while Tsoukalis's wide-ranging analysis of the European economy (1993) gives minimal transport coverage; and in his otherwise useful text, Stephen George (1991) omits it altogether. As if to drive home the point by exclusion, a massive reference compilation on the EU (Drost 1995) has entries for every major common policy—except for transport.

On the other hand, recent trends do indicate somewhat greater appreciation of transport as a policy concern, and several works give separate chapter treatment. Owen and Dynes (1989) gave a (brief) chapter overview of Single Market-led changes in the transport market. Anderson and Eliassen (1993), analyzing the evolution of European-style policymaking, give transport prominent consideration, though focused on high-speed rail development. Delamaide (1994) shows transport's crucial role in yet another area, regional development; Vickerman's edited volume (1991) does so in more scholarly fashion. Recent economics texts have included chapter-length treatments of transport (e.g., Lee 1994), as does the Barnes's EU textbook (1995), which devotes its first policy chapter to transport issues.

Those texts dedicated to transport also vary considerably in approach and emphasis. Two broad-based studies, Abbati (1987) and Whitelegg

(1988) are now dated. More recently, Masser et. al. (1992) deal with transport within the context of European geography and specifically as a question of future spatial development. Similarly, Strohl's exhaustive study of European high-speed rail development (1993) approaches transport as a question of "geo-economics." The co-edited volume by Giannopoulos and Gillespie (1993) stresses the positive impact of technology on transport systems. Button (1993; 1994) has made two notable recent contributions, the former as a revised transport economics text, and the latter aiming to generate a conceptual framework for future European transport planning. Both works emphasize a gradualist approach to transport reform, suggesting a broader application of cost-benefit analysis (CBA) to decisionmaking.

In contrast, Whitelegg (1993) emphasizes transport's growing social dimension, via an exhausting litany of traffic-related consequences for European quality of life and a damning critique of notional EU efforts to promote transport sustainability. These contributions notwithstanding, Vickerman concludes in a recent survey (1994b) that the extant transport literature neither fully grasps the consequences of the EU's geographic expansion nor amounts to an adequate working model for the future of European transport—difficult though this latter task may be.

Recently two other volumes have emphasized transport's prominence in broader European development. One, edited by Hayward (1995) focuses on the internationalization of European industry, with two illustrative chapters on the air industry and one on the Channel Tunnel. Banister, Capello, and Nijkamp (1995) analyze transport-communication links in European networks development of recent years. As edited collections, both underscore the complex nature of Europe's transport conundrums, the difficulty of the trade-offs involved, and the lack of clear answers. Thus while coverage is improving, the surfeit of technical and economics-based works is not yet sufficiently counterbalanced by attention to policy and political elements of transport.

This varied and uneven treatment of the transport problem is less the result of analytical confusion than of the inherent, and growing, synergy between transport and numerous other related policy areas. The mere inclusion, in the Rome Treaty, of a designated Common Transport Policy does not necessarily indicate easily identifiable parameters to it; indeed the treaty's notorious vagueness on transport questions (discussed in Chapter 2) has likely contributed to the subsequent confusion. Button (1994) in fact notes seven different aspects or levels of transport integration: (1) of international transport systems within Europe; (2) of different national transport policies; (3) of European policy with global trends; (4) vertically within countries; (5) horizontally across the transport modes; (6) temporally, linking transport policies over time; and (7) between transport and other policy areas. Any coordinated strategy on transport questions must take due account of other sectoral interests, as discussed next.

POLICY LINKAGES AND SPILLOVERS

EU attention to transport issues has evolved in three aspects: first, through redoubled efforts to realize CTP provisions in their own right; second, by addressing gaps in Europe's transport systems, such as industry liberalization and filling missing links, as a means of achieving broader Single Market aims; and third, as a key linkage policy area, interfacing more or less explicitly with numerous other issues. This last point has great implications for institutional (EU) efforts to promote overarching policy solutions because it complicates the task: even as the CTP's own profile is raised and sharpened, it becomes harder to distinguish it and treat it in isolation. Transport has emerged as a fulcrum around which other policy areas increasingly revolve, both functionally and in a policymaking sense, as seen below.

a. *Industrial policy*. The relationship between transport and heavy industry dates from the early industrial period when access to ports, increasingly provided by rail links, enabled consolidation of cottage industries such as textiles. Rail growth opened up hinterlands, and itself stimulated iron, steel, and coal production to meet expanding infrastructure and operational needs. The same was true for the once-mighty shipbuilding industry and its heavy requirements for these commodities. Later, the displacement of rail by the more flexible auto and truck industries shifted industrial patterns, although the macroeconomic linkage remained intact; even today, durable goods orders (e.g., cars, planes) are closely watched leading economic indicators of national industrial health.

Auto and truck manufacturing remain crucially important industrial sectors, stubbornly maintaining their positions, even in private hands, as indicative national champion industries in many countries (Renault and Peugeot in France; Fiat in Italy; Volkswagen in Germany; Volvo in Sweden). To a surprising degree, national economic power continues to be measured largely in terms of the industrial muscle wielded by such (often heavily subsidized) monoliths. Intriguingly, the Hayward volume (1995) indicates that, within an identifiable overall shift in Europe from national to international champion industrial strategies, the transport sector remains a considerable exception. Even so, emphasis is increasingly on the role of small and medium-sized enterprises (SMEs) in transport development, as with the "car of tomorrow," a centerpiece of the EU's fifth R&D framework program for 1998.

b. *Competition policy*. Movement on transport issues in the 1980s was prompted mainly by Single Market-led denationalization of the various industrial sectors and the introduction of greater competition in services. The ongoing, if often painfully slow, breakup of national transport monopolies is the result of a growing corpus of EU legislation predicated on the notion that transport, constituting a service like any other, should be opened up to allow foreign (European) operators to compete with do-mestic providers on a more level playing field. Accompanying this trend has been a growing movement to separate infrastructure from operating services, the latter being pried open to greater competition, notably in rail.

The European Commission and its Competition Directorate (DG IV) emerged, under Peter Sutherland in the mid-1980s and subsequently under Leon Brittan, as a vigorous investigator of industrial mergers. Liberaliza-tion of one entire sector, the airlines, has resulted from application of com-petition principles of the Treaty of Rome (Art. 116) rather than via the CTP, which had left air policy to one side (see Chapter 2). Intra-Commis-sion personnel changes reinforced this linkage, as Karel Van Miert shifted from Transport to Competition commissioner in the late Delors era, carry-ing with him a backlog of cases (e.g., mergers, state subsidies) requiring at-tention.

DG IV's determination to vet individual cases has dramatically raised its profile; in one view (McGowan and Wilks 1995) competition has even emerged as the EU's first truly supranational policy area.[4] The Commis-sion's joint Transport-Competition undertaking in June 1996 to investigate six transatlantic air alliances—marking the first application of Treaty Art. 88—further reflects a frequent coincidence of objectives. And Van Miert's vigorous campaign for a formal Commission investigation into the mooted Boeing-McDonnell Douglas merger in the U.S. amounted to an extraterri-torial thrust for EU competition policy.

c. *Regional policy.* The CTP far pre-dates Community attention to problems of uneven and lagging economic performance in peripheral and declining regions. Specific regional policies were introduced only in the mid-1970s, via a package deal in association with Britain's EEC entry, and had no formal legal foundation until the 1987 Single Act. Nonetheless re-gional funding has increased faster than any other single EU item, via the three main structural funds (European Regional Development Fund, or ERDF; European Social Fund, or ESF; and European Agricultural Guid-ance and Guarantee Fund (EAGGF), which together account for nearly a third of all EU spending (Hooghe and Keating 1994).

The unevenness of European development patterns, exacerbated by four EU enlargements, has focused attention on deficiencies in transport infrastructure; and individual transport projects themselves are convenient instruments of regional aid and cohesion policy. The relationship between the two areas works both ways; as CTP issues increasingly have a spatial and structural dimension, so too is EU regional policy becoming more ex-plicitly linked with, and its success measured in terms of, development of large infrastructure projects. This synthesis is strengthened by the trans-Eu-ropean networks (TENs) initiative and the establishment of the Cohesion Fund alongside the existing structural funds (see Chapter 7).

In a recent essay, Vickerman has even asserted that "the spatial development of the European Union is . . . perhaps even *the* major issue, which has moved to the forefront of the policy debate in the post-Single Market, post-Maastricht era" (1994b: 249). Delamaide cites transport systems as crucial to the creation of European "superregions" as a new political form; and institutionally, the EU's (still only advisory) "Committee of the Regions" now gives expression to regional needs, which are shaped largely by concerns about access to the European core.

d. *Energy policy.* Like transport, energy issues have figured in the European enterprise from the outset; and subsequent EC treatment of both areas has been strikingly similar[5]—not least because of heavy politicization and slowness in achieving common ground. Only with the 1994 Energy Charter and a 1996 agreement on partial liberalization of electricity markets was a breakthrough of sorts achieved. Yet energy initially was thought so crucial that it warranted a separate institutional structure, the Atomic Energy Community (Euratom), created alongside the European Economic Community itself. Nuclear energy questions, however, quickly became detached from collective consideration because of France's post-1958 nuclear development program and wider Cold War pressures.

Joint consideration of nonnuclear energy and transport issues emerged in the wake of the 1970s oil shocks, partly because greater intra-Community movement has meant that transport takes a large, and disproportionate (around 30 percent) share of Europe's total energy requirements. Its usage is twofold: either directly, by the burning of fossil fuels in internal combustion or jet engines, or indirectly, for example via railways' use of electricity, which still requires oil- or nuclear-fired energy plants to produce it. Thus electricity policy is a crucial "downstream" energy question with transport implications (McGowan 1995). One transport sector, shipping, is doubly tied in with energy issues, responsible for delivery of crude oil and refined products for other uses while also burning its own share.

Shifting use to more wasteful air and road sectors contributed both to the growing energy requirements of transport and to perceptions of European dependence on foreign suppliers and vulnerability to external shocks. This was a major stimulus for creating the International Energy Agency (IEA) in 1974, though it concentrated on securing supply rather than promoting conservation. However, growing environmental pressures caused attention gradually to spill over to questions of fuel use and savings, which heightened a perception, not only of a transport-induced energy crisis but of an alarming disjunction between what was needed (attention to energy conservation and efficiency) versus what was actually happening (relentless expansion of less efficient modes). Energy policy moved to the fore in two ways: by increasing high-level political attention at European summits; and "from the side," as an offshoot of attention to other, energy-related policy areas including the environment (DG XI) and transport itself (DG VII) (Andersen 1993). Programmatically, the two sectors are tied both in the internal market (Joule and Thermie programs) and via networks-related energy and transport projects with an external dimension.

e. *Environmental policy.* This constitutes the third leg of a policy triad linking also the energy and transport sectors. The absence of Rome Treaty environmental provisions reflected lack of international attention to issues handled (if at all) at national or local levels. Yet already by 1967 the EC was issuing its first environmental directive, and by the 1970s this led to a series of environmental action programs designed to raise awareness of the issues involved. The SEA in 1987 formally introduced environmental quality as a Community objective, via a reformulation of Article 100A, helping to counterbalance the economic focus of the Single Market with a clear social agenda.

The Maastricht Treaty explicitly sets out environmental concerns as "a component of the Community's other policies" (Article 130R), and its follow-up Fifth Environmental Action Program, for 1993–2000, identifies transport as key to its sustainable development strategy. Every major new transport project is now, in accordance with two (1985 and 1993) EU directives, automatically subject to a comprehensive environmental impact assessment. The treaty also gives the EU the right to take specific "measures at the international level to deal with regional or global environmental problems" (Article 130R), suggesting scope for extra-European activism. Environmental legislation has been often transport-related, as with the 1989 Small Car Directive and with the recent (but abortive) carbon tax proposal. The EU is committed to stabilizing CO_2 emissions at 1990 levels via cleaner transport, though budget cuts in the EU's Save II energy program have cast doubt on the efficacy of this aim.

f. *Telecommunications policy.* Transport and communications systems long have been regarded as twin elements of a logistical network (Bruinsma et al. 1991). Government regulation of both sectors has been tight (though telecoms liberalization, slated for 1998, is coinciding with the ending of transport cabotage restrictions), and transport operators are often official agents for communications functions such as postal carriage. The EU has underscored this fundamental symbiosis by programs aimed at incorporating information technologies, initially promoted separately via ESPRIT, into future transport planning, as part of the growing "soft" infrastructure links. Recent corporate developments as well, such as the Mannesmann-Deutsche Bahn joint telecommunications venture (DBKom Gmb H), aimed at competing directly with the privatized Deutsche Telekom, illustrate the ongoing restructuring of traditionally segregated industrial sectors.

g. *New technologies.* The traditionally theoretical focus of European scientific research, typified by Euratom and the Center for European Nuclear Research (CERN) in Geneva, has gradually shifted toward the applied side, reflecting national treatment of transport companies, which prioritized new technology as a means of expanding transport's own boundaries (CEC 1993a). The belief in the transformative possibilities of applied transport-related research flows from *dirigiste*-oriented policies in France, which pioneered technical advances in aircraft (the Concorde, jointly with Britain) and more recently in rapid rail (TGV). Indeed the French initiated the intergovernmental EUREKA program for European research cooperation, which by 1992 was targeting 12.6 percent of its budget for transport (Lee 1994).

Not surprisingly, the EU Commissioner for Research and Development (DG XII) since January 1995, Edith Cresson, was a high profile political appointment. Under her watch DG XII has given increased emphasis to coordinating applied research in Europe; and out of the six designated priority topics, four are directly transport related. Under the Fourth Framework Program (1994–1998), budgeted at ecu 12.3 bn ($15.6 bn), the EU's Training and Mobility of Researchers (TMR) initiative has focused on seven different areas in the field of transport research.[6]

Given the inherent difficulties of reducing traffic usage, attention is increasingly focusing on incorporating new technologies as supporting instruments for transport. Projects such as DRIVE, drawing on ESPRIT's progress, aim to develop new technologies (telematics, or integrated telecommunications and information systems; computer-guided highways and "smart" cars; driverless trains) to ameliorate problems of overcrowding and unsafe roads through efficiency gains. This growing EU attention to cross-border scientific collaboration has major, if little recognized, implications for sovereignty itself; some twenty years ago Kintner and Sicherman (1975: 142) noted the paradoxical effect of technology on international relations, in which "the sensation of increased sovereignty is sustained by technology even as the nation-state's effective control over its destiny is sharply undermined."

h. *Foreign policy*. While hardly the stuff of superpower summitry or even a central focus of the EU's common foreign and security policy (CFSP), transport questions are impinging increasingly, and with growing urgency, on the international policy debate. This tendency, however, has deep roots; the manufacturing industry's 19th century shift from coal to oil power put oil diplomacy on the international agenda long before 1970s oil politics, and dictated, for example, western interests in the Middle East and the disputed Mosul territory even before World War I.

More recently, Brussels has recognized transport's impact on EU external relations; its transport action program for 1995–2000 (CEC 1995b) set out the external dimension as one of the CTP's three central components. Transport's international impact is manifested in at least four ways: (1) at the bilateral, intra-EU level, either directly between states (UK-French collaboration on Channel Tunnel operations) or between the EU and member governments (struggles over state subsidies to carriers); (2) at the bilateral, extra-European level, such as open skies air talks with the U.S., Korea or Japan; (3) as an instrument of wider European development, either programmatically (TENs) or via special linkages to member states (Greece's interest in the Danube bridge project); and (4) as a feature of a wider, multilateral trade regime, as with the problem of shipbuilding subsidies left aside from the 1995 WTO treaty.

Transport links are commonly used by states as instruments of political leverage, to compel policy shifts in other, often unrelated areas (i.e., linkage). The Berlin crisis of 1948–49, for example, was precipitated by a transport action (the Soviets' blocking of ground access to West Berlin), and resolved by another (the American-led airlift). More recently, both the American and Chinese governments have used transport decisions as leverage against allies and foes alike.[7]

Within Europe itself, the EU's awkwardly truncated geography long has highlighted the sensitivity of access to the land transport systems of three central but non-member states: Switzerland, Austria (prior to its 1995 accession), and (former) Yugoslavia—all crucial for north-south trade flows. Environmental restrictions on heavy lorry traffic across the two Alpine states created major tensions between themselves and Brussels, and in Austria's case, emerged as a contentious issue in its drawn-out entry negotiations in 1993–1994. Recent Swiss transit restrictions on lorries have targeted transport concerns as easily the biggest single obstacle to closer Swiss-EU relations (see Chapter 7). External commercial considerations relating to the burgeoning duty-free industry (with its $5 billion annual turnover) in turn raises the profile of sea and airport operations.

Globally, the trilateral economic nexus between the U.S., Europe, and Japan has often revolved around transport concerns, especially as the Rome Treaty has increasingly been interpreted as giving the European Commission certain competences to conduct external commercial negotiations on the EU's behalf. The tables are, however, often turned the other way: Europe is an emerging battleground for industry supremacy and for testing new strategies, such as the recent mini-car venture between General Motors and Suzuki. European and U.S. interests have clashed directly in the air sector, regarding landing and "beyond" rights for their carriers, and within GATT and WTO over subsidies to Airbus Industrie in its competition with Boeing in the international airframe market.[8] And fears of losing Europe's auto market led to a series of voluntary export restrictions on Japanese car sales within EU territory. Disturbing allegations in late 1995 about surreptitious CIA involvement in U.S.-Japanese negotiations over opening up the Japanese auto market—though with, perhaps, predictably little effect on their outcome—were a further high-profile example of transport questions being raised as national security concerns.

The overlapping of transport questions with international security issues is reinforced by the inevitable targeting of transport systems by terrorists, given their sheer visibility as mass movers of humanity. Yet another linkage is the national gate-keeping function of customs officials at border entries, a task becoming both more difficult (because of rising passenger volumes) and more urgent (due to stricter European asylum policies). Passport checks at airline check-in counters have become a familiar element in an ongoing trend for airline companies themselves to shoulder the burden of vetting travelers perceived as possible trouble-cases (e.g., economic refugees). Airlines have long balked at performing such border duties, though they seem to have little choice in the matter.[9]

Other Linkages

One of the crucial past and present themes of transport's policy profile is fierce state protection of transport industries based on their strategic value. Civilian-military spillovers and the sharing of technology have marked the airlines sector almost from the outset; early nationalization of rail industries was based on a similar muddling of the private/public divide, as is the maintenance of large merchant navies for possible requisitioning in a crisis, similar to Britain's use of the *QE2* in the Falklands campaign. Excessive focus on the national dimension of transport, however, has hindered attempts to promote international governance of what is an increasingly international industry; for example, high profile industrial accidents (highlighted by the *Amoco Cadiz* disaster of the 1970s and more recently the *Exxon Valdez* spill in Alaska), have raised still largely unanswered questions about excessive demands on the shipping industry and its aging fleet. Within Europe itself, these tensions exert themselves in, among other ways, Commission-Council disputes over the scope for a specific Community dimension in transport policy.

At the opposite end, transport plays a crucial role in individual decision making. Unlike food, which accounts for a small and declining percentage of household budgets (a fact with major implications for CAP reform), transport demands on individual schedules and household budgets are growing. Average overall household expenditure on transport rose from 8 to 14 percent between 1960 and the mid-1980s (Molle 1990: 353); the average European now spends about one hour in transit daily. Though attention gravitates to the concerns of long-distance and "visible" transport (air, high-speed rail, etc.), the vast majority of trips remain short, local and road-based, implying that urban public transport requires greater scholarly and policy attention than it typically receives (Holzapfel and Schallabock 1994). Despite reams of EU transport studies, the Commission produced its first policy document on public passenger traffic only in late 1995 (CEC 1996a).

Transport's impact on individual decision making further contributes to its salience as a public and political issue. Human sensitivities seem to be heightened in motion, a reality keenly appreciated by the burgeoning tourism industry. Indeed, few policy areas so directly determine the functionality and livability of societies, especially in urban areas; John Whitelegg is surely right in asserting that transport has a major say in what is possible and not possible in society (1993: 1). For all the emphasis in the social sciences on formal and informal institutions, agenda-setting and relative competencies, European societies are, in the end, judged by the workability of transport systems as much as by any other single factor. Transport issues impel attention in the behavioral sciences no less than in applied technology.

Most European citizens are now within reach of a greater variety of transport services, and at higher levels of speed, comfort, and efficiency, than has ever been the case before. Specific transport advances such as TGV, the Concorde and the Channel Tunnel remain technological, if not economic, European achievements of the first magnitude, providing a source of considerable (though arguably underexpressed) regional pride. Despite this, transport issues frequently appear intractable in the public debate because they arise in greatest force when problems occur. Modern society's prevailing assumption that getting around should be easy, punctual, and inexpensive—itself a function of past successes—focuses attention on system breakdowns. The worldwide ridicule of the Atlanta organizers of the 1996 summer Olympic games centered on lapses in transport services that otherwise would have gone unnoticed. If complaint is an innate human characteristic, it is hardly less natural to direct it at the systems of movement.

Transport issues can be, further, heavily symbolic elements of a national consciousness-shaping nature, assuming an importance far out of proportion to their economic impact. Transport's spatial elements make them, equally, territorial questions, directly bound up with terrestrial boundaries, territorial waters or airspace, all crucial definers of the bounds of sovereignty. As a quintessential "turf issue," transport is often minimally conducive to cooperation and compromise. Transport issues can become so entwined in the national fabric, and thus so emotive in content, as virtually to rule out in advance the imposition of compellingly logical reforms (e.g., raising gasoline taxes in the U.S., or establishing a speed limit on Germany's autobahn). Perceived deficiencies in national transport infrastructures can even evoke defensive outbursts of national pride.[10] There are occasions when nationalism trends into romanticism with almost comical overtones, as when the Major government postponed the sale of Dover's port operations after the combined "political" intervention of Dame Vera Lynn and the Queen Mother, to keep the white cliffs of Dover safely in British hands (FT, 3 Nov. 1995: 8).

Transport decision making within industry is hardly less affected by public perceptions far removed from realities. Air operators, for example, have long known that backward-facing seating increases crash survivability, yet have allowed consumer preferences for traditional, forward-facing arrangements to prevail over public safety concerns. Indeed the traveling public tends to regard airlines and ships as risky modes and tends to feel safest when behind the wheel (and ostensibly in control), in the face of overwhelming evidence of the relative safety of airplane and shipboard travel (both up to 26 times safer in terms of passenger fatalities; CEC 1996a: 31) compared with the risks of auto use. Reliance on the transport sector as a testing-ground for rational choice expectations has its definite limits.

In short, the "reach" of transport issues is both horizontal, touching on much broader economic and political questions, and vertical; the transport industry is a manufacturing colossus, yet also a provider of services of peculiarly personal relevance to the individual traveller (CEC 1993a: 10–11). Frequent use of transport metaphors in defining the overall integration enterprise[11] further indicates the sector's sheer pervasiveness in the European discourse.

THE NATURE OF THE TRANSPORT CRISIS

Decades of inexorable growth in European travel, reflecting cross-border ties as well as growing domestic mobility, have heightened concerns about the overall capacity of the system to cope and have highlighted its significance as a policy issue. Indeed most independent analysts, regardless of modal specialization, nationality, or political persuasion, seem to find agreement on one crucial point: that European transport is in a state of crisis, and moreover one that seems destined to worsen in coming years as an expanding economy, and growing mobility of people and goods, increase pressures on existing infrastructures. Werner Weidenfeld warns that European transport is "close to collapse" (1994: 12); Klaus Kammerer that the German railways are "on the verge of collapse" (1990: 31); and slightly less alarmingly, Heinze and Kill state that the "structural weaknesses of the traditional modes of transport will increase" (1994: 132). There are increasing references in the literature to the German term *Verkehrsinfarct* (roughly, "traffic blockage"), although the awkward English reference to "infarction" has anatomical rather than economic connotations.

Nor are these views limited to isolated alarmists or a gloomy German school of thought; an expert study group convened by the European Commission in the late 1980s to analyze the transport problems of Europe (the "Group Transport 2000 Plus") referred to "the crisis which is threatening the European transport system" and even to its "direct threat" to the Community's main objectives (Transport 1990: 5, 7 and passim). Conclusions by targeted expert groups, such as the airlines "wise men" (*Expanding*

Horizons 1994) have been hardly more salutary. The situation is essentially one in which the overall problems of transport (overcrowding, time
wasted, pollution, inefficiencies, lack of intermodalities, underinvestment),
compounded by mode-specific problems (e.g., the lack of a single European air traffic control system), have outstripped the capability of the system, either via industry self-regulation or via overarching political authority, adequately to address, much less resolve, those problems.

Along with overburdened infrastructures, Europe's transport operators face global competitive pressures, forcing reactive policy responses at
national and EC levels. Fear, a powerful driving force in all human endeav-
or, has been at the heart of industry changes to meet the challenge of loss of
competitiveness. Heavy operating losses in key transport industries and
worsening debt burdens are key factors behind shifts in industrial and national strategies and in forging new types of government-industry relationships.

Not surprisingly, the refrain "we are all reformers now" characterizes
much of the debate; the differences lie not in whether reform is needed, but
rather in the perceived urgency of the problems and the speed with which
they require attention. Independent analysts tend to fall into one of two
categories: cautious and bold reformers. The former tend to emphasize efficiency, growth management, and the need for each mode to reflect its true
costs; the latter advocate more rapid reform aimed at addressing environmental concerns and limiting or even reducing traffic in accordance with
notions of sustainability. Both approaches have their critics; the former for
excessive prudence, the latter for being tempted by quick-fix solutions that
may prove damaging in the long term. Thus agreement on the nature and
extent of problems themselves is a necessary, yet only preliminary, step toward viable policy responses.

This divergence in the analytical debate speaks to the messy nature of
the trade-offs inherent in transport prioritizing.[12] After all, few could reasonably dispute either the intrinsic value of healthy, competitive transport
companies, or the need to check the worst social effects of ever-growing
traffic. Still, the assumed depth of the problem is such that analyses often
focus not on materially improving the system, but only on slowing the deterioration—reminiscent of the annual American ritual of debating the federal budget deficit. It is, of course, often politically useful to overstate the
magnitude of problems; in addition, it is hard to deny that the detritus of
transport overuse is a by-product of EU success in promoting greater mobility. Transport-related ills may be a "cost of non-Europe," but equally,
they are a sign of Europeans on the move as never before.

For present purposes, key transport problem areas fall into three general groupings: economic problems, social concerns, and policy issues. As
the complicated nature of the transport policy environment warrants separate treatment in Chapter 2—with one observer lamenting "the absolute

policy failure in the direction of an EC [transport] policy" (Kammerer 1990: 33)—discussion here focuses on the first two.

The *economic problems* of European transport derive from an industry being squeezed from both ends. On the demand side, the relentless expansion of traffic and overall mobility has greatly increased pressures on existing infrastructures and services. In goods transport, intra-EC volume increased by over 60 percent from the mid-1970s to the mid-1980s, from 630 m tons per kilometer (t/km) to over 1 bn t/km (Weidenfeld 1994: 12). Auto traffic in each of the four major EC countries (Britain, Italy, France, Germany) increased by at least 75 percent between 1970 and 1987 (Button 1994: 29). European airports face severe capacity constraints that raise safety concerns, especially at heavily used airports such as London's Heathrow and Milan's Malpensa. Serious as they are, current problems will pale in comparison with the expected doubling of air traffic within the decade, which will not be matched by a like expansion of airport capacity (of major cities, only Athens, Paris, and Berlin are planning new airports). Road congestion costs are estimated at up to 3 percent of European GDP, or ecu 120 bn each year.

Despite prevailing mindsets that have favored infrastructure expansion rather than traffic limitation, one ironic offshoot of governmental protectionism of different transport industries has been a marked decline in infrastructure spending. It is estimated that total capital invested in transport infrastructure declined some 22 percent in real terms from the mid-1970s to the mid-1980s, with the overall percentage from national budgets declining from 1.5 percent to around 1 percent (Weidenfeld 1994: 12; CEC 1993a). Urban transport systems have felt cuts particularly strongly, with consequent drops in services and quality. And despite a growing EU role in infrastructure development, there is no question of meeting projected needs of the 21st century, nor even of making up for national or regional funding shortfalls.

In turn, operators face growing pressures associated with ongoing liberalization of the transport sector and the ending of domestic monopolies in services. State-run transport industries, long accustomed to a favorable policy environment at home, have felt the pressures of EMU-generated budget cuts particularly strongly, and have faced wrenching political challenges in tackling problems of overmanning and high fixed costs. In 1995–96, Air France and SNCF, France's national rail system, both came perilously close to bankruptcy, with SNCF suffering a series of high-profile embarrassments (see Chapter 3), that severely dented its reputation as a world-class rail operator.

Competitive pressures since the late 1980s, and more broadly, the changing operational environment of European industry, have left no European country, industry, or company untouched (Hayward 1995) and have forced a number of adaptive measures:

a. Partial or wholesale privatizations of state-run operators, along with loss of their monopoly positions, especially for north European airlines, with their southern counterparts still lagging;

b. Stringent cost-cutting in public and private companies alike, in which pay freezes, early retirements, and no-new-hire policies have become the rule, not the exception;

c. Bankruptcies and receiverships for many heavily subsidized companies, particularly shipyards (Germany's Bremer Vulkan yards; Denmark's Danyard and Burmeister and Wain; Greece's Skaramanga and Elefsis) to an extent unthinkable in earlier times;

d. Corporate restructurings, whereby European transport companies are increasingly focusing on core businesses, selling off unprofitable subsidiaries (e.g., Daimler-Benz's unloading of loss-making aircraft makers Fokker and Dornier), undoing mergers (Saab-Scania's breakup) or hiving off ill-fitting parts (e.g., Daimler's sale of AEG white goods), which may herald the ending of an era for European transport conglomerates;

e. Introduction of profit incentives and attention to shareholder (or "stakeholder") value in private companies, and streamlining corporate practices in publicly subsidized ones (Airbus Industrie);

f. Global alliance formation, especially in airlines but also in car manufacturing and shipping lines, as a survival tactic and a way to gain access to foreign markets;

g. The ending of "full-service" companies with significant outsourcing and franchising for auxiliary supply functions, leading to intriguing possibilities of the "virtual transport company" with a minimal core, of which British Airways may be a forerunner.

Such adaptive strategies have been forced by growing international competition and heavy financial losses at some of Europe's flagship transport companies. Germany's Daimler-Benz lost DM 5.7 bn ($3.8 bn) in 1995, and France's Alcatel-Alsthom $5.7 bn, each the heaviest year-on-year corporate loss in their respective country's postwar history, which came in vivid, and unwelcome, contrast to a period of record profits for Detroit's Big Three automakers.[13] As it followed a decade of wrenching changes in the 1980s, Detroit's resurgence fueled pessimistic views that European industry was a decade or more behind its American (and Japanese) competitors.

Yet unlike previous years, companies can no longer look to their governments for favorable treatment because of the European Commission's increasingly vigorous application of competition principles in the transport sector. The war of words in mid-1996 between the German government and the EU's Competition directorate over subsidies to Volkswagen in Saxony *Land* illustrated that no government is immune from intense EU scrutiny over public subsidies. Europe's state-run airlines, notably Greece's Olympic, Air France and especially Belgium's Sabena, have attempted to maintain full services despite severe cash-flow problems, and their governments have locked horns with the Commission over reducing costs and debt.

Indeed with governments racing to meet EMU convergence criteria, the question of overall national debt (in many cases, substantially a function of heavy transport subsidies and debt) has, itself, been institutionalized as a political issue at EU level, since the choice of countries to join the currency union will be, in the end, a largely political one. At the Florence European summit in June 1996, Europe's political leaders underscored the linkage between high transport costs and overall, Euro-related budgetary rectitude by vetoing additional EU expenditures on transport infrastructure.

Secondly, the transport industry faces growing public scrutiny of the *social problems* of transport use. Traditionally, the main concerns of European transport planners have been efficiency-oriented, while the social elements of transport date from post-1970s concerns, associated with the growth of Green parties in northern Europe, notably Germany. Two caveats, however, can be interjected here. One is that (national) transport planning has always had a strongly social/distributional function (Gwilliam 1983; Lodge 1989). Transport operators often labor under implied or formal public service obligations by governments anxious to maintain services, which partly accounts for the tenacity with which governments have fought EU encroachments on what they have long considered national turf. The difference is that current attention focuses on the social costs of overuse, rather than benefits of use. For a time, the weak and fragmented nature of the international environmental lobby limited its influence at EU level, although post-Maastricht changes in EU governance, particularly the strengthening of the European Parliament, is increasing the possibilities of Green expression and impact.

The second caveat is that transport has always had negative consequences and side effects; transport-related pollution is hardly a new phenomenon, and indeed in some modes, like rail, it has been reduced substantially due to widespread rail electrification in Europe (now approaching 40 percent of all lines). New generations of jet aircraft are quieter and more fuel efficient (e.g., the Boeing 777 versus the 747). Increases in auto emissions due to escalating traffic volumes would have been much greater if not for technological breakthroughs on a single unit basis, such as the development of cleaner burning engines and fuels and obligatory use (from 1993 for all new cars) of catalytic converters; tailpipe emissions on new cars today are some 90 percent less than cars produced in 1970. The increasing litany of identified problem areas that long remained implicit (such as visual, noise, and even time pollution), thus inflation of the relevant vocabulary, has not itself worsened these problems, but undoubtedly has focused attention on them and their perceived urgency as policy concerns.

The many social problems of transport overuse have been documented in devastating detail by authoritative public reports (CEC 1993a and 1996a; Transport 1995) and analysts (Whitelegg 1993) alike. Transport operations, mainly road-based, account for an inordinate amount of fuel use and is a major source of harmful emissions, including over half of all Europe's nitrogen oxide emissions, nearly half its hydrocarbon emissions, over eighty percent of its carbon monoxide emissions, and smaller amounts of sulphur oxides and particulates. Fuel use/wastage is most marked in the air, as the typical commercial jet uses up to thirteen times the amount of fuel per passenger kilometer as do land-based modes. As noted, however, pollution intrudes in many ways, and the increasing pressures on the environment due to encroachment on Europe's limited land space by expansion of infrastructure (airports, rail lines, motorways) add to noise and visual pollution levels, all related to the quality-of-life debate. Poor air quality in major cities, traffic noise, and the like need no statistical corroboration to be acknowledged as urgent problems.

Yet another consideration is safety, or lack thereof, again with special relevance to the road sector; upwards of 45,000 fatalities and 1.5 m injuries occur on Europe's roads and motorways yearly. Safety deficiencies of roll-on, roll-off ferries, highlighted by the Baltic sea disaster of fall 1994, demonstrated the inherent risks of movement in any form, even in the safest modes. Indeed, industry liberalization and growing traffic are raising fears that safety concerns will be downgraded in the emphasis on economic viability.

The Politicization of Transport Questions

These twin problem areas, and their interrelationship through what Gunther Topmann (1994: 185) aptly calls "the tension between ecology and economy," indicate the growing complexity of Europe's transport policy-making environment. To be sure, politicization of such issues is far from new;[14] Philip Williams (1972) notes the collapse of a French government back in 1952 over the question of railway reform. Even so, two key shifts in the debate appear to have occurred. One is that, whereas specific projects have drawn intense, short-term political opposition, transport questions across the spectrum have intruded into the political debate on a more regular and consistent basis. A second change is the emergence of transport questions, once limited to local or at most regional concerns (bridge-building, airport extensions), as bona fide national and even international questions.

Timothy Garton Ash (1993), for example, traces the "web of interdependence" between East and West Germany in the 1970s and 1980s, strengthened by an increasingly dense network of human contacts, back to a lowly 1972 transit agreement allowing personal visits across the Berlin Wall.[15] In their recent study of European transport and communications networks, Banister, Capello, and Nijkamp (1995) suggest that the politics of European transport, via "the impact of political changes on transport systems" and "the role of new actors," is a crucial area of future research. One of the few studies in their volume directly examining transport decision-making processes (Lemberg on Denmark's Great Belt project) exposes a wide array of intriguing elements at work that fairly beg for more extensive analysis of the impact of politics on transport prioritizing and policy-making, and vice versa.

The scope for overt politicization of transport issues has grown along with increasing EU attention to two key transport elements: structural policies, and competition rules aiming at ending national monopolies. Large-scale transport works inevitably draw attention because of their great expense, long gestation periods, social nuisances, and sheer visibility, particularly for those that cross sensitive geological (marine, alpine) areas or that threaten lifestyles in urban or privileged rural settings. The concentration of resources needed to complete them requires difficult choices over the allocation of scarce resources—"political" in the classic Eastonian sense of the term. And insofar as European transport infrastructure is assuming increasingly international dimensions, via completion of the Anglo-French Channel Tunnel and through progress on projects such as the Öresund bridge-tunnel project in Scandinavia, cross-border high-speed rail links, and transalpine road/rail projects, the threat of political "spill-up" to the international dimension, and the intensity of the conflicts themselves, is correspondingly increasing (Andersen and Eliassen 1993; Ross 1995).

Less often realized is the inherently political nature of the Single Market project itself, and its attendant effects on the liberalization of European industry. It is often said that the Single Market initiative reflects essentially economic and commercial, rather than political, aims, in distinct contrast to the heavily political, quasi-federalist content of the Maastricht Treaty; the elimination of borders was designed to help European industry rationalize internally in order to help it compete in the global marketplace. While it may be true, as Moravcsik (1991) has argued, that the Single Market was not the result of neofunctionalist spillover or evidence of growing federalist powers in Brussels vis-à-vis the national capitals or the Council of Ministers, the Cockfield/Delors initiative was nonetheless suffused with political and distributional considerations, and it reflected a clear prioritization of the policy agenda. Many of the reforms attributed to Maastricht were, in fact, initiated in the SEA (Tsoukalis 1993).

The push toward deregulation has reflected a distinctly and heavily political objective of industrial interests, working both at national levels via influence in Departments of Transportation (DOTs), and at the European level via separate modal interests and the European Round Table of Industrialists (ERT). The deliberate focus on enhancing Europe's competitive position (as opposed to promoting, for example, full employment or environmental protection) reflects the organizational prevalence, and efficacy as a lobby, of industry interests at both national and international levels.

Streeck and Schmitter (1991: 137) note, for example, that out of a total of 654 interest associations registered in Brussels in 1985, some 471 were either industry- or commerce-oriented, while just 99 were professional or union organizations—an imbalance that has prevented, in their view, the emergence of neo-corporatist arrangements at the European level. That these (industry) interests could prevail even under the supposedly left-leaning Commission under the Socialist Delors merely corroborates the point; and despite the subsequent advocacy of the Social Charter in the late 1980s by then-Social Affairs Commissioner Vasso Papandreou, noneconomic issues clearly played a secondary role to the internal market project's rationalization, cost-saving and competitiveness objectives. Some states, notably Britain, managed entirely to remove transport elements from social policy in their European calculations.[16]

A further problem is industry's reluctance to accept the natural consequences of liberalization, namely exposure to external competition, and there are wide variations between, and even within, different modal interests regarding the elimination of barriers and the ending of heavy state subsidies. Large national champion firms, such as car manufacturers and national airlines, have been notably reluctant reformers. Their angling for continued state aid via "one more heave"-type delaying strategies, and strongarm tactics to maintain market share, provides strong evidence of a keen awareness of self-interest, and of an ability to project those interests through the political system at various levels. In contrast, smaller companies (such as regional airlines) have welcomed the creation of a more level playing field, even though industry consolidation ultimately may increase their vulnerability as takeover targets. Attempts to designate one group or another as unified actors inevitably become overgeneralized and therefore limited as analytical tools.

The increasing internationalization of transport politics has two important effects. First, it adds to the overall scope and number of potential political forums in which transport questions figure as contentious issues. Table 1.4 indicates a vertical hierarchy consisting of four separate levels at which contention can be manifested, namely the international/global level, the European (Union) level, the (intra-)national level, and the modal level. Nor are these levels comfortably self-contained; the spill-up political tendencies accompanying the growing international dimension of transport policymaking[17] indicates that the divisions are not so much glass ceilings as

Table 1.4
Transport Politics: Eleven Dimensions

I. The International Dimension
   A. Inter-regional conflict (U.S.-Europe-Japan/East Asia)
   B. European intergovernmental conflict, including:
      1. Large vs. small states; 2. producer vs. nonproducer states; 3. central vs. peripheral states; 4. EU states vs. nonmember states

II. The European Union Dimension
   C. Intergovernmental vs. supranational interests (European Council vs. European Commission, Parliament, Court)
   D. Parliamentary vs. collective/consensual interests (European Parliament vs. European Commission)
   E. Intra-Commission rivalries, including:
      1. Between the Directorates-General (Transport, Energy, etc.);
      2. Within DG VII (Transport) over modal priorities

III. The Intra-state Dimension
   F. Government vs. opposition priorities
   G. Intra-coalition pressures (both across and within parties)
   H. Bureaucratic pressures (inter-departmental rivalries)
   I. Local and regional vs. national priorities

IV. The Modal Dimension
   J. Intermodal rivalries (rail vs. road)
   K. Intramodal rivalries (large vs. small carriers; state vs. private operators)

mere lines in water. So constituted, this political hierarchy also increases the web of complexity across and between the various levels, in which new political dynamics emerge. One important indication of this trend is the growing regional lobby in Brussels, in which like-minded regional bodies often bypass national governments altogether in hopes of securing greater access to policy channels (and, naturally, to funds) in Brussels.

The second major effect of transport's growing international dimension is to raise the overall political stakes involved. As discussed above, transport issues are emerging as highly sensitive matters of trade diplomacy with major implications for the World Trade Organization (WTO) as well as for bilateral intergovernmental relationships. Within this changing milieu, the role of international institutions, and specifically those of the European Union, becomes crucial. The EU emerges partly as an arbiter of different and conflicting concerns; just as importantly, it becomes a political actor—or more precisely, a series of actors—in itself, with interests that increasingly conflict with entrenched industrial or political agendas, with traditionally ascendant national transport authorities, or even with each other.

It is possible further to isolate, within the fourfold hierarchy, at least eleven different, though overlapping, arenas in which political disputes over transport issues can be, and are being, manifested. Several of these arenas have further subdivisions, depending on the multiplicity of actors and interests involved. For example, within the European dimension, at least four different arenas of conflict emerge, including European interstate relations; member state-EU relations; interinstitutional EU relations; and even intrainstitutional (e.g., Commission) relations. Further, the political expression of different interests is not limited to public governing bodies but also takes place across, and even within, individual modes themselves, which can in turn influence the way governing bodies react and prioritize.

Within this overall schema, the traditionally single most important European political dimension, namely class politics via the left-right spectrum, is but one of many factors. The transport sector is by no means immune to employer-worker conflicts and industrial action; European rail and air strikes continue to make headlines and cause financial losses, and often involve intensely political questions. Local industrial actions from the Gdansk shipyards in the early 1980s to Renault's Belgian operations in 1997 have escalated into international politcal issues.

Even so, transport industrial action is often bound up in broader questions; even the crippling 24–day French transport strike of December 1995 originated in the contentious nature of the social security cutbacks instituted by the Juppé government, which in turn had transport implications (via proposed reforms of SNCF). This factor is partly the result of overarching modal self-interests, whereby union/industry conflicts over working conditions are often overridden by the greater (perceived) need to make common cause in defense of the mode they both serve and benefit from. The combined economic and social/distributive functions of transport systems has promoted this perception of common cause. Organizational conflicts over policy priorities also play a crucial role, both by involving international institutions (the EU, the WTO) in transport issues, and by linking newer, post-industrial (environmental) policy concerns with traditional, class-based issues.

This work is less interested in determining the relative importance of these different elements (which at any rate varies according to issue) than in underscoring the cumulative effect of the expansion of transport's political scope, and its complicating consequences for the growing European dimension in transport planning. Nonetheless, as policymaking has become more "Europeified," so too has the political process affecting it, both internally (within Europe) and externally (between Europe and the rest of the world). Transport has increasingly become a question of "high politics," even while it remains a key policy concern at the subnational level and a sensitive touchstone for subsidiarity principles. Thus, far from removing politics from transport policymaking, the growing involvement of EU institutions, and Europe's projection as a global economic power, have expanded the overall potential for politicization. The various manifestations of these points of conflict will be dealt with in subsequent chapters.

Thus, in brief and preliminary summary, the analytical perspective of this work can be summarized as follows:

1. Transport has shifted from a peripheral to a central aspect of European integration, highlighted by the Single Act and Maastricht Treaty revisions and accompanied by considerable task expansion of the EU;
2. Increasing policy attention at various levels, engendered by economic and social concerns, has intensified the degree of politicization of transport issues;
3. Transport politics are increasingly complicated by the multiple levels at which issues are addressed, ranging from local authorities to global institutions;
4. The growing "spill-up" and "spill-down" pressures between these levels, along with an increasing intensity of the issues and webs of interrelationships, are adding new arenas of confrontation while not eliminating traditional ones;
5. Governments and states still matter in determining priorities and in shaping policy outcomes, though often negatively, as a hindering influence on common policy-making;
6. Non-governmental bodies and public institutions also matter, both via pressure groups and via EU institutional pressure on states to reform (European Parliament, Court, Commission), as well as via policy spillovers (e.g., transport privatizations spurred by EMU-induced pressures on national budgets);
7. Industry changes are complicating policy solutions, stemming from intermodal competition for resources and increasingly from intramodal competition as well, such as between large and small operators;
8. The emergence of transport politics at the international level—symptomatic of the EU's emergence as an economic and (partly) political actor on the world stage—is adding to European sensitivity and vulnerability to extra-European developments.

IS TRANSPORT A SPECIAL CASE?

Notwithstanding the policy interlinkages discussed earlier, Europe's transport debate has been influenced, complicated, and even plagued by a widespread attachment to the belief that transport problems are, by nature, unique. Many in industry and government have claimed that, due to the sector's innate characteristics, the application of broader EU principles (such as competition rules) could even lead to prescriptions worse than the disease itself. The problem is compounded by the EU's considerable task expansion, leading to what many regard as inherently incompatible transport objectives of facilitating mobility (via industry liberalization and structural policies) alongside sustainability objectives that presuppose limitations on traffic.

The Rome Treaty is not helpful on the point. While it noted the importance of common action in transport for broader economic convergence aims (Art. 74) and established the legal foundation for common policies (the CTP), it also specifically cited "the distinctive features of transport" (Art. 75). It was not until key ECJ rulings in the 1970s and 1980s that transport came to be treated as "just another" service industry in terms of European legislation (see Chapter 2)—which, ironically, then paved the way for more substantial CTP progress. In a wholly separate context I have argued that joint international actions can be jeopardized by the granting of special dispensations for individual purposes (Ross 1989), but the logic of exceptionalism gives the point relevance here as well.

Economically, a case can be made that transport does have distinctive features not replicated in other policy spheres. Klaus Kammerer (1990: 29) notes five peculiarities of the sector: (1) the tendency toward a ruinous competition; (2) the tendency toward a structural monopoly; (3) competitive distortions; (4) irresponsibility of transporters for the overall economy; and (5) treatment of transport infrastructure as a public good. He holds that point (1) relates to the problem of long-term overcapacity, punctuated by temporary bottlenecks (severe undercapacity); this problem results from the great gap between high fixed, and essentially nonrecoverable, capital costs of transport infrastructure (roads, railways), as compared with relatively low operating or marginal costs (also Abbati 1987: 20).

The question of competitive distortions arises because each mode differs in the way its costs are borne. Whereas rail suppliers have carried the bulk of their own costs (a major reason for the heavy debt load of Europe's national rail systems), road use carries significant non-internalized social and economic costs (pollution, time lost) borne by society at large. Privatization, especially in the air industry, has transferred these divergences within single modes; a growing complaint of commercial airlines is predatory pricing by state-owned European carriers. This (costing) point is symptomatic of even more fundamental modal differences: in their industry structures, policy environment, physical reach, and even vocabulary. Some (e.g., rail) require straightforward coordination of (mostly still) monopolized national systems; others (road, inland waterway) affect numerous private operators; still others (air, shipping) involve global operations that defy purely European solutions. Unquestionably, diversity remains a key defining characteristic of the transport sector.

As for Kammerer's last two points, there is a natural disjunction between the interests of individual transporters aiming to protect their own market share and maximize revenues, and the greater public good, however defined. To this could be added that without prompting from above, there is often little incentive either for intermodal cooperation or for individual behavioral changes, with their marginal costs to society at large (Nijkamp and Vleugel 1995a). Each mode has its own natural advantages and drawbacks, and has pressed its own case for fair (read favored) treatment, but these differences are exacerbated by a policy process which has tended to reinforce intermodal competition. All this hinders system efficiency and inhibits rational, overall CTP strategies acceptable across the European board.

Another factor here is the common interest by EU member governments, despite substantial differences in transport needs and philosophies, in promoting home transport industries via favorable policy environments and often subsidies. Such support has two powerful historical antecedents, which will be developed in the modal chapters. One is that transport systems have been key instruments of societal development and modernization at *national* level; the other is their role in promoting states' *international* expansion and/or prestige, as reflections or expressions of broader national economic and political capabilities. The very term "flag carrier" and reliance on increasingly outdated national champion strategies illustrate the stubborn persistence of these historical linkages even in cutting-edge industries.

Within this context, states have promoted development in differing ways. One line of analysis distinguishes between "Continental European" philosophies, particularly in France and Germany, which have tended to regard transport as a vehicle for social integration and maintain public service obligations formally in public law;[18] and an "Anglo-Saxon" approach, stressing efficiency-oriented marketplace considerations in determining priorities (Button 1994: 52–53; Molle 1990: 340). Abbati (1987) refined the distinction by placing the Low Countries, with their dense traffic networks and small sizes, in the latter category, while considering France somewhat less interventionist than Germany (though recent developments would undoubtedly switch the two in his analysis).

The growth of transport franchising and especially telecommunications deregulation in Finland and Scandinavia put those countries closer to the Anglo-Saxon model, defying widespread assumptions about the inherent centralism of Nordic welfare states. Thus in some respects there is also a classic north-south split between liberal (market-oriented) north European approaches and interventionist policies in the "olive belt," though again with exceptions (e.g., Greek shipping). Recent characterizations of a "paradigm shift" from Keynesian to neoliberal approaches to European industry (Wright 1995) may be broadly correct, but the transport sector has emerged as an increasingly awkward exception.

In light of the formidable set of factors ranged against advocacy of common transport decisionmaking, it is not surprising that progress has been limited. The CTP has been cited as one of, if not the, least successful of all the EU's major policy areas (Owen and Dynes 1989); that the legal authority for a common transport policy has been on record (via the Rome Treaty) since the outset merely adds insult to injury. Even so, dismissive summations should be treated with caution. First, the EU's relatively passive pre-1980s approach to transport questions may reasonably be thought inadequate, but this has not meant a lack of policy per se, nor of political pressures and interests. Indeed state-level resistance to common rules may have added to the overall number of incrementalist Community regulations and directives, aimed at chipping rather than sweeping away existing (monopolistic) practices, the result being not so much policy as policies in the plural.

Second, progress has been achieved along many fronts, although advances have been underappreciated because of their piecemeal nature and generally noncontroversial, often technical, content; unhelpful foot-dragging by governments in implementing EU directives has also contributed to perceptions of lack of progress. Even so, a single glance at a recent EC compilation of transport legislation through 1992 (CEC 1993b) suffices to dispel any myth that the EC has overlooked transport as such. And third, such criticisms lose much of their validity after the early 1980s; since that time the Community's transport policy debate has been transformed almost beyond recognition, as if making up for lost time.

Part of this growing attention has been stylistic, in which a whole new transport lexicon has been introduced, including such concepts as "citizens network," "combined transport," and "global strategy," all elements in the debate over sustainable mobility. Insofar as rhetorical overreliance on such terms can imply a lack of operational guidelines, the EU can open itself up to charges of tokenism. Even so, the rhetorical attention is increasingly backed up by specific actions: by new programs involving substantial EU financial commitments; by the firm application of competition principles to an industrial sector long cosseted as a privileged monopoly; and by the zeal with which Commission regulators have pursued governments in cases of alleged rule breaches and over-subsidization. The many ramifications of this newfound attention will be spelled out in the remainder of the volume.

NOTES

1. C. Northcote Parkinson's classic formula ("work expands so as to fill the time available for its completion") was applied to the transport context by A. Downs in 1978, who held that traffic naturally expands to fill existing infrastructure (cited in Button 1994: 94, n. 154).

2. *The Economist* (Broadening 1991) estimates that leisure travel accounts for between two-thirds and three-quarters of all world travel by volume, the great majority of which is to domestic, rather than foreign, destinations.

3. See Urwin (1995) for a comprehensive EU bibliographic essay.

4. The number of competition cases rose from 1081 in 1994 to 1472 in 1995, due both to the 1995 enlargement and to the expanding gamut of policy areas (e.g., media, banking).

5. Andersen (1993: 146) notes the EC's parallel treatment of transport and energy policy via (a) early hopes followed by neglect, (b) recent renewal of interest in common policies, (c) divergent national priorities, (d) strong influence of the European Parliament, and (e) general assumptions about both policy areas as "too special to be left to market forces." Arguably, energy is more distinctly national insofar as some member states (Britain, the Netherlands) produce and export energy, while most others rely on imports. Neither the SEA nor the Maastricht Treaty elaborated specific European energy policies, further corroborating the point.

6. The seven projects include strategic research; rail transport; integrated transport chains; air transport; urban transport; waterborne transport; and road transport (The Fourth 1994). Transport is one of fifteen sectoral activities of the program.

7. The decision by the U.S. Transportation Department in March 1996 to affix a safety warning on air tickets to Greece, due to alleged security lapses at Athens's Hellenicon airport, was decried in the Greek press as a misguided attempt to push the Simitis government into a more accommodating stance vis-à-vis Turkey. The decision was lifted just a month later. Washington has used air sanctions against Colombia's Avianca in an effort to stem drug trafficking from Bogota (IHT, 5 August 1996: 7).

China's decision in 1995 to purchase Airbus instead of Boeing craft for its national airlines was a very public slap at American criticism of its (China's) trade stance and human rights record.

8. On the political consequences of Airbus subsidies, see Tyson (1992). American suspicions of Airbus practices were fueled by allegations (later judged baseless) that former Canadian prime minister Brian Mulroney accepted bribes in return for agreeing to purchase Airbus jets for Air Canada.

9. For example, British Airways has been fined 2000 pounds per passenger arriving at British airports without proper immigration papers. Security lapses that possibly led to the downing of TWA Flight 800 in July 1996 will no doubt reinforce pressures on the airlines for vigilance in passenger scrutiny.

10. The British government claimed broader EU goals of reducing transport subsidies as a defense of its decision (later partially reversed) not to commit public monies to build a high-speed Channel Tunnel rail link. In another case, Greek officials angrily denied allegations of safety lapses at Greek airports by Danish and German pilots' associations, claiming surreptitious aims of undermining Greek tourism and economic well-being.

11. The Maastricht-inspired metaphor of choice was an "express train leaving the station," which would-be EU members were advised to join before it was too late. More recently, discussions of variable geometry and multi-speed Europe led John Major to reject "a single train with all carriages moving at the same speed" (*The Economist,* 20 June 1996), and Helmut Kohl in contrast rejecting the notion

of a "convoy moving at the speed of the slowest carriage"—as if it could move at any other speed.

12. "Few issues are more important to national prosperity, yet harder to resolve, than an effective transport policy." FT editorial, 6 Feb. 1995: 15.

13. Chrysler Corporation, for example, after achieving record profits for 1994 ($3.7 bn) recorded a best-ever second quarter in 1996, with profits totalling $1.72 bn.

14. I am grateful to an anonymous reviewer of the *Journal of European Public Policy* for clarification on this point.

15. Though Ash's reference is to the transit agreement's humble origins, the opposite implication could be drawn: of the great, if bottom-up, integrative potential of noncontroversial measures designed to facilitate human movement.

16. Following Britain's November 1991 opt-out from the EU Social Charter, negotiations over the so-called "working-time directive" were held up by British insistence on exemptions for its transport sector, and its workers in the rail, road, sea, air, and inland waterway and lake transport businesses were exempted from the measures passed in November 1993. Even so, Britain abstained in the vote and took the issue to the European Court, amidst accusations of negotiating in bad faith. FT, 21 June 1996: 13.

17. This reference to "spill-up" tendencies is similar to what Peterson (1995: 74) calls the "bidding-up process," in which institutional actors vie for identification with innovative policy solutions, such as the strengthening of EC-level auto emissions standards in the late 1980s.

18. Treatment of transport as a "public service" is true of both France (as a *service publique*) and Germany (*öffentlicher Dienst*), where both the airways (Lufthansa) and the railways (Bundesbahn) have had obligations under the German constitution, or Basic Law, to another state monopoly, the postal service (Bundespost). See Abbati 1987: 21–22. A similar situation exists in Spain, Italy, and Greece with respect to ferry services. EU legislation periodically has upheld such obligations, though the recent trend has been to allow exceptions based on more circumscribed public service contracts.

Chapter Two

The Common Transport Policy: The EU's Unfinished Legacy

> When our human methods of transport are so
> perfect that physical laws no longer regulate our
> journeys by land or sea or air, why, then we shall
> have outgrown our planet.
>
> —FREYA STARK
> *The Journey's Echo*

The previous chapter set out transport's general characteristics and discussed its significance for the European political economy. This chapter looks specifically at the problem of shaping common policies within the Community's institutional framework, focusing especially on the challenges of breaking down the numerous barriers, both natural and artificial, to cross-border cooperation on transport issues. Two primary questions inform the discussion. First, why was the EC chronically hindered in its earlier attempts to establish common rules for transport? Second, what accounts for the resurgence of transport as a policy focus over the past decade? A third line of inquiry—to what extent has general enthusiasm translated into specific progress?—is also broached, though the modal chapters examine the relevant policy developments in greater detail.

Sustained initiatives, whether within sovereign national settings or within looser organizational frameworks such as the EU, require the confluence of many factors collectively exerting a powerful influence on the policy process and on the institutions and individuals involved in it. Naturally, the EU elicited more analytical interest due to the advances of the late

1980s compared with the previous decade, often dismissed as a period of "Eurosclerosis," even if the distinction between the two periods is often overdrawn.[1] Obstructed progress, however, reflects a different dynamic, in which various factors such as lack of operational guidelines, disruptive efforts by any single (national) actor, or a general apathy that prevents follow-through of initiatives can all play a part. One characteristic of the CTP's evolution is that both phenomena—stagnation and rapid advance—can be examined comparatively over time as well as across the modal divides.

The European transport policy context divides roughly into three eras: first, from the early 1950s to the early 1970s; second, from then up to the mid-1980s; and third, from that time to the present. Though both failure and progress punctuated the continuum in each period, the first was characterized generally by initial high hopes, incremental progress, and frequent setbacks; the second by an expanding gamut of policy concerns and crisis-generated initiatives to break policy logjams; and the third by Single Market-inspired liberalization and structural initiatives in every mode. The 1986 shipping regulations, the first air liberalization package of 1987, the freeing of road haulage, and the enunciation of a high-speed rail network, all date from this period. The ending of cabotage, or domestic monopoly, restrictions by the late 1990s will represent a (delayed) culmination of these 1980s initiatives.

Given this development, several prevailing general characterizations of EC progress have limited applicability to transport. The "stop-and-go" process mentioned by Schneider and Cederman (1994) does not account for the lack of sustained high-level EU commitment for the better part of three decades. Neo-functional emphasis on spillover processes is also limited, since the Community's recent push is partly a question of making up for lost time and of riding the wave created by overall Single Market progress.

Many have argued that momentum on transport policy has economic and technical origins, as industry advances have spilled up and gained attention in Brussels. But transport's macroeconomic importance has been consistent, even if understanding of it has advanced; while the great postwar technological breakthroughs, such as the invention and commercial application of turbofan and turbojet engines in aviation, and of high speed engines in the rail sector, were fruits of sustained research efforts in the 1950s and 1960s, rather than later (Tyson 1992; Dunn and Perl 1994). What changed, rather, was the political context within which these advances were taking place: the emergence of new institutional advocates of progress; the globalization of the political economy; the political assertiveness of Brussels vis-à-vis national capitals; and the wider integrative thrust from which transport, despite claims to a special status, could not remain immune.

THE EARLY PERIOD: BEGINNINGS AND SETBACKS

For all its recent progress, the EU's overall transport legacy is not particularly auspicious, and at times the CTP has rivaled the unloved common fisheries policy as a source of sheer institutional frustration. This decidedly mixed legacy also indicates the tenuous linkage between the theoretical and developmental perspectives of the EU. Initial creation of the customs union presupposed the parallel development of a single market in transport, via "joint action in the form of systematic legislation at Community level" (Abbati 1987: 16), as opposed to mere coordination of national policies (as under Articles 6 and 105 of the Rome Treaty).

A second linkage is that between economic coordination and the emergence of common political structures, which lay behind German insistance at Maastricht that political union (EPU) and monetary union (EMU) provisions be placed on an equal footing. Such assumed linkages have long European precedents; just as the 19th century German *Zollverein*, reinforced by developments in rail, telegraph and steamship, had a transitional role in Germany's political unification, so too did many regard a common approach to transport questions as instrumental to Single Market progress and a step toward true political union—even if the parallel is limited in other ways (not least because the federalist model has receded rather than advanced).

There are two alternative ways of looking at the CTP. As Vickerman (1991) rightly notes, there is a means-ends distinction between, on the one hand, transport cooperation as a means of enhancing broader integration goals, and on the other, CTP progress as a necessary goal in its own right. The distinction is not merely semantic, but has also had major policy implications. In the early years the latter assumption prevailed, that neither a single market in goods and services nor even a customs union was possible without a parallel single transport market (Lindberg and Scheingold 1970), presumably with overarching (EC) regulatory authority extending across modal divides and national borders.

By the late 1960s, however, lack of progress effectively dashed hopes for a genuine CTP, and focused efforts on harmonizing different national practices. Nicholas Moussis (1996) has characterized this shift as one from common policies to a Community policy, based on mutual cooperation rather than coordination. This shift also paralleled the replacement of "positive" with "negative" integration—the move from active shaping of common policies to the gradual, and more modest, task of removing artificial distortions and barriers. It also paralleled shifts in other areas (e.g., professional qualifications) from harmonization to mutual equivalence and compatibility. Transport (and other policies) came to be regarded as means toward a broader end of economic integration, though even here one must be careful; as Amitai Etzioni once argued (1965), economic integration itself is a process as well as an end-state, a means to advance the long-term well being and security of Europe's citizens: a point often overlooked in the Europhoric zeal of the late 1980s, when the "1992 project" came almost to be regarded as desirable and necessary in itself.

The April 1951 Treaty of Paris, which created the European Coal and Steel Community (ECSC), aimed at integrating those two key strategic industries as a means of averting future Franco-German (hence European) conflict. Its transport provisions, mainly Art. 70 of Chapter IX (Title Three, economic and social provisions) called for "the application of such rates and conditions for the carriage of coal and steel as will afford comparable price conditions to comparably placed consumers" (Treaties 1979: 79–80). The treaty treated transport in a "negative" fashion, aiming mainly to eliminate obvious pricing discrepancies. This approach reflected a limited philosophical view that transport was a source of distortion in trade, rather than a potential facilitator of it (Lindberg and Scheingold 1970). Other commercial elements of transport were left untouched.

In contrast, the Treaty of Rome (1957) clearly regarded the transport sector as an integral component of the common market, in three ways. One is its importance as a vehicle for broader EEC policy advances. European integration can be pursued via any number of means, but the ones mainly emphasized have been the creation of the common market; the development of common institutions; and the creation of common policies—the last of which proving to be, over time, the most problematical (Hooghe and Keating 1994). Still, at the outset great hopes were placed on progress in the "lesser" policy areas, including transport, as a launching-pad for bolder advances in other fields, no doubt reflecting functionalist notions concerning gradualist integration. Such a strategy was also dictated by the fact that the "big issues" effectively had been downgraded as integrative vehicles because they were either (a) co-opted by other international organizations (e.g., monetary policy by the Bretton Woods institutions), or (b) ruled out for political reasons (e.g., defense and security cooperation after the French National Assembly's 1954 rejection of the European Defence Community).

A second general element is transport's prominence as one of only three common policy areas (Article 3) (the others being the common agricultural and common commercial policies). This parallel treatment of the transport and farm sectors is both striking and paradoxical, in light of the excessive subsequent attention given to agriculture, which attracted so much budgetary largesse and political rancor within the Community and in the GATT and WTO.[2] In comparative terms, transport was not only given more space (ten articles in all, as opposed to nine for the CAP provisions), but was considered, post-ECSC, as an even more likely focus of European agreement.

Such early optimism found expression in the ambitious (but abortive)

Bonnefous Plan for creating a separate European Transport Authority linked to the Council of Europe (Urwin 1995: 58–9). A reading of the treaty itself will indicate that the framers intended transport cooperation as no less crucial to a single economic market than the "four freedoms" (free movement of goods, services, capital and labor) themselves; and in the chapter on services, operative Article 61 deliberately omits transport because it is the subject of special and separate provisions.

The third major characteristic of the treaty's transport provisions was their relative vagueness, coupled with decidedly uneven modal treatment. Articles 74–84 include both common rules applicable to international transport and conditions under which nonresident carriers could operate services within member states (cabotage). The provisions are couched in the form of general principles aiming at an overall policy framework, in which negative discrimination against foreign carriers would be abolished, along with positive discrimination favoring domestic operators. The Council, acting on Commission initiative, was responsible for specifying and carrying out these objectives.

The original CTP provisions pertained mainly to freight transport, and were directly applicable to just three major modes, namely rail, road, and inland waterway. All were deemed crucial to the initial customs union, and with few exceptions had special relevance to the initial EEC6 (France, Germany, Italy, Belgium, the Netherlands, and Luxembourg). However, two other sectors, air transport (at that time still in its infancy as a mass passenger carrier) and the maritime sector (shipping), were marginalized in the sense that the Council, acting unanimously, was to determine the extent to which CTP provisions should apply to them (Article 84); this in reality was little more than an "agreement to agree" on common principles.

As regards inland transport, the treaty seemed to provide a double guarantee for action, since above and beyond the CTP framework itself, the transport sector (on one, Commission-based, interpretation of the treaty) was also subject to the more general treaty principles, such as the common commercial policy and in particular its rules on free and fair competition (Articles 85–90). Competition rules applied in three senses: the right of free establishment, the prohibition on competition-distorting state aid, and the prohibition on agreements impeding intra-EEC trade or allowing the abuse of a dominant position (Treaties 1979; Molle 1990: 344). This application of general (competition) principles to inland transport subsequently has been reinforced by Court of Justice rulings, and in a celebrated 1986 ruling (the *Nouvelle Frontières* case) it upheld their applicability to air transport as well; and the general trend has been to give a liberal, rather than restrictive, reading of these elements of the Rome Treaty.

Despite their seemingly unassailable place in the treaty, the transport provisions were marked by a number of gaps which subsequently helped justify inaction. Indeed one may reasonably interpret the "original intent" of the treaty as being a statement of principles rather than a plan of action. "Transport" itself was not defined, nor were its policy effects, direct and indirect, properly explicated. The treaty provided no operational guide-lines, actual or provisional deadlines, or provisions for punitive sanctions against states thwarting progress.

The EEC's institutional role was also left vague, with numerous "im-plied competences" but few actual ones. Still another problem was proce-dural; the reliance on Council unanimity on transport issues in both the first and second stages of the EEC's evolution gave each state an effective veto in the making of common rules and ensured that progress would be hindered by the chronic need for lowest-common-denominator consensus-building. It was only with the SEA that Council voting on some transport issues, as with a growing number of other policy areas, reverted to QMV (qualified majority voting) principles.

Yet another serious structural problem, mentioned briefly in the pre-ceding chapter, derived from the treaty's reference to "the distinctive fea-tures of transport" (Article 75). This seemingly innocuous wording seri-ously eroded the logic of its intended symbiosis between transport and wider common market principles; and it undercut the Commission's sub-sequent attempts to lay the groundwork for international cooperation leading to common policies. Article 75 was intended to account for long-standing public service transport obligations nationally, which the treaty itself cited as a legitimate reason for state subsidies; and in a 1969 regu-lation (no. 1191/69) the Council reinforced states' rights to guarantee public transport services in the inland modes. These acknowledged loop-holes were later, and amply, exploited by protectionist-minded govern-ments.

Still another problem, though hardly unique to transport, has been the chronic difficulty in translating legislation into action. States have a verita-ble armory of methods to limit or forestall the impact of Community legis-lation even short of deliberate noncompliance (e.g., delayed or partial en-actment of Community directives). Even formal ECJ rulings are hindered by the absence of an automatic sanctioning mechanism, making compli-ance a traditionally awkward Community issue.

A number of important reforms were proposed in the early years, in-cluding a formative Commission "memorandum on the general lines of a common transport policy" of April 1961, and its follow-up action plan a year later. The memorandum laid out three separate and detailed policy options, including (1) basing transport development on competition princi-ples and reliance on market forces; (2) organizing the market by harmoniz-ing modal operating conditions and putting them on an equal footing; and (3) establishing a genuine Community transport market. This document examined all aspects of the (still limited) CTP, which, it concluded, em-braced four main issues: supply of services, overall market organization, harmonization of competition principles, and transport infrastructure (Abbati 1987: 56–57).

A common policy would be based on five principles: (1) all users should be free to choose among means of transport, and suppliers to charge what they like; (2) all forms of transport should be treated equally, mainly in financial questions like taxation; (3) all forms of transport should pay their own way; (4) users should share the cost of maintaining and developing transport infrastructure; and (5) new transport investments should be coordinated.

To these ends the Commission proposed a system of "forked tariffs," with upper and lower limits designed to prevent both cutthroat competition and exploitation of monopoly positions (Lindberg and Scheingold 1970: 164). Despite its thoroughness, this Commission initiative was never acted upon by the Council of Ministers, and indeed it was opposed by the Dutch, whose efficient transport industry was seemingly best positioned to take advantage of integrated transport markets. Thus the Commission proposals languished as a set of virtually nonoperational guidelines. In particular, the third point (regarding modal coverage of own costs) has only recently been taken up again.

In this atmosphere, progress on transport questions tended to be sporadic, piecemeal, and generally limited to noncontroversial technical harmonization (such as emissions standards and axle sizes), and social concerns (e.g., lorry drivers' hours). It would be inaccurate, however, to assert that the member states were united in across-the-board opposition to common action. In 1962 the Council created a procedure for examining and consulting on any laws or provisions adopted at state level which were "liable to interfere substantially with the implementation of the common transport policy" (Abbati 1987: 58). Though nonbinding, this procedure did enhance the sharing of information between states and Brussels, as well as between the Commission and Council, and was later expanded in different directions, including infrastructure and shipping.

Similarly, in May 1965 the Council agreed on harmonizing certain provisions affecting competition in the three inland modes, particularly in terms of social legislation, taxation, and state aids (Moussis 1996: 388). This step later had implications both for railway management and for harmonization of commercial access to road networks. Progress was temporarily thwarted by the 1965 crisis resulting from France's Council walkout, alleging an erosion of national sovereignty, and the subsequent reinforcement, via the "Luxembourg compromise," of the national veto over Council (hence effectively, EEC) action in all fields. One key issue—access of European road hauliers to other EEC markets—was left hanging, although a new initiative to apply commercial principles to the inland sectors was underway by 1967.

The vivid contrast between early farm (CAP) guidelines and spending increases, and lagging progress in transport, drew attention from analysts. Lindberg and Scheingold (1970) concluded that CAP progress was facilitated by the early creation of a powerful coalition for change ("policy community" in the contemporary lexicon), in which one powerful and self-interested state (France), with a clearcut domestic agenda of farm supports, guided a policy acquiesced in by the other states because because none perceived it as inimical to its basic interests.[3] The CAP also benefited from an indicative treaty timetable and somewhat greater overall specificity.

The CTP, however, languished because no forceful, self-interested advocate of common rules emerged (apart from the Dutch, who at any rate had expended most of their political capital in the CAP debate). Meanwhile, other EEC governments were divided by entrenched differences over transport regulation, ownership, and financing. The differences were at two levels: between governments, at loggerheads due to what William Wallace calls a "structural and geographical block" (1994: 62–63) between the Germans and the French, reinforced by a common interest in keeping strong national control over vital transport sectors (Germany in the rail industry; France over national road licensing and border controls). Second, major modal interests were scarcely motivated to work for the abolition of a policy environment which sheltered them from exposure to outside competition.

The absence of leadership—whether by a single state, industrial sector or the Commission itself—thus prevented the emergence of a winning coalition and hindered the sorts of processes (side-payments, log-rolling, and positive feedback) typically associated with a dynamic policy process. In short, there quickly arose a fundamental gap between stronger status quo interests in state protection and separation of modal carriers, and the broader but weaker economic concerns of the Community as a whole which argued for liberal reform based on equal treatment and nondiscrimination and intermodality.

THE TRANSPORT POLICY CONSTELLATION

Progress on the CTP has been complicated by the transport industry's heterogeneous nature, which more properly should be regarded as separate market and policy environments. The fragmentation of organized interests, even at the national level, has also reflected these different modal characteristics and priorities. The transport policy network includes numerous regulatory and advisory bodies at different levels (regional, local, national, international), as well as private industrial and separate modal interests, all of which retain considerable influence over the policy process as well as a direct stake in its outcome. The multiplicity of interested actors, in turn, increases the interlinkages and connections between and across the different players in the process. At the national level, this often refers to "the relationship between the state and organized interests" (Collins and Louloudis 1995: 95). But at the international level the situation is much more complicated, requiring as it does cooperation between self-interested states as well as a panoply of international bodies.

The organizational problems of transport are compounded by the involvement of separate institutions, often with similar tasks, overlapping memberships and limited mandates. Despite its prominence, the EU is far from the only international organization with a hand in European transport questions (Abbati 1987). Indeed, many initially argued that the EEC was a wholly inappropriate forum in which to attempt common policies, and that the CTP amounted to a case of institutional overreach by a six-member grouping without any evident claim to being a natural market. This situation in turn strengthened the hand of other international bodies, many predating the EEC, vying for a say in European transport governance. These bodies are of two types: (1) general organizations with a transport interest, and (2) modal-based transport authorities with technical regulatory powers.

Among the first category, the United Nations has a hand in transport issues via its Economic Commission for Europe (ECE), the most inclusive of the European-based bodies, involving all the European members of the UN, as well as the U.S. and Switzerland, even though the latter is a UN nonmember.[4] The ECE holds institutional ties with the EU, specifically the Commission, through Article 229 of the Rome Treaty (Treaties 1979). Periodically the ECE has succeeded in pushing through technical reforms, such as speeding up customs formalities in rail transit and in the standardization of codes; it also advocated early EC network development in motorway and rapid rail systems. Despite this, the ECE has no decision-making powers on transport (or other) questions. Another body, the European Conference of Ministers of Transport (ECMT) has a similar intergovernmental, non-decision-making role predating the EEC itself, having been established in 1953. Though limited in its functions, it has played a useful role via quality published reports and suggestions for infrastructure and operational improvements, especially in the rail sector.

A third, still older body is the Coal and Steel Community (ECSC), dating from 1951, though its specialized nature and limited charge excluded it from involvement in commercial transport questions. The independent powers of the ECSC's High Authority were sectorally narrow, extending only to two industries, and even these powers were not translated to the European Commission in the Rome Treaty (Abbati 1987: 29). The ECSC did play a little-noticed role in financing early French TGV rail development and the extension of TGV Atlantique services westward from Paris. Even so, the termination of its fifty-year mandate in 2002 ensures its peripherality in future transport issues.

As for the second category, there are numerous modal-specific international bodies. In inland waterways, the Convention on the Canalization of the Moselle (dating from 1956), and the much older Central Commission for the Navigation of the Rhine (CCR), established in 1868, have both indicated the value of regime formation for European waterways (Abbati 1987: 23–24). The Community of European Railways (CER) acts as an advocate for that industry, along with the broader International Union of Railways (UIR). In the air sector, the International Civil Aviation Organization (ICAO) plays a multilateral regulatory role, while a separate grouping (the International Air Transport Authority, or IATA) pursues an industry agenda. The International Maritime Organization (IMO), a specialized UN agency, plays a role in shipping similar to the ICAO in air policy—both sectors (air and shipping) thus defying narrowly European solutions to broader issues (Schiavone 1983).

However, given the CTP's pride of place in the Rome Treaty, the EU remains the most important international body dealing with European transport questions, and the only one claiming broader, supranational powers. But the Community itself has been splintered organizationally. Its overall treatment of transport, charitably describable as inconsistent, results from differences in organizational interests, national approaches, and other elements negatively impinging on attempts to forge common ground. Worse, these differences intensified over time, contrary to expectations aroused by theoretical discussions of "spillover" and the benefits of the "habit of cooperation" leading to a convergence of expectations and attitudes.

Transport is not, of course, the only policy area that suffered lack of movement in the 1960s and 1970s due to the unanimity principle (and its reinforcement of tensions between Council and Commission), but the politics of transport were complicated further by a wide variation in national attitudes even among the original EEC6. Important countries remained outside the Community; two centrally located nonmembers, Switzerland and Austria, left EEC territory badly truncated; and the seven original members of the European Free Trade Association (EFTA), a looser free-trade organization led at the time by Britain, were virtually untouched by EEC transport decisions (at least prior to the pathbreaking European Economic Area (EEA) agreement of 1993), as was the whole of eastern Europe.

The 1973 enlargement (bringing in Britain, Ireland and Denmark), and those of 1981 (Greece) and 1986 (Spain and Portugal) had a mixed effect on EC transport governance. While additional members attenuated the structural problem of the EEC's deficiency as a natural transport market, they complicated matters in at least four different respects. One was the *spatial problem* of adding new, noncontiguous territories. Britain and Ireland were island polities for which continental access was a major trade concern; Denmark's scattered territories, separated by water, raised special problems; and Greece's remoteness from the European core required external transit agreements with Yugoslavia, its main land link to Europe (not least because of Yugoslavia's separate border restrictions as a non-democracy, even before its breakup into civil war). And Spain and Portugal faced problems of remoteness, the Pyrenees mountain barrier, and a wider rail gauge. The fourth (1995) expansion, bringing in Finland, Sweden, and Austria, increased EU territory by 40 percent, but its population by under 5 percent.

Secondly, the successive enlargements exacerbated state *differences in transport philosophy*. Britain's entry in particular strongly reinforced the liberalists' hand, and even during the Labour-led governments of the 1970s Britain's economic approach to transport tended to be more market-oriented than were those of its continental counterparts. An Anglo-Dutch transport alliance of sorts began to emerge in the 1980s,[5] following in the footsteps of the binational oil giant Royal Dutch-Shell. Britain's philosophical differences with other European states became political ones following Thatcher's election victory in 1979; and they highlighted modal differences, in particular Britain's strong prioritizing of the road sector, in contrast to tangible efforts to maintain a viable rail alternative on the continent.

The third change, ushered in by the two Mediterranean enlargements, involved *diverging levels of development*, reflected in deficiencies in the new members' transport infrastructures. The need to redress these deficiencies resulted in the huge new thrust in the 1980s, begun with the Integrated Mediterranean Programs, toward regional spending, which as indicated in Chapter 1 (and 7), were targeted increasingly at transport projects and programs. And fourth, the enlargements *shifted states' modal concerns*, highlighting the two areas shunted aside from the initial CTP, namely shipping (an especially crucial Greek concern) and air transport (Lodge 1989: 91).

THE 1980s: A POLICY OF MOVEMENT

Formative Policy Influences

Just as factors were ranged decisively against transport reform in the EEC's early years, the collective calculus began shifting as a result of policy and institutional as well as technical factors, and due to national as well as international developments. Two general points stand out in this shift in policy priorities. One is the sheer contrast between the passivity of previous years and the activism increasingly evident from the mid-1980s. The second is the broad sweep of policy issues to which this newfound activism was directed, encompassing liberalization initiatives in all the major operational modes (air, shipping, road, and, somewhat later, rail) as well as overall infrastructure planning. These initiatives had multiple origins including the following:

(1) *Institutional.* Many observers have laid the lack of CTP progress squarely at the door of the Council of Ministers and therefore of obstructionist national governments; others (e.g. Abbati 1987: 44) are somewhat more circumspect in blaming the general (read loose) institutional framework of the EU. In earlier years, the Commission itself came under sharp criticism for failing to follow up on its initiatives or to provide general leadership (Lindberg and Scheingold 1970). Yet eventually if paradoxically, the endless deadlock between a reform-minded but timid Commission and a status quo-oriented Ministerial Council enabled broad reform.

One quite unintended consequence of the "leadership deficit" was to elevate the significance of three other organs normally peripheral to EC policymaking. One was the European Parliament (EP), relegated early on (as the Assembly) to mere consultative status. Despite this, the EP has lobbied effectively for CTP progress, both collectively and via its transport committee, and has rarely hesitated to goad other organs into action. It has also engaged in important technical and preparatory work; further, its inability to control the process created possibilities of taking a longer-term view and developing areas of expertise that worked to its advantage in an increasingly complicated policy sector.

One source has summarized the EP's overall role in transport questions as "extremely good" (Abbati 1987: 45). Transport was one issue in which the EP had a direct stake in progress, in light of its expensive, time-consuming and (many have argued) wastefully peripatetic nature, dividing its work between Brussels, where most MEPs reside and where most committee work gets done, Luxembourg, where its secretariat is located, and Strasbourg (France), where it meets monthly in plenary session. Transport is an immediate problem for the EP as it is for no other institution. Furthermore, the Maastricht provisions for co-decision require the EP's input in future transport legislation.

A second interested body is the Committee of Permanent Representatives (COREPER), which carved out a niche for itself in filtering Commission recommendations and making them palatable for the Ministerial Councils. In transport, the failure of ministers even to meet regularly shifted much of the preparatory and deliberative work onto COREPER, which enhanced its expertise and agenda-shaping capabilities. Third, the advisory Economic and Social Committee (ESC) has been consulted frequently on transport questions by the Commission prior to its tabling formal proposals. Occasionally the ESC has made its presence awkwardly felt, as in a 1990 report sharply criticizing the Commission for failing to consider the wider European consequences of Channel Tunnel development (EC 1990).

Even so, the ESC's long-term usefulness in the EU's institutional galaxy is being increasingly challenged.

Another institutional push came from the previously low-key but newly galvanized Directorate-General for Transport (DG VII) under the energetic leadership of the Belgian Socialist Commissioner, Karel Van Miert. His attention was prodded by a growing consensus among informed outsiders and industry leaders that lack of progress in common transport policymaking was becoming a drag on progress toward the 1992 Single Market project, and even a growing threat to its ultimate success. These were among the conclusions of an independent advisory group, the "Group Transport 2000 Plus," which he convened in 1989 (Transport 1990). DG VII initiatives coincided with activism by the competition directorate in challenging monopolistic practices, and by the environment directorate in responding to Green political pressures.

Finally, transport reform emerged as an important focus of a quasi-institutional body from the 1980s, the European Round Table of Industrialists (ERT). Spurred by the 1973 oil shock and the subsequent recession, European business leaders began calling for a more activist European regulatory dimension for industry and for transport infrastructure upgrading. Their initial publication, *Missing Links* (1984), called for more European infrastructure spending, and the ERT effort itself was pushed by an auto executive (Pehr Gyllenhammar of Volvo). Later, in March 1994, the ERT established a European Center for Infrastructure Studies, a nonprofit think tank, in Rotterdam (Cowles 1995).

(2) *Legal developments.* Arguably the most profound institution-generated shift in CTP priorities has been the pivotal involvement of yet another, namely the European Court of Justice (ECJ), the EU's legal body.[6] Though not particularly well positioned for judicial activism, the ECJ waded into the transport debate with two key transport rulings at the time of the first enlargement and another a decade later, in both events stimulating new movement. In case 167/73 it held that the general treaty provisions (taxation, right of establishment, free movement, aid policy, competition), even if left out of Title IV, were applicable to the transport sector since no genuine CTP existed. A year later (April 1974) it ruled that these general rules also applied to the maritime and air sectors. And as Burley and Mattli (1993) have argued, ECJ activism reflects its wider, unexpectedly strong impact on political integration via its ability to transform legal issues into political questions.

No doubt the most important ECJ ruling came in 1985 (re case 13/83), following a legal action under Article 175 brought by the European Parliament with Commission support against the Council, alleging systematic failure (citing at least sixteen specific instances) to introduce common policies or even to lay down the framework for creating them. The court's limited ruling favored the plaintiffs, which due to its binding force (and nonappealable procedures) thereby required subsequent Council action to liberalize transport services and introduce rights for nonresident operators.

Though the ruling's scope was limited by the specifics of the case and by the court's acknowledgment of insufficiencies in the treaty itself, it was unprecedented as an interinstitutional legal action, and its outcome galvanized CTP promoters. It also indirectly, along with two isoglucose rulings in the late 1970s, tangibly raised the profile and, eventually, the political clout of the EP (Pinder 1991: 33). The 1985 transport ruling, along with the earlier *Cassis de Dijon* ruling (case 120/78) regarding EC-wide mutual recognition of national regulations and standards, represented crucial steps toward wider application of single market principles. Even so, the ECJ can never be a true advocate of policy activism beyond that specified in the treaties, as shown in its annulment of the earlier Eurovignette ruling (directive 93/89/EC), laying down common rules for taxes and road haulage charges (CEC 1996b: 58).

(3) *Movement toward the Single Market.* France's presidency of the European Council in early 1984, culminating in the Fontainebleau summit, is frequently cited as a breakthrough for the European idea following years of budgetary wrangles, British obstructionism and overall lack of direction. Subsequent progress toward the Single Market (and the Anglo-French symbolism of the Cockfield-Delors White Paper) fed into the transport debate, as did resolution of the vexing question of Britain's budgetary contribution. Bilaterally it paved the way for the landmark Franco-British agreement (November 1984) to build a cross-Channel fixed link. The Commission's 1985 White Paper on Completing the Single Market (CEC 1985) cited the "necessity of making rapid progress in this [transport] area" (item 108), as freer movement would have major economic and trade consequences.

Accordingly, the White Paper specified the need for Council action with varying deadlines, including freedom of sea transport (end 1986); greater freedom of air services (1987); phasing out of quantitative restrictions (quotas) and measures on cabotage (the operation of nonresident carriers within another state) by 1988; freedom of services in road passenger traffic (1989); and freedom of services, including cabotage, in inland waterways (1989). Though these putative deadlines became starting rather than ending-points, the very act of setting them as targets produced its own momentum, as did the December 1992 deadline for the Single Act, and those regarding the CAP in the 1960s.

Even so, the White Paper's proposed measures were uneven; curiously, they totally excluded rail from consideration (a vivid indication of the tight grip of governments in that sector), as well as other related issue areas such as state aid policy, infrastructure planning and investment, and harmonization (Butler 1986). The Commission's clear emphasis in the 1980s, bolstered by the 1985 ECJ ruling, was on gradual liberalization of services;

the 1987 Communities Bulletin (BEC 1/1987) spoke modestly of "efforts to secure gradual application of the principle of freedom of services and elimination of distortions in competition." It was not until the early 1990s, under the trans-European networks initiatives, that the old concept of harmonization was resurrected as a Community priority, this time with ambitious spending plans to back up planning efforts.

Single Market progress was also broadly relevant to intra-EC institutional relationships, including state-EU relations, since the SEA expanded QMV principles into an increasing array of policy areas. Commission President Delors stated in 1988 that within a few years, 80 percent of all legislation would originate in Brussels—a claim which attracted much criticism even as it was proved broadly accurate. By allowing state majorities to determine Council (hence EC) policy, the EC paved the way for much more rapid progress across the board: not only via elimination of states' veto in internal market questions but secondly by enhancing the positions of smaller, reformist-minded governments holding disproportionate power in the weighted QMV system. Nonetheless most states continued to oppose rapid liberalization and outright privatization. At least the Single Act created a more positive policy climate, allowing old deficiencies to be addressed in new ways.

(4) *External pressures.* Slow EC progress in tackling inefficient transport practices has given outside states an unintended catalytic role in introducing far-reaching reform. Button and Pitfield (1991) have emphasized that European transport deregulation has been part of a much wider, indeed global trend in which the EU has been compelled to follow suit. Indeed Zacher (1996) argues that transport (and communications) deregulation initially began in the far East, with only subsequent policy effect in the U.S. and (still later) in Europe. U.S. airlines deregulation in the late 1970s led to a major industry shakeup, including bankruptcies of traditional market leaders (Pan Am, TWA, and Eastern), and to the rearrangement of traditional flight patterns to the now-common hub-and-spoke system, which Delta subsequently attempted to introduce in its European services (Staniland 1995). Airline subsidies entered into the GATT discourse and also affected bilateral transatlantic relations.

Other, less noticed changes late in the Carter administration involved both the rail sector (via the Railroad Transportation Policy Act and the Staggers Rail Act) and roads (via the Motor Carrier Act, all in 1980) (Kammerer 1990: 31–32). Cross-Atlantic sharing of market philosophies between Reagan's America and Thatcher's Britain also ensured that the more purist American interpretation of state-market relations found an outlet directly into the EC debate. By the late 1980s, further pressures from non-EC states came in the form of pioneering attempts to break up national rail monopolies, boosted by denationalization trends as far away as the Antipodes. In Europe, partial rail liberalization including operator franchising was pioneered by Sweden and by other EFTA states (e.g. Austria and Switzerland) connected to the EC grid.

(5) *Developments at national level.* The main factor here was rapid French progress in translating high-speed rail technologies, developed initially in the 1960s, to the operational phase. Between 1981 and 1983 the French opened the breakthrough Paris-Lyon *train à grand vitesse* (TGV) sud-est line, which immediately leapt into profitability despite its inordinately high development costs. The EC itself, pressured by rail bodies like the UIR, began to capitalize on TGV's unexpected popular success by promoting rapid rail as a Europe-wide means of tackling problems of air and motorway overcrowding. The renewed CTP activity in the mid-1980s was a result, as much as a cause, of these and other technological breakthroughs, funded from national budgets and not from EC coffers.

Similarly, the binational Channel Tunnel endeavor galvanized EC thinking in at least four senses. First, it illustrated the increasingly cross-border needs of transport infrastructure if a seamless network were to be realized. Second, its macro-economic and developmental effects were potentially great, even in areas far removed from the fixed link itself, a point painstakingly brought home in a lengthy study commissioned by DG XVI, the Commission's Regional Directorate, on the effects of Chunnel development (The Regional 1992). Third, the project's success hinged on private-sector funding, as governmental underwriting was ruled out in the 1986 Chunnel Treaty itself; at the time this represented genuinely new thinking in a sector (infrastructure) which traditionally relied on national governments and public purses. And fourth, the Chunnel's inherently multimodal nature, connecting both rail and motorway systems between the two countries, indicated the growing need to transcend single-mode planning for Europe's transport needs.

THE COMMON TRANSPORT POLICY: NEW DIRECTIONS

Following publication of the White Paper, EC Transport Ministers agreed (November 1985) on the necessity for (a) a free transport market without quantitative restrictions, and (b) liberalization aimed at ending distortions in competition, both by 1992. In 1986 the Commission published the first of a series of CTP-related reports, namely a medium-term transport infrastructure program encompassing, in contrast to earlier efforts, all the transport sectors (CEC 1986a). This led, in 1988, to a far reaching Action Program in the sphere of transport, including intercity links and efforts to integrate the European periphery; though the following year (CEC 1989a) the Commission scaled down this ambitious proposal in order to concentrate its efforts. The Commission set out seven priority projects, which it intended to designate as projects of European interest:

1. The high-speed rail link Paris-London-Brussels-Amsterdam-Köln (PBKAL network);
2. The high-speed rail link Lisbon-Seville-Madrid-Barcelona-Lyon;
3. Modernization of the Alpine transit axis (the Brenner route);
4. Improvement of the European air traffic control system;
5. Modernization of the British road axis toward Ireland (the A5/A55 north Wales coast road);
6. Completion of the Scanlink;
7. Reinforcement of land links in Greece.

These proposals led to an important Council regulation establishing an Action Program designed to complete the Single Market in the sphere of transport (CE 1990b). Herein was formally established the principle of "Declaration of European Interest," opening the door to direct EU funding for projects considered by the Commission to have EU-wide importance.[7] The Council approved a slightly altered list of major projects; though it left out the air traffic control problem (point 4 above), it included two other elements, namely (a) contributions to the combined transport network of Community interest, and (b) trans-Pyrenean road links (Somport).

The Commission's publication of a wide ranging communication on the future development of the Common Transport Policy (CEC 1993a) represented a major step toward defining overall CTP goals, and further underscored its own role in establishing priorities.[8] This newly activist stance, emboldened by the post-1989 upsurge of optimism in Europe, included a wide range of previously neglected policy issues warranting closer attention: the transport of dangerous goods; health, safety, job security, and other social concerns; and an explicitly external dimension via its so-called "global approach." The Commission regarded the year 1992 as

> An important turning point in the evolution of the CTP, from a policy which has aimed essentially at the completion of the internal market through the elimination of artificial regulatory barriers . . . towards a more comprehensive policy designed to ensure the proper functioning of the Community's transport systems, on the basis of an internal market in which any remaining restrictions or distortions should be eliminated as rapidly as possible, while taking into account the new challenges likely to confront transport policy in the post-1992 period. (CEC 1993a: 5)

Even discounting the rhetorical elements and the use of more dynamic language (e.g., emphasis on transport coordination rather than mere cooperation), the Commission clearly had a more comprehensive grasp of the multiplicity of issues involved and no lack of ideas about how to tackle them. Its approach was set out in a five-step proposed CTP action program: (1) development and integration of Community transport systems based on the internal market;[9] (2) safety; (3) environmental protection; (4)

Table 2.1
Seven Pillars of the Common Transport Policy

A. *Quality Improvement*
   1. Systems development (integration of modes; new technologies; infrastructure; public transport; competition)
   2. Environment (lessening transport's impact; reconciling demand for mobility with environmental sensitivity; modal shift toward "greener" modes)
   3. Safety (harmonization of rules; overall improvement; better monitoring; maritime improvements; air control; equal accessibility)

B. *Single Market*
   4. Market access and structure (enforcement of state aid rules; improving maritime competitiveness; liberalization in other areas; structural adaptation; elimination of overcapacity)
   5. Costs, charges and pricing (harmonization of charging systems within modes; reducing differences between modes)
   6. Social dimension (harmonization of safety and health conditions; better living and working conditions; working time regimes; better accessibility for the handicapped)

C. *External Dimension*
   7. (Ending of bilateralism vis-à-vis third countries; identification of bases for common action; strengthening mandates with third countries and with international organizations)

Source: CEC 1995b.

a social dimension; (5) external relations. Inherent in the discussion was a shift away from strict separation of modes to one addressing cross-modal concerns.

In late 1995 the Commission adopted a CTP policy agenda for 1995–2000, together with a designated action program (CEC 1995b). The document's seven different elements are set out in Table 2.1, under three headings: improvement of quality via integrated systems; maximizing efficiency of the Single Market; and broadening the external dimension of the CTP. The program reiterated the many cross-policy issues such as environmental and social policy. It also appeared to break new ground by emphasizing measures to shift traffic away from roads; promoting universal access to better public transport via a "Citizens Network"; promoting single Community solutions vis-à-vis third countries; and harmonizing charging systems both across and within modes. This last (pricing) issue was addressed in detail in a 1996 green paper (CEC 1996b), which also specified the need for Community action in transport in four circumstances: cross-border externalities; effects on the internal market; possible economies of scale; and policy spillovers (p. 56).

The overall European transport policy context has entered into a new phase as a result of greater Community assertiveness. CTP development was long hampered by two elements: lack of long-term strategic vision, and lack of political will, either to fulfill the initial CTP provisions or to provide an alternative vision and see it through. Strategic vision was long hampered by the complexity of the issues themselves, competing modal interests, and the vagueness of the very guidelines intended to provide an overarching policy thrust. These problems were complicated politically by governments' determination to control transport policy themselves, and they were relatively free to do so in the absence of a forceful Commission or individual state promoter of an EC dimension.

To a marked degree, both problems have been addressed, yet neither has been overcome. The outline of a strategic plan seems to be emerging (1992, 1995), and the Commission itself is much more active in shaping CTP guidelines by asserting its existing investigatory and regulatory powers and pressing for additional negotiating authority. In the process the CTP, not long ago characterized by passivity only occasionally interrupted by incrementalist advances (Lodge 1989: 91) has emerged, belatedly, as a substantive and high-visibility policy area.

Unresolved Problems for the EU

Despite the EU's intention to remain ahead of the curve in the transport debate, its efforts to coordinate future direction remain in the realm of ambition as much as reality, and it faces numerous unresolved concerns that threaten to make madness out of the incipient method. The very newness of Commission activism is reason enough to maintain a healthy skepticism about the potential pace and depth of change, and thus the "sustainability" of its own efforts. Some of the major problems include:

1. *EU non-universality.* As an international agreement, the Rome Treaty and its SEA and Maastricht revisions are nonbinding on outside states. Extraterritorial enforcement of transport rules remains highly problematic, especially in shipping (Chapter 6), and Europe's vigorous condemnation of American efforts, via Helms-Burton legislation, to impose sanctions against third countries doing business with selected countries (Cuba, Iran, Libya) illustrates the great problems of coordinating like-minded international efforts. Even within Europe, EU nonmembers hinder common policymaking, though the problems were ameliorated by the 1993 EEA agreement extending Single Market principles to the EFTA states. But Swiss voters' rejection in December 1992 of the EEA agreement, and with it full EU membership for the foreseeable future, complicated Swissair's efforts to find an EU-based partner and had major transport implications regarding north-south, trans-alpine traffic. Since then the Swiss have taken exception to EU demands for road access, both by restricting lorry traffic and by mandating greater use of piggy-back rail systems (see Chapter 7).

Moreover the uncertainty over which east European states will join the EU, and when, has further challenged EU attempts to develop a comprehensive European infrastructure policy. An interesting development in this context was the agreement by four non-EU states (Albania, Bulgaria, Turkey, and the Former Yugoslav Republic of Macedonia [FYROM]) to develop an alternative major highway system, the East-West Axis, to attract road traffic between the Adriatic (via the Albanian port of Durres) and both the Black Sea (via a trunk line to the Bulgarian port of Varna) and the Middle East via Istanbul. This agreement has been alternatively dismissed by Greek officials as a "para-Egnatia" and feared by them as a challenge to EU sub-regional development in the Balkans, since the 660 km Egnatia road project across northern Greece to the Bulgarian and Turkish borders, is a priority European infrastructure project.[10] U.S. interest, post-Dayton, in helping finance this new system via its Southeast Europe Cooperative Initiative is an additional concern, although Albania's implosion in early 1997 put the project on hold indefinitely.

Cooperation among these non-EU countries is now extending to rail and air links as well, for example with the late 1995 agreement to build a direct rail link between Sofia and Skopje, FYROM's capital. The EU has stepped up efforts to promote infrastructure development in the east, for example by its recent promotion of an ambitious road link between the Baltic (Helsinki) and the Mediterranean (Alexandroupolis).[11] Even so, the problems of coordinating such various pan-European efforts will be Herculean, particularly if the CCEE's EU entry is delayed much beyond 2000.

2. *Diversity of EU decisionmaking procedures.* Commission efforts to centralize coordination of transport policy in its DG VII continue to be hindered by the complexity of EU policymaking channels. Ironically, the same pressures that initially involved other EU organs (especially the Court and Parliament) have also emerged as potentially complicating factors in future reform efforts. The Maastricht Treaty formalized this diversity of involvement in two additional ways, one minor and one major. The minor change was creating the Committee of the Regions, with its required (if only advisory) input. The major change is the introduction of co-decision procedures which directly involve the European Parliament in transport-related decisions, including those on structural questions. Given the EP's longstanding reformist impulses, this change is important for three reasons.

First, it makes EP input a regular, consistent, and across-the-board presence, as opposed to its ad hoc involvement of previous years. Second, it likely will slow rather than facilitate passage of new legislation, which must now follow a lengthier process involving formal parliamentary readings, debates, and votes. Third, it may well affect intra-EU political dynamics. Traditional divisions between "European" organs (EP and Commission) and the national representation of the Ministerial Councils, which tended to link Parliament and Commission in a natural alliance, may be evolving toward greater confrontation between a Parliament pushing for faster change than the more cautious Commission desires. This greater diversity of the EU policymaking matrix (see also point 3 below) was reinforced by a European Court ruling, in regard to the GATT Uruguay Round agreement, that the Commission must share responsibility with member states in certain policy areas with trade implications, including transport (FT, 10 Dec. 1994: 2).

3. *Intra-Commission rivalries.* The consensus-oriented nature of the College of [currently 20] Commissioners masks the often intense rivalries between the different directorates-general that form the Commission bureaucracy. Peterson (1995: 74) aptly notes that the Commission is "more a political system in itself than a single-minded actor." Even with the growing importance of DG VII (Transport), which now also has primary responsibility for trans-European networks, the transport-related activities of other directorates—reflecting, institutionally, the policy overlaps discussed in Chapter 1—have increased the scope for differences in priorities and duplication of efforts. For instance, DG XII (Science and Research) increasingly has a hand in development of new transport-related technologies, while the Maastricht-based requirement for environmental scrutiny of new projects gives DG XI (Environment) a direct transport role as well.[12] This requirement effectively hinders a basic DG VII aim, namely a seamless transport network, since it requires separate consideration of individual projects.

Further, the watchdog efforts of the Competition directorate (DG IV) to prevent oligopolistic mergers often conflict with efforts to promote cross-border activity in transport markets and establish a stronger EU presence in the sector. On the question of continued subsidies for state-run airlines, DGs IV and VII have clashed publicly (e.g. over Spanish aid to Iberia in 1994). Indeed in its efforts to establish negotiating authority for European air policy, the Commission has cited the Common Commercial Policy rather than the CTP provisions; and the Commission's decision to investigate the mooted American Airlines-British Airways partnership was generally regarded as a competition rather than a transport initiative, even though it was presented as a joint effort.

The Regional directorate (DG XVI) has also been increasingly involved in transport questions. The establishment of the Cohesion Fund directly links transport infrastructure and regional development in the four recipient states (which prior regional initiatives, such as the ERDF, had left indirect). Still other public bodies associated with regional development have a more or less direct hand in transport questions, notably the European Bank for Reconstruction and Development (EBRD) and the European Investment Bank (EIB). Future progress in transport networks (see Chapter 7) hinges on a careful balancing act by the Commission (with its own diverse priorities) and a growing range of other actors.

4. *The historical legacy.* EU efforts to promote coordination of transport systems will continue to be hindered by national-based priorities. One insidious legacy of the CTP's long neglect is the deep entrenchment of prevailing attitudes and practices that have reinforced states' hesitancy to cede the Commission more regulatory authority. In return, the Commission is compelled to fight a continual rearguard action to maintain its hard-won authority.

There is in fact a double-barreled yoke on progress in the form of twin, long-held national commitments to transport systems as (a) instruments of social distribution and not merely as determinants of economic efficiency, and (b) elements of national security, in which relinquishing control over national transport services is often regarded as tantamount to ceding sovereignty itself. The post-Maastricht debate has demonstrated the potential power of national recidivism; patterns are reversible, and transport may well be as vulnerable to backsliding as any policy area. Attention to subsidiarity issues further hinders harmonization efforts. A recent ECMT report ("Poor Response" 1995) highlighted these problems and lamented the deficient monitoring of international traffic flows and the lack of a multimodal database.

Two developments in the first half of 1996 neatly encapsulated the halfway status of transport in the EU policymaking milieu. In May, the Council finally agreed to Transport Commissioner Kinnock's longstanding demand that the Commission be granted authority to conduct air negotiations with outside parties. The following month, however, the European Council at Florence refused to support another Commission transport initiative, namely Jacques Santer's proposal to shift unspent budgetary funds (ecu 1.2 bn) to infrastructure development to help fight unemployment. If not for recent Commission efforts to forge an overarching CTP outline, the perception might well obtain that the EU has tied itself up in knots on transport issues.

Despite continuing national differences and needs, recent years nonetheless have brought about an increasing awareness of similar, pan-European pressures of traffic overcrowding, aging infrastructures, pollution, and longterm debt in national transport industries, which was becoming a sectoral drag on national budgets and, even further afield, a problem for EMU itself. Due to these worsening problems, justifications for Community action increasingly became demands for reform. While attempts at creating an overarching reformist policy community still fight a stiff headwind, a "negative" agreement informed by a wide perception of crisis, and belief in the usefulness of coordinated efforts to counter it, was growing.

In brief summary, the main substantive changes in the EU's approach to transport issues have been as follows: (1) a shift from a reactive to a proactive approach, reflecting the growing strategic role of transport; (2) explicit linkage of transport with other sectoral policy areas in addition to traditional Single Market concerns; (3) enlargement of the CTP's scope to include air and shipping policy along with the inland modes; (4) application of broader treaty (e.g., commercial) principles to the transport sector; (5) new emphasis on structural development in conjunction with liberalization in services; (6) EU financial commitments for transport-related spending in research, infrastructure, feasibility studies, and the like; (7) attempts to bridge the modal divides with a more holistic, multimodal and environment-friendly approach; and (8) attempts to assert EU authority in conducting Europe's external transport relations.

NOTES

1. Despite 1970s growing pains associated with two oil shocks and a 50 percent rise in membership, the EEC initiated new regional policies, the European Monetary System, and direct Parliamentary elections. In contrast, the highly touted Single Market initiative involved policy (and even institutional) changes, particularly the four freedoms already enunciated in the Rome Treaty.

2. The CAP quickly emerged as the main line item in the EEC budget, attracting at one time close to two-thirds of appropriations. Even after the 1980s reforms and attention to inefficiency and outright fraud (reputedly over 10 percent of expenditures), the CAP still accounted, as of 1995, for 52.2 percent of all EU spending (CEC 1995d).

3. The EEC is often presented as a direct Franco-German trade-off: agricultural programs to mollify French concerns in return for lowering industrial tariffs, a key German aim. William Wallace (1994: 62), however, asserts that it was Dutch pressure to open German markets that initially put agriculture on the agenda, which only later emerged as a Franco-Dutch coalition.

4. Switzerland, the only state voluntarily to forswear UN membership, did become a party to the Statute of the International Court of Justice (ICJ) in 1947 and accepts its compulsory jurisdiction clause. In a crucial 1986 referendum, a large majority (75 percent) of the Swiss public rejected a government-sponsored motion to accede to the UN Charter.

5. Britain and the Netherlands first broke the mold of state control of air markets with their pathbreaking bilateral air agreement of 1984. More recently, P&O and Nedlloyd have combined their container shipping operations. The two states also share similar policy approaches in, for example, worker-generated pension schemes.

6. The Luxembourg-based ECJ is to be distinguished from the European Court of Human Rights at The Hague, which despite a prominent international profile has no direct EU role.

7. Funding for pan-European projects was however limited to 25 percent of actual costs or up to 50 percent for feasibility studies, with the rest from other sources (private industry, governments, regional authorities).

8. For example, the 1993 report held that, as for both the internal market and third country relations (areas of "exclusive power"), the Community "is obliged to realize the objectives assigned to it." Moreover, even in areas of "shared power"

(such as cohesion and environmental issues), "the [Commission's] political commitment to Community action is very strong" (CEC 1993a: 14). Even with due reference to principles of proportionality and subsidiarity, the report's proactive intent is fully apparent.

9. Integrative measures were to include an economic and regulatory framework; technical harmonization; research and development; and network development. CEC 1993a: Annex III, p. 71.

10. Greek fears were fueled by the presence of EU Foreign Affairs Commissioner Hans van den Broek at the signing ceremony for the East-West Axis, which conspicuously took place during the UN's fifty-year celebrations in New York in October 1995. The Commission, however, insisted that its support was mainly symbolic, and that the project would get only token EU funds (*Kathimerini*, 26 Oct. 1995).

11. This north-south Baltic-Mediterranean road project emerged from the second pan-European transport conference in Crete in 1994. If and when completed, it will pass through St. Petersburg, Moscow, Kiev, Odessa, and Bucharest, requiring the agreement of Finland, Moldavia, Belarus, Bulgaria, Lithuania, Romania, Russia, Ukraine, and Greece, as well as the European Commission.

12. Maastricht Article 130r obliges the EU to integrate environmental protection into the definition and implementation of other policies, including transport. In 1993 the Commission (via COM(93) 575 Final) modified the landmark 1985 environmental directive, proposing that all projects bearing on environment-based Community directives be assessed; Europe 2000+ 1994.

Part II
MODAL DEVELOPMENTS IN EUROPEAN TRANSPORT

Chapter Three

Iron Roosters:
The Railroads

No change of pace at a hundred miles an hour . . .
will make us one whit stronger, happier, or wiser.
The railways are nothing more than a device for
making the world smaller.
            —JOHN RUSKIN, quoted in J. J. Norwich
                              A Taste for Travel

The analysis of separate modal developments finds its natural point of departure with the rail industry. More than any other mode, rail's varying fortunes over its 170-year history have been directly bound up with modern industrial development and its main accompanying elements: the shift away from agriculture-based primary economies and toward secondary economies more reliant on manufacturing; heavy industrialization; the growth of mass markets; rapid urbanization; increasing societal mobility; and the accumulation of wealth. In Europe as in few other places, rail has been a crucial agent of modernity; by the same token, its problems in recent decades reflect many of the broader dilemmas inherent in the post-industrial transition of mature economies.

European rail development merits close and separate scrutiny in the overall transport context for five major reasons:

(1) Its crucial state- and nation-building role, fostered by a keen appreciation by governments of its strategic capability in consolidating national territories. Rail thus has been a true touchstone for broader CTP struggles between vociferous state protection and cross-national cooperation in Europe;

(2) Its precipitous postwar loss of market share to other modes, especially road. Rail's decline is thus symptomatic of wider dilemmas in the overall European transport industry;

(3) Its recent regeneration as a potential integrative force, as the EU has targeted intercity rail links as a key to transcending boundaries, solidifying the European market and fostering pan-European cooperation, all while encouraging sustainability;

(4) The emergence of high-speed trains (HSTs) as technological breakthroughs with widespread commercial application. HST growth, notably in the EU's two key integrationist states (France and Germany) has provided a proverbial shot in the arm for the industry, widely heralded as transformative;

(5) Its characteristic distinctiveness as the most "European" of all the modes. Unlike the increasingly globalized auto and airlines industries, rail development remains an identifiably European issue, crucial to domestic and regional economic activity but much less salient in terms of outside export markets. And unlike other transport sectors where Europe struggles to remain competitive, rail is one area where Europeans arguably still maintain a technological lead and competitive advantage over all comers.

This chapter first examines rail's historical role in European politico-economic development, and the reasons for its postwar decline. Then it discusses recent EU efforts to enunciate a more coherent and comprehensive European rail strategy. Third, it examines HST initiatives at both national and international levels, and their relationship to wider questions concerning rail competitiveness and transport intermodality. It concludes by discussing nascent rail privatization trends, with special reference to the recent pathbreaking selloff of British Rail (BR).

RAIL IN EUROPEAN HISTORICAL DEVELOPMENT

The rail industry's traditional defiance of far-reaching EU harmonization or liberalization efforts reflects its historical role as a crucial determinant of national development. The symbiosis between transport and overall national economic health dates back to the sector's origins, associated with the takeoff of European industrialization by the 1830s and 1840s. The modern problems of rail not only stem from rigid and inefficient state organizational structures but from attitudes and transport philosophies that developed over a long period and have proved extraordinarily resistant to change.

The long-term macroeconomic significance of rail can be seen in two ways. First, its early growth was partly a consequence of the growth of long-distance trade, itself a function of early mass production techniques and the need, due to overproduction of goods, to seek out new export markets. Economic growth fueled demand for faster, more reliable transport, and early rail developers found a niche in servicing these needs. Second, rail itself became a causal factor of development. Regular extensions of national track length, coupled with operating services on a semiregular basis, enabled rail to stimulate the growth of other, once-localized industries and indeed to provide "a general stimulus to the whole economic system" (Thomson 1966: 179).

As producers could now serve more distant markets, sectoral growth facilitated wider regional, and ultimately national, economic development. Rail's great strength, apart from speed, was its ability to carry heavy goods over long distances. Thus began an early association between rail and heavy, "dirty," industries (iron and steel; coal) which has lingered into the contemporary era with negative consequences for the industry's public image, as closely linked with the gritty industrialization of the past as with the service-oriented, flexible present.

Early rail development was almost exclusively funded from private sources, with governments only later, and in stages, taking an active role. Early rail lines and services were built and operated by a relative handful of family concerns, and the nascent industry was adventurous and rife with speculative risk in which great fortunes were won and lost almost overnight (1847 being an especially disastrous year). In the U.S., rail companies dominated emerging capital markets; Charles Dow's original "Customer's Afternoon Newsletter," forerunner of the *Wall Street Journal,* quoted eleven companies, fully nine of which were railway enterprises.

Another 19th century characteristic was intense intermodal conflict (setting a pattern still evident) between rail interests and those promoting road and canal development as providers of local and regional services. The inaugural Liverpool-Manchester railway opened in 1830; in twenty years Britain had close to 10,000 km of track in operation. Germany's first rail line (Fürth-Nürmberg) opened in 1835, and by 1850 Germany had around 4500 km of operative track, and France another 3000 km. A later building surge quadrupled the European network between 1870 and 1900.

Though hesitant to commit itself early on to rail development, Germany arguably derived greater benefits from rail expansion than did other states, as it helped transcend physical limitations of a coastline restricted to the Baltic Sea to the north, canals that inconveniently froze in winter, and a poor and badly eroded road network. There were clear parallels between the removal of natural divisions by rail and artificial divisions between the German states by means of the 1849 *Zollverein* (customs union) (Thomson 1966; Pinson 1966). And insofar as the *Zollverein* itself facilitated political as well as economic integration in Germany by 1871, the expansion of rail was a crucial, if indirect, state-building element in Germany.

The same association was evident early on in Belgium, which in post-independence zeal after 1830 rapidly centralized a national plan for its railroads. Larger states had an even greater domestic political stake in rail consolidation. Russia's construction of the trans-Siberian railway, finally completed in 1902, opened eastern parts to goods trade and human migration. Rail development was even instrumental in introducing into Russia a money economy (Thomson 1966: 332). This development was as momentous as its western expansion counterpart in the U.S. (Joll 1976: 87–89), where completing the transcontinental rail link became the stuff of national lore; whistle-stop train tours are an age-old American political tactic, from Lincoln right up to Clinton in 1996.[1] To the north, the Canadian-Pacific railway ("Canada's spinal cord") opened up vast new tracks to the west; completion of the Trans-Australian (Perth-Sydney) Railway in 1917 shaped Australian national consciousness strongly as well.

Rail's inexorable expansion, and the economic stimulus it provided, led to equally profound changes in thinking. In David Thomson's felicitous phrase, rail "symbolized the conquest of space and of parochialism" (1950: 42); countries and peoples began regarding their own position in terms of an increasingly wider world. Rail-inspired linkages between transport and communications also led, inevitably, to a growing association with nationalist politics. Nation-state consolidation in Europe in the 19th century "from above" became linked with control over railway operations, seen increasingly as industries with overtly strategic implications and military applications.

Soon after German unification under Prussian rule in 1871, the railways were moved (1879–1884) under regional control. As early as 1873 a Reich railroad bureau was established, even earlier than the *Reichsbank* or the Supreme Court (Pinson 1966: 163), although wholesale nationalization came later, with the creation of the *Deutsche Reichsbahn* via the 1919 Weimar constitution. Similarly, British pre-World War I strategic thinking incorporated rail; Winston Churchill, ever the grand strategist on both sides of the aisle, was advocating Britain's rail nationalization as early as 1906 (Thomson 1965: 243).

In Russia, the trans-Siberian line also had strongly strategic overtones, partly as a means of protecting the nation from imperial British designs but mainly as an instrument of Russian expansionism in the Far East, of which the Russo-Japanese war of 1904–1905 was a major consequence. Later still, the system could be exploited for domestic political purposes; Russia's rail network became a key instrument in the Bolshevik revolution via so-called Agitation-Propaganda ("Agit-Prop") trains, fitted out in art-deco style and used to spread leaflets and revolutionary propaganda into remote areas.

Such attitudes were part of a much wider trend in which rail expansion became caught up in the pre-WWI scramble for colonial territories. Kaiser Wilhelm II's wooing of late Ottoman Turkey reflected a desire to gain railway concessions in the Mideast for a Berlin-Baghdad line; this German-Turkish tête-à-tête over rail development was symbolic of a cultural clash between pan-slavism and pan-germanism, with direct implications also for German-Russian tensions. Conversely, Cecil Rhodes's (unrealized) plan for a Cape-to-Cairo railway aimed at keeping Germany's African designs at bay (Thomson 1966: 518).

The war itself vindicated these strategic considerations, particularly for Germany in its constant shuttling of troops between its eastern and western fronts, and later for Russia in its post-revolution haste to abandon the war effort in the west. Even outside Europe, the importance of rail in the reverse sense (its strategic vulnerability in remote areas) was keenly perceived by T. E. Lawrence, whose contributions to early guerrilla warfare and munitions deployment in the Mideast played a considerable, if arguably overstated, role (a pernicious effect of popularity in film and print) in determining the course of the war.

After the war Britain's 1921 Railways Act consolidated its system into four regional (but still private) railroads, with outright nationalization coming in 1947 under Attlee's Labour government. Centralization in France came more slowly, due to its greater success in road building and early auto production; the national railway company, SNCF (*la Société nationale des chemins de fer*) was created only in 1938, and even then was a mixed, rather than purely public, enterprise (Dunn and Perl 1994). In the postwar formation of the German Federal Republic (FRG), its Basic Law (*Grundgesetz*) specifically recognized a national role for the railroads, in contrast to the role of the *Länder* (states) in executing federal law in other transport modes (motorways, inland waterways). Meanwhile, in France postwar national control over SNCF operations was consolidated in stages before the introduction of market considerations in the mid-1960s (Dunn and Perl 1994).

By the early postwar period, Europe's rail systems had become closely associated with strict political control by governments, and with domestic market monopolies. These elements were reinforced physically by the prominent urban siting of railway stations in most European cities; in turn, rail siting determined urban development patterns, via tram lines extending spoke-like from the center, fostering urban growth alongside expanding rail networks. All this was in contrast to, for example, sea or airports, which due to either geographical imperatives or to space needs and other factors (e.g., noise) are shunted to the urban periphery.

Thus rail terminuses are uniquely capable of visibility, a factor recognized by Mussolini in constructing Milan's cavernous central station; and a workable Italian railway system became a powerful instrument in his propaganda machine, still frequently identified as one of the few positive legacies of the Fascist period.[2] And in Helsinki, Eliel Saarinen's imposing pink granite masterpiece is a prominent focal point architecturally as well as locationally, as was London's St. Pancras in earlier times. The expensive recent overhaul of Waterloo Station in south London to accommodate Channel Tunnel trains further indicates that use of rail stations as grand, and very public, urban symbols is by no means a phenomenon of the remote past.

RAIL'S PARADOX: PROTECTED DECLINE

I have dwelt at some length on the national roots of rail development because this legacy has hindered more recent attempts to promote an international dimension for the mode. History has determined rail organizations, structures, operations, budgetary and accounting procedures, and mindsets. As rail planning has proceeded along national lines, there has been precious little incentive to shift concerns to the international network or to broader European interests. Cross-border rail travel has long been possible across the continent because of standard coupling methods and, with certain exceptions (Ireland; Finland; Iberia) rail gauges (track width); even so, crossborder cooperation has remained firmly arms-length, hindering, for example, attempts to standardize rail power supplies.

European governments' tenacious grip on rail systems has been highly paradoxical in light of the glaring inefficiencies, heavy debt burdens, overmanning, and declining investment levels characterizing the sector. Indeed the post-1945 fortunes of Europe's rail industries have been determined primarily by two elements: state monopolistic protection of national rail networks as strategic and public service industries; and declining demand due to shifting industrial and consumer patterns.

Until the 1950s, rail accounted for over half of all European haulage and transport-related employment; its percentage then dropped to well under a fifth by the 1990s. In vivid contrast to relentless expansion of roadways, the length of the overall rail network actually declined by some 20 percent from the 1950s to the 1980s, due to the closure of lines, and the number of wagons fell by a full 30 percent (see Table 3.1). Some figures are even more telling; for example, the railroads by 1986 carried just 9 percent of Europe's freight tonnage, far below sea, road, or inland waterway modes (Molle 1990; CEC 1989a). By the 1990s rail accounted for under 7 percent of the European passenger market. Such figures indicate continued

TABLE 3.1
European Railway Use (EC 12), 1950–1985

Category	1950	1960	1970	1980	1985
Coaches (1000s)	113	102	79	76	70
Goods wagons (100,000s)	15	13	11	9	7
Track length (1000s kms)	163	148	136	129	127
Electric multitrack (1000s kms)	10	18	27	34	36

Source: Molle 1990.

overmanning of the industry despite major recent downsizings (see also Tables 1.1–1.3). Table 3.2 further indicates the decline of rail goods traffic in absolute as well as in relative terms over the past quarter-century; a remarkable statistic in light of the rapid overall expansion of trade during this period.

Simultaneously, financial problems accrued from the generous application of preferential user rates; such preferences are among the three most common means of rate manipulation (the others being export subsidies, or reduced rates for exports, and external tariffs, or increased rates for imports). Rate preferences have favored key industries (coal in Germany; machinery in Italy), as well as fares for selected passenger groups, notably youths and pensioners. Extraordinarily, they also include foreign (even non-European) users via discount programs such as the Eurail and Interail pass systems. In some countries users have paid as little as 20 percent of actual costs of travel (Roundtable 1993). Though such preferences added to deficits, any shortfalls were masked by the railroads' internal financing and by considerable use of cross or hidden subsidies. By the 1980s the railroads' financial position was precarious, requiring annual subsidies of about DM 14 bn in Germany, FF 50 bn in France, and L 11,500 bn in Italy.

In Germany, chronic overmanning and heavy R&D costs associated with the separate (and competing) development of "regular" high speed intercity (ICE) services and futuristic magnetic levitation trains have led to a severe financial crisis. Annual losses at the Bundesbahn (DB) exceed DM 7 bn, with a total accumulated debt of a staggering DM 70 bn, requiring some DM 12 bn in annual interest payments—and this before the expen-

TABLE 3.2
Goods Traffic via European Rail, 1970–1990 (EC 12; in thousands of tons)

Country	1970	1975	1980	1985	1990
Bel	71,778	59,381	71,457	67,047	62,533
Den	8,050	7,209	6,460	5,724	5,576
Ger	377,141	314,364	349,576	315,955	294,919
Gre	2,953	4,034	3,646	3,999	3,603
Spa	N/A	N/A	36,529	31,683	25,717
Fra	249,662	217,383	207,854	154,474	134,277
Ire	N/A	3,440	3,629	3,379	3,278
Ita	57,780	43,161	56,349	48,336	59,180
Lux	20,072	16,828	17,401	12,727	13,191
Neth	26,743	17,736	22,142	19,921	18,190
Por	N/A	N/A	3,736	5,262	5,940
UK	208,700	176,454	154,671	141,388	139,163
Totals:	N/A	N/A	933,450	809,895	765,567

Source: Eurostat: Transport Annual Statistics 1970–1990 (1993).

sive formal linkage of DB with the former east German Reichsbahn (Ross 1994). Italian rail is the most heavily subsidized in Europe, with German, Belgian, Dutch, and French systems much less so; British Rail (BR) has been by far the least subsidized, even before its recent splitup and selloff. But in light of Germany's leading role as an advocate of tight money as a basis for EMU, the ballooning of its rail debt—now the third largest contributor to the overall German federal deficit—naturally becomes a touchstone for Europe's wider rail dilemma. And the problem is hardly limited to Europe. In Japan the main debt overhang from the 1980s stems from two institutions: mortgage-lending institutions (*jusen*) and Japan National Railways.[3]

The problems at France's SNCF have been hardly less acute, as 1995–1996 saw a traumatic succession of crises that undermined its reputation as an expertly run state industrial company. Rail services were crippled in December 1995 by a demoralizing, 24-day strike of SNCF's 180,000 employees, which nearly brought down the Juppé government. This action led to a management reshuffle in which chairman Jean Bergougneaux was replaced by Loik Le Floche-Prigent, who engineered a dramatic rescue plan involving government relief of most of SNCF's TGV-related longterm debt (amounting to $25 bn, or FF 125 bn), in exchange for internal reforms;[4] French rail unions, however, have rejected the proposal to abandon five-year renewable state contracts.

Amidst the acrimony, Le Floche-Prigent was arrested and charged with fraud (though in connection with his earlier chairmanship of Elf-Acquitaine, a French oil giant, and not SNCF). With his replacement by Louis Gallois, SNCF had its third chairman within eight months. Few observers believe that these mounting problems are resolvable in the near future, especially as France's Transport Minister under Juppé, Bernard Pons, was much less proprietary toward SNCF than his predecessors had been, calling it "the most indebted, most subsidized company in France" (IHT, 25 Nov. 1995: 13).

Despite declining rail use and growing debt, the EC remained decidedly reluctant to tackle the problems of rail throughout the 1980s. Whereas rail had figured directly in the original CTP provisions of the Treaty of Rome, with sea and air sectors marginalized, the reverse was now the case. The 1985 internal market White Paper simply sidestepped rail reform in concluding that, while the CTP extends to rail questions (such as improving rail financing), these "other measures . . . are not of direct relevance to the internal market" (CEC 1985, item 112). Two years later the EC's Official Bulletin limited its main rail objective to the financial reorganization of the railways, namely separate passenger and freight accounting (BEC 1/1987), which in itself was merely a continuation of several other recent EC initiatives.[5]

HIGH-SPEED RAIL: TO THE RESCUE?

The EC's timidity in addressing pressing rail issues, however, has contrasted with a growing across-the-board interest in one special sector, namely rapid rail (HST) systems. The late 1980s saw a dramatic upsurge of interest in HSTs as a commercially viable technology, particularly on intercity routes, and as a genuine alternative to road and even air use. High-speed rail facilitated a shift from passivity and even fatalism to a renewal of optimism about the overall industry. The old thinking reflected rail's declining use, and intermittent hopes for an EC role in managing that decline; the new thinking revolved around the promotion of HST as a new, pathbreaking, and (notwithstanding the precedent set by Japan's *Shinkansen*, or "bullet train"), a discernibly "European" development. This view has evidently gained many adherents; for example, the publication accompanying the second World Eurailspeed Conference, at Lille in October 1995, held that HST is "increasingly perceived as a new high-performance transport system" by all the major interests (railway companies, policymakers, finance, private industry, and other modes) (HSR 1995).

In fact, HST has been regarded, in economic terms, as a triple catalyst: (1) as a way to shake the rail industry out of its seemingly terminal decline by "providing full incentives for the development of most of the conventional rail networks" (CEC 1990: 27);[6] (2) as a means of injecting new vitality into the CTP itself, transforming its stodgy image so as to realize its originally intended role as an integration catalyst; and (3) most broadly, as a creator of demand, new markets, and hence overall growth and development, and even, as a European Parliament report suggested, "a major weapon in fighting unemployment" (EP 1989: 250).

For the Community, promotion of rapid rail was not just a question of higher speeds and relative efficiencies; rather, HST tended to be hived off as a qualitatively different issue, vigorously promoted even as efforts to harmonize regular rail systems lagged. Its series of reports dealing with the vexing question of gaps ("missing links") in the infrastructure network have often paralleled more specific HST-related proposals. For example, its important 1986 report proposing a Medium-Term Action Program on Transport (CEC 1986a) was released alongside a specific endorsement of a European high-speed rail system (CEC 1986b). Subsequent Community documents underscored this pivotal role of HST in promoting Community-wide transport projects of declared European interest (CE 1990b). More than any other single development, HST spurred, paralleled and reflected the overall regeneration of the Common Transport Policy.

The speed and extent to which a pro-HST policy community coalesced suggests a multiplicity of pro-integrative factors collectively at work.

Blum, Gercek, and Viegas (1992), for example, posit the interplay of economic, social, and political factors: (1) scale economies of transport systems; (2) global environmental pressures; and (3) pressure from the rolling stock industry. The Community envisioned HST as the proverbial white knight in transport planning because of its promise of multiple advantages vis-à-vis other modes. One factor was that rapid rail represented a clear break with the past, one that required new locomotives, rolling stock, and, in the French case, entirely new track in order to maximize its greatest single asset, speed. Fast it certainly is; French TGV services top out commercially at 300 kph (186 mph), set to rise to 350 kph; commercial speeds of up to 500 kph are now thought feasible within two decades, and France's TGV Atlantique has been tested as fast as 515 kph. HST's novelty became its own attraction, as the EC, goaded on by international rail bodies like the CER and UIR, spotted a new area ripe for forging new policies from the ground up, and one less tainted by the wearisome burdens of national rail systems.

Second, HST dovetailed nicely with the EC's increasing emphasis on scientific R&D, aiming for European technological breakthroughs with broad societal applicability.[7] Third, along with its economic potential as a generator of revenues and demand, HST has been promoted as an environmentally sound alternative to Europe's increasingly burdened transport systems. Not to be discounted were factors such as lingering embarrassment over earlier Community neglect of the CTP, and a growing sense of crisis in competing (road and air) modes. New rapid rail alternatives could help the railways overcome their traditional "relief function" for other overcrowded modes (Munch and Walter 1994: 172), which had tended to understate rail's own intrinsic value.

In this aim, Community interest paralleled its growing concern with two related policy sectors: the environment and energy (see also Chapter 1). Environmental groups have long promoted rail as a superior alternative to the road and air sectors, helping to check the seemingly relentless growth in motorway and airport construction (infrastructure) as well as in fossil fuel consumption (operations). The Green-inspired tightening of European environmental standards (a focus of the 1990 Dublin declaration even preceding the Rio environmental summit) was indeed behind an important, but seemingly little noticed, shift in the EC's rail emphasis, from narrowly financial to broader environmental concerns.

Whereas in the late 1980s it emphasized only the need for financial reorganization of the railways and the abolition of competition-distorting subsidies, the EU began to recast the CTP in environmental terms as "sustainable mobility" became the transport policy equivalent of calls for sustainable economic development (CEC 1993a). DG XI (Environment) efforts have included advocacy of rail and on punitive measures (e.g., the carbon tax proposal) in the road sector. Similarly, the lower energy requirements of rail, particularly with electrification of rail lines for most high-speed use, links energy concerns with shifting modal priorities.

The European Commission played a central, even if not critical, role in focusing attention on infrastructure gaps and the potential of fast trains in filling them. Much of the new dynamism can be attributed to the activist transport commissioner in the late 1980s, Karel Van Miert from Belgium (which operates the world's densest rail network). Even so, the HST initiative benefited from a powerful policy community, with backing from national, industrial, and institutional players, including the following:

(1) French rail (SNCF) inaugurated Europe's rapid rail age with the staged opening (1981–1983) of the TGV Sud-Est line between its two largest cities, Paris and Lyon. In 1989 TGV Atlantique services opened, linking Paris, via two trunk lines, with Tours and Le Mans to the southeast. The domestic orientation of these two services was counterbalanced by French plans for international HST links, centering on its ambitious TGV Nord initiative. The initial trunk route, between Paris and Lille to the northeast (opened in May 1993) was envisioned as the basis of an international intercity network designed to take advantage both of the proximity of major cities in adjacent EC countries (hence the designation PBKA, for Paris-Brussels-Köln [Cologne]-Amsterdam), with future plans to link fast services with the British network via Channel Tunnel trains to London and points beyond, and to Germany via TGV Est.

French planning has also taken on increasingly intermodal dimensions; for example, the November 1994 opening of a rail junction directly at Roissy-Charles de Gaulle airport outside Paris allowed travelers to skirt the capital itself. (Other European airports have done similarly, including Amsterdam's Schiphol, and Geneva's Cointrin.) This is part of a much wider French "master plan," given government approval in April 1992, for sixteen projects totaling some 4700 kilometers of new line and serving a network of 11,000 km. These plans have increasingly international links as well.[8] The French so far have spent over $25 bn in TGV development.

The French example proved instructive to the EC for two key reasons. First, it resulted from deliberate planning over a long period, aimed at creating a Europe-wide HST network centering on and emanating from the French capital. Second, TGV proved a great commercial success, generating a return on capital of close to 15 percent on the Paris-Lyon route, and between 9 and 16 percent on all routes together. Particularly surprising to many outsiders (though not to system planners) was that TGV operations created substantial new demand above and beyond straight passenger shift from other modes (Dunn and Perl 1994).

A longer term developmental effect has been a transformation of regional centers into bona fide transit and industrial hubs. Three in particular—Nord-Pas de Calais, centered on Lille; Bourgogne, centered on Dijon; and Rhône-Alpes, centered on Lyon-Grenoble—have all developed into viable economic centers to match the Mitterrand-inspired political devolution efforts of the 1980s, substantially as a result of TGV access.[9] The French have strongly defended high TGV development costs by the macroeconomic, regional, and social gains generated by new transport links;[10] a tendency to quote (French) distances in travel times rather than kilometers also speaks to TGV-inspired changes in thinking.

(2) Organizational promotion of HST. The Community of European Railways (CER) began floating ideas for a pan-European rapid rail system as early as 1984; and in January 1989 it submitted a formal proposal for the creation of a European HST network (CER 1989). The European Commission not only referred to this report as a catalyst in its own thinking but included the CER's report, together with amendments, in its own proposals to the Council of Ministers. The CER's proposal was based on seven elements by which HST would contribute to European integration.[11] The CER has been joined by other railway and economic organizations, including the UIR, the Union of European Railway Industries, the ECMT, and the European Round Table, in advocating HST.

(3) The European Parliament. In September 1987 the EP passed a wide-ranging resolution on a European high-speed rail network (OJ 1987), calling high-speed train development "of decisive importance for the revival of passenger and goods transport by rail on the continent of Europe as part of a strategy of harmonious development and integration between the various modes of transport" (p. 72). EP enthusiasm was also tempered with realism, advocating HST but not "at the expense of the existing public transit network"; and it emphasized HST progress as an integral part of the Community's scientific and technical research (COST) efforts. It also promoted research into alternative HST technologies based on magnetic levitation in addition to conventional wheel-on-rail systems.

The EC also emphasized HST development because of expected knock-on effects on industry and trade. Though HST services are usually passenger-oriented, their positive effect on rail goods haulage should not be overlooked. The "capacity argument" holds that HST services, even on dedicated track, free up capacity for goods transport on the regular rail network. The international effect would then be considerable, since rail freight is increasingly competitive with road haulage at long distances. And HST systems are vital high-tech industries in their own right, via the production of new rolling stock and complex engine technologies, such as the Eurostar engines on Channel Tunnel services, which had to be designed to run on three separate power-supply systems. Industrial spin-offs to other high-tech sectors, such as semiconductors, are also considerable.

Major private companies have been involved in HST development, on contract from national governments and increasingly via cooperative alliances. These include Siemens and Daimler's subsidiary AEG, developers of Germany's ICE system; GEC-Alsthom, a conglomerate of General Electric in Britain and France's Alcatel-Alsthom, and builder of TGV and Channel Tunnel trains; and Asea Brown Boveri (ABB), created when Sweden's ASEA bought out Switzerland's BBC in 1988, forming a third major player in the intensely competitive rapid rail market. ABB has since aligned with Daimler-Benz to form ABB-Daimler Benz Transportation (Adtranz), to manufacture and modernize rolling stock.[12] Further afield, Mitsubishi helped develop Japan's *Shinkansen*, though again with a purely national orientation.

Train system types have varied in consequence. French TGV systems are whole train-sets operable on regular track but not capable of exploiting top speeds (currently up to 186 mph/300 kph) unless on dedicated (straighter, more level) new lines. In contrast, German ICE trains use upgraded regular track and benefit both passengers and freight. Sweden (the X-2000) and Italy (the Pendolino), on the other hand, have pioneered "tilting" technology, with the Italians in the midst of an ambitious $10.4 bn plan (the *treno alta velocita* or TAV) to link Turin with Naples by 2001. German interests, led by AEG's 611 series, have begun developing tilting trains which can even run on diesel fuel, similar to fast trains developed in the 1980s for Britain's east coast line. Swiss rail is also coming to rely on Adtranz-built tilting trains on its mainline (St. Gallen-Zürich-Geneva) route, for economic and geographic reasons (FT, 6 July 1996: 3).

Finally, HST has drawn attention as part and parcel of EC structural policy, designed to connect Europe's disparate and often isolated regions via new and upgraded infrastructures. Thus the focus on "missing links," especially those crossing national boundaries and often across geologically sensitive (marine, alpine) areas, which otherwise fell through the cracks in an investment structure designed solely on national lines. High-speed intercity links were one of five priority concerns for the EC's 1988 revised transport priorities, which were then formally accepted as EC aims in the important 1990 Council regulation establishing the Declaration of European Interest for infrastructure (CEC 1988; CE 1990b).

In this context, an explicit linkage was created between rail transport issues and center-periphery Community concerns, in three ways: improved transport links would (1) draw individual EC regions closer to each other, (2) draw them collectively toward the European core, and (3) stimulate intra-regional development. Even so, the dynamics of demand in core areas are very different from those in peripheral areas, where lower market demands mean that firm political backing is needed for development, thus feeding concerns about the essential unevenness of rail-related spatial development (Blum, Gercek, and Viegas 1992). And perhaps inevitably, growing EC involvement drew national critics in more road-based states like Britain; a more practical problem involved duplication of Community structural efforts.[13] These (structural) linkages are examined more closely in Chapter 7.

Progress and Problems in High-Speed Rail

There is little doubt that HST development has exceeded many European expectations, or that the Commission has chosen wisely in targeting this segment of the transport market for future growth. Still, the widespread assumption that HST is a viable integrative vehicle for overall European economic integration is not totally cut and dried. Despite their intercity, cross-border potential, the longer distances at higher speeds they cover, and the mobility of people and (indirectly) goods they generate, HST systems thus far have proceeded first and foremost at state level, reflecting national plans long predating the Single Market initiative. Rather than conforming to the cooperative or spillover integrationist models, early HST development in fact tended to confirm the competitive model and to perpetuate traditional national champion strategies in new forms.

The HST literature has noted at least three separate competitive strands: between passenger-only and combined passenger-freight usage, focusing on French and German systems; between 'tilting' technology (based on new train-sets) and systems that also require track upgrading or new track; and between rail funding and developmental philosophies, highlighted by divergencies between French and British approaches.

The two binational comparisons merit special consideration. The French and German examples raise numerous dissimilarities in both conception and application of HST systems, which stand out with more force because both countries embarked on HST research programs at around the same time. France's TGV development resulted from a strategic shift in rail thinking, based on the internal Nora report of 1966, which introduced explicitly commercial principles into the monopolized SNCF's framework. The resulting TGV program was a carefully targeted, state-sponsored venture aimed at strict cost containment and ultimate commercial viability, based on a narrow and homogeneous policy network which excluded extraneous elements such as environmental groups. As such, TGV development could proceed apace as a "dramatic public enterprise initiative" along the lines of the Concorde supersonic aircraft before it (Dunn and Perl 1994: 321), and now firmly established in the best Gallic tradition of high profile, state-sponsored technological endeavors.

In vivid contrast, Germany's simultaneous HST development was delayed by a much more nebulous and heterogeneous policy network, reflecting traditionally sectoralized interests and corporatist practices there. The Germans opted for a multipurpose ICE system, operational for both passengers and freight use, and usable along existing (upgraded) track. In fact, freight use, rather than the French-style passenger focus, was the main German developmental emphasis. ICE train sets were also designed to be uncoupled to form trains of varying lengths, adding flexibility and facilitating repairs to individual (car) units, thus causing fewer service disruptions than is the case in France (Strohl 1993).

Yet another difference was the development of an alternative policy network in Germany in the field of mag-lev rail technology, which the Ministry of Research and Technology pushed strongly as an alternative to the Bundesbahn's conventional wheel-on-rail system. After years of experimental development, the Transrapid mag-lev system was demoted in favor of ICE, largely because of its incompatibility with the normal rail network and entirely new infrastructure requirements.[14] However, German reunification increased demands for new transport alternatives, and mag-lev development was resurrected by Thyssen, a German conglomerate. In 1994 the first commercial line was commissioned by the German government, along a 284 km (170 mile) corridor between Berlin and Hamburg (Magnetschnellbahn Berlin-Hamburg GmbH). A total price tag of DM 5.6 bn is envisioned, funded jointly by the government and the contractors as a public-private partnership (FT, 15 Dec. 1994: 18). Once completed sometime after 2002, Transrapid services are expected to connect the two cities in under an hour, at speeds of up to 450 k/hr (320 mph); a prototype has already achieved speeds up to 400 kph (280 mph). The emergence of a separate HST alternative again contrasted sharply with the French experience, in which early mag-lev development (the Aérotrain project) was ultimately sabotaged by SNCF, with its TGV focus (Dunn and Perl 1994).

Aside from these discrepancies in mag-lev development, the emergence of competing strategies in conventional (TGV and ICE) systems has raised technical issues of cross-border operational complementarity. Even more widely, they represent essentially alternative visions for the focus and direction of Europe's future rail network. Indications for coordinated rail development in Europe thus far are not particularly encouraging. Whereas French progress on HST, and its international TGV-Nord and PBKA intercity linkages were clearly predicated on Paris as the locus of a north-south directed international network, the post-reunification shift of German interests toward the east has highlighted Berlin's role as a new European transit hub and key to the growing east-west transport dimension.[15] Huge new financial commitments to upgrading transport infrastructure in Berlin Stadt and Brandenburg Land, amounting to DM 20 bn,[16] and the 1994 relocation there of Siemens's headquarters illustrate this shift in focus and its Europe-wide implications.

Another competitive element has emerged in the small but growing export market. Although HST development has been primarily domestic in orientation, the gradual fulfillment of the most urgent needs at national level has increased pressures to sell rapid rail technology abroad, in order to justify high initial development expenditures. So far the French, given the head start of TGV and backed by a relentless promotional campaign, have had the most success in selling rapid rail systems elsewhere, but even this impact has been small, limited mainly to neighboring states.[17]

In the late 1980s great hopes were placed on American enthusiasm for rapid rail, such as in Florida, Texas, and along the northeastern corridor linking Washington, D.C. to Boston via New York. A major contract to link four Texan cities via "TGV Texas" fell through when investors were unable to come up with the initial capital ($170 m) on which state government approval of the $7 bn project hinged. In the northeast corridor both French and German systems were bypassed in favor of Swedish pendular trains that lean into curves but do not require new track; even so, progress has been slowed by funding problems and delays in electrifying the New York-New Haven leg. Several predictable factors combined to puncture much of this newfound rail enthusiasm: tight government budgets at all levels, the perennial problem of attracting private capital to rail development, fierce competition from no-frills regional airlines (such as Southwest), deficient urban transport systems, and the auto-based needs of a highly mobile society have all played a role.

Thus the initial burst of enthusiasm for HST development at the outset of the Clinton administration rapidly deteriorated into heavy Congressional cuts in financial support for Amtrak, the national passenger rail system. The situation worsened further with the Republicans' capture of both Congressional houses in November 1994. The melancholy conclusion for European would-be rail exporters can only be that the U.S., otherwise one of the world's most lucrative export markets, is marginal when it comes to marketing high-speed rail technologies. Awkwardly and in return, American freight rail exporters are increasingly challenging European manufacturers on their own soil.[18]

Equally instructive was the intense Franco-German competition to sell HST technology to South Korea for its Seoul-Pusan line in the early 1990s. After a two-year struggle, Korea's Highspeed Rail Construction Authority awarded the $2.1 bn contract to the French-led bid by GEC-Alsthom, although on slim margins and at a contract price well below the original bid ($2.4 bn); and post-contract demands by the South Korean government for local content of components diminished the deal's effect further (*The European*, April 22, 1994: 18). This failure proved a bitter blow to Siemens, the main German rail manufacturer, which has yet successfully to break into the export market. Even for GEC-Alsthom the experience tempered hopes for selling into the growing east Asian region, principally Taiwan and China, or even to large, more developed states such as Australia or Canada.

To many, the South Korean experience demonstrated the necessity of pooling resources among the two giants for a joint European train project with export potential, and proposals for such an "Airbus on wheels" have been floated, though joint development remains far off.[19] Aside from the fact that such collaboration presupposes rough equality between the partners (whereas GEC-Alsthom is far ahead of Siemens in operationalizing its technology), any attempted merger within the already small pool of major manufacturers is likely to meet resistance from the EU's Competition directorate.

In turn, the French and German approaches differ substantially from the British. Dobbin (1993) argues that, in the rail sector, common assumptions about French statism versus British market-oriented approaches are largely inaccurate; France's TGV was thoroughly rooted in market principles along with a belief that the state itself can influence those markets by generating top-down demand, whereas British high-speed rail development has languished because of an assumption that travel demand is more or less a zero-sum dynamic whereby demand emanates solely from civil society and private market forces and not from state manipulation (i.e., "from below" rather than "from above").

Thus ironically (at least, before BR's privatization), it was French HSR development, and not British, which has involved the markets for the provision of seed capital; and it is British development, not French, where political intrusion and interparty wrangling over national rail policy has been a drag on development. Such contention, for example, contributed to Britain's (and to America's) failure to convert early research progress in developing (diesel-powered) high-speed engines for the commercial market, allowing European competitors a step up in electrified systems.

A prime, if melancholic, case in point is the series of attempts in Britain to commit to construction of the 70-mile, $4 bn dedicated high-speed rail line from the Channel Tunnel to London. Much of the initial investment and interest in the Chunnel project was predicated on prospects of linking London to Paris and Brussels by uninterrupted fast train services, but these hopes have been repeatedly dashed on the British side by a combined effect of politically well-placed "conservative green" environmentalism in Kent, public planning rows between the government and (then-public) British Rail over the proposed route, and Thatcherite insistence that the British public should not subsidize international rail services. Years of delaying any decision, compared to France's completion of its high-speed link to Calais in May 1994, have invited endless public and press ridicule, although a consortium (London and Continental Railways) is now in place to help fund its construction and operate the system once completed sometime early next century.

All these differences in HST approaches give ample reason for caution over whether the EU will, in fact, make good on its aim of coordinating the future growth of the European HSR network (Dobbin 1993), and on whether its vaunted shift to a pro-activist HST strategy is more rhetorical than actual. The Commission moved to solidify the EU's stake in the HST network through its April 1994 proposal for a Council directive on the interoperability of European high-speed trains, concerning design, construction, and putting into operation an overall network, though the states remain responsible for funding development. Any such advances thus remain modest, and the bulk of developmental efforts remain geared to meeting domestic needs, a point lamented by the Commission (CEC 1994b).

There is some progress in the most recent generation of HSTs to enable interoperability across borders; for example, Italy's ETR 460 has been built to run under French power supply, which will facilitate the Lyon-Turin/Milan link; Swiss rail (SBB) can now accept both French TGV and German ICE trains on certain routes. In addition, the continuing consolidation of European rail manufacturers is largely a reflection of ongoing, cross-border standardization of rail equipment. Such standardization (such as ABB's move from six European locomotive types to a single one now) augments the EU's own ongoing promotion of technical harmonization in rail systems.

Progress has also been forthcoming in the development of standard signaling and control systems, a key EU priority, via the new European Train Control System as a basis for future rail traffic management. Such steps are vital in rail freight, where Hermes, the manually-operated computer information system for rail operators, is widely considered inadequate. A new freight tracking system is being developed for Channel Tunnel use, using transponders to allow automatic tracking of freight parcels (FT, July 4, 1996: 10), although use is likely to remain voluntary. Indeed, despite deep discounting, Chunnel rail freight has proved a disappointment (even before the disastrous fire in November 1996 aboard a Chunnel freight train), and BR's earlier 500 m pound investment in freight services has already been written off.

The political impact of Green opposition to HST links in southern England, as well as in southern France and in Germany, also broaches the question of whether fast trains in fact offer the environmentally sound rapid transport envisaged by its promoters. In comparative modal terms, HST is without peer; rapid trains use a fraction of the energy of an airplane on a per-kilometer basis (a key budgetary consideration for oil importers), and produce far lower CO_2 emissions than do individual road vehicles carrying the same number of passengers. France's SNCF estimates that TGV is 2.5 times more efficient than private cars per passenger km, and 4 times more efficient than air services (Mathieu 1995). Overall rail services account for only 4 percent of total transport-generated CO_2 emissions in Europe, and just 2.5 percent of its energy requirements, both figures far undercutting its importance in freight or even passenger traffic. Building new rail lines to accommodate fast trains (a prerequisite for optimal TGV use) also requires up to two-thirds less land-take than does a motorway with similar capacity.[20] Rail's relative safety levels—estimated by industry analysts at some six times greater than for road use (CEC 1996a)—notwithstanding newsworthy accidents (Italy, Spain) in winter 1996–1997, is a major additional pro-rail factor. Clearly any viable, concerted effort to promote modal shifting must center on promotion of the rail, and by implication HST, alternative.

Even so, the efficiency vs. environment trade-off is not quite as straightforward as many suggest. The electricity requirements of HST are considerable; their visual and noise impact is evident even if hard to quantify; and the straighter, more level track they require for optimal usage often means localized construction nuisance in building tunnels and bridges. Though French TGV development was facilitated by favorable topography, this may be an exception rather than the rule; the more undulating German territory (aside from stronger Green politics) requires more tunnel-building and much higher total costs.[21] Other social costs of HSR include increased vibration at high speeds, with its resulting structural damage to buildings in urban areas, given the inevitable focus on intercity services. Whitelegg (1993) even contends that HST's environmental savings are fictitious, since they imply more leisure-time use of the automobile. And HST systems without doubt benefit developed core regions more than peripheral ones.

Nonetheless, the relatively lower social costs of rapid rail gives it strong comparative advantages, especially considering the frame of reference; the middle-distance passenger market, chiefly competitive with the airlines, offers a trade-off overwhelmingly in HST's favor. But while air-to-rail switching may be a viable aim in this market segment, freight modal switching efforts (road to rail) will require substantial changes in road-use charging. In the final analysis, one of the most powerful factors in favor of modal switching may be not only the relative merits of rail, but deteriorating conditions in other modes (airport delays, traffic congestion), in which time savings emerge as pivotal factors in consumer and industry choice.

REORGANIZING THE RAILWAYS: IS PRIVATIZATION ACHIEVABLE?

The coalescing of a pro-HST European lobby (despite the fragmentative tendencies noted above) has tended to hive off HST questions from those regarding regular rail services. Nonetheless, the highly publicized successes of rapid rail services in France, Germany, Sweden, and Italy, particularly in terms of profitability and increasing ridership, has refocused attention on the broader question of reorganizing national railway companies internally, together with greater coordination between them externally. Past neglect of the rail sector by the EU has meant that efforts toward both harmonization and liberalization have had to be addressed together.

The problem of harmonizing rail services throughout Europe is a complex one, insofar as it involves the three elements of technical coordination (electrical systems; aligning track and loading gauges especially in eastern Europe);[22] economy (sources of investment; internalization of costs); and regulatory power (national governments, international bodies, or both). Domestic rail services traditionally have linked both infrastructure and operations under one authority, but growing European treatment of transport as a service which must be opened to competition has given rise to EU measures aiming at the decoupling of structures and operations and, ultimately, at the breakup of national monopolies themselves. As early as 1989 the Commission's Communication on Railway Policy (CEC 1990) indicated moves in this direction.

Of pivotal importance here is the Council Directive of July 1991 (CE 1991), which aimed to enhance the efficiency of European railways and to adapt them to the demands of the Single Market. It called for the separation of rail infrastructure and operations (mandatory for separation of accounts, though still optional in organizational terms), and to "ensur[e] access to the networks of Member States for international groupings of railway undertakings." Thus the aim was not only to open up closed domestic networks to outside competition (but excluding regional, urban, and suburban services), but also to encourage international cooperation in providing those services. The new guidelines allow managers to charge user fees and allocate capacity on a nondiscriminatory basis aiming at maximizing efficiency (CE 1995b). Simultaneously the Council included an arrangement whereby rail operators can apply for a license in the state in which it wishes to operate, with that license valid throughout EU territory (CE 1995a). Both undertakings underscored the Commission's intent to give independent rail companies more freedom to operate services on the various national rail networks.

On the other hand, many governments had initiated rail decentralization well prior to the 1991 directive, and impetus for change has come largely from outside the EU. New Zealand was one of the first to detach operations from infrastructure, along with Australia, Japan, Switzerland, and Norway. In Germany, movement has occurred in both directions. The east-west (Reichsbahn and Bundesbahn) merger was followed (1994) by a splitting of the national network, into three different businesses (for track, passenger services, and freight). Another step came in 1996 with the "regionalizing" (*Regionalisierung*) of rail regulatory authority to the *Länder* (CEC 1996a). The government has even announced tentative plans for privatizing DB in 1998.

One of the boldest experiments has come in Sweden, a latecomer to rail nationalization (1939) but which is often noted more for the generosity of its public services than for its commercial flair. By 1988 its Transport Policy Act separated the organization and management of *Sveriges Järnvägen* into infrastructure and operations, now respectively handled by the national rail administration and "Business-SJ," while also granting regional authorities much more leeway in determining services and prices. The act further separated the rail network in terms of both type of services (passenger, with more flexibility, and freight, still within the aegis of SJ), and function (main lines versus county lines) (Larsson 1993). The success of these reforms[23] has led directly to deregulation in other transport sectors, including aviation services in 1992, and in telecommunications as well. Finland too has decoupled its rail system in line with the 1991 directive, with one company (VR-Rata) responsible for track and infrastructure maintenance, and a separate operating company (VR) which, unusually, also runs two road haulage companies.

The opening up of domestic rail services to competition should not be seen, however, as the first step down the slippery slope toward outright mandated privatization of rail monopolies. A 1990 ECMT conference on rail privatization strongly underscored the numerous problems requiring attention before it can even be attempted on a wide scale (Round Table 1993); and the Community of European Railways (CER) opposed the Commission's first tentative steps (taken in 1989) in this direction. On the contrary, the 1991 Council directive specifically holds that the building and maintenance of rail infrastructures (track, signaling systems, and other fixed installations), by far the greatest cost of any rail system, is to remain the prerogative of national governments.

Unsurprisingly, opposition to relinquishing state control over rail systems has been strongest in southern Europe. Even Italy's flagship high-speed TAV intercity project retains a controlling stake for the government, which also has major (60%) funding obligations. It has also delayed its infrastructure division, and the uncovering of a rail embezzlement scandal in mid-1996 may well delay it further. And the late 1995 French railway strike, following proposals to reform SNCF, likely will have a chilling effect on the pace of denationalization there as well. The French have fiercely opposed such an operational separation (although separate accounts were agreed to), and completely ruled out a selloff of SNCF; and it may take years of Commission cajoling and ECJ rulings to impel the French to allow other countries' operators to run along its rail lines, even if the technical problems are overcome.

At the other extreme, Britain has moved furthest toward full denationalization, since it has not only introduced competition in rail operations but actual private ownership of the network itself. However, it also provides an instructive example of the difficulties inherent in a gradualist process, and of the bad political tempers that seem specially reserved for public discussions about national rail policy there. Problems over BR services led to widespread reductions in services from the early 1960s, the so-called "Beeching cuts" after its Railway Board chairman—a severance with Britain's proud industrial past that was presided over, ironically, by its last elected patrician Prime Minister, Harold Macmillan (Horne 1989:

250–252). BR went through extensive reorganization in the 1980s, including sales of railway property and trunk lines, while escaping a wholesale selloff under the Thatcher knife.

The 1993 Railways Act provided for the creation of a national rail infrastructure company, Railtrack, and broke up BR's services monopoly into three rolling stock leasing companies ("roscos"). The aim was twofold: to get the physical infrastructure (track, stations, signaling systems) out of the public sector, and to promote competition in services between franchising and independent operators. The transition, however, is cushioned by long-term contracts for train operators, and Railtrack's continued, if private, monopoly position. The rosco sales were announced in November 1995 by Transport Secretary Sir George Young, as a first step toward the sale of Railtrack itself.[24] Chancellor Kenneth Clarke's December 1994 budget focused on rail as a prime component of his Private Finance Initiative (PFI), designed to attract market capital to traditionally public services. Most (80 percent) of contracts thus far have involved rail, road, and air traffic control, giving PFI an essentially transport focus. Success so far, however, has been mixed.[25]

Predictably, BR's gradual privatization became caught up in interparty politics, in both directions. The Major government appeared to gear up the process in advance of the spring 1997 elections, for example completing the May 1996 stock flotation on terms widely thought excessively generous to investors.[26] The opposition Labour Party capitalized on the issue's considerable controversy[27] in its vague threats to reverse the breakup should it retake office; and Labour spokesmen, notably Claire Short and Glenda Jackson, continued verbally to assault the BR privatization.[28] Other, non-party opponents of privatization, led by "Save our Railways," also challenged the issue in court due to alleged governmental misrepresentations over the extent of future cuts in services and safety trade-offs. By early 1996, however, Labour was backing away from its renationalization threats and began calling for a "publicly accountable railway," a much tamer prospect; and Tony Blair as Prime Minister appears to have dropped all notions of reversing BR's private course.

CONCLUSIONS

Britain's problematic rail privatization may well remain the European exception. For most countries there remains a great distinction between opening up services to franchisers and creating a separate infrastructure body (quasi-privatization), and the more far-reaching creation of a bona fide company with majority control held by private entities. A major problem and legacy of the past is that rail systems continue to have explicitly social connotations for states as distributive mechanisms (via underused rural lines, privileged fare structures, and the like) alongside efficiency-based needs.

A second problem is that rail planning, not only building infrastructure but the creation of manufacturing facilities for rolling stock, is a time-consuming process measured in years and even decades. However, introduction of private capital into the process will focus attention on short-term, bottom-line considerations, which could well hinder necessary long-term horizons for wider network planning. Additionally, the cost of financing private rail investments is inevitably higher than for state-owned enterprises protected by an implicit recognition of protection from default, just as large enterprises in other sectors (e.g., banking) are assumed to be more insulated than smaller ones. SNCF has long benefited from such assumptions in tapping France's domestic capital markets.

Third, even under an "open" system, state rail operators will continue to enjoy considerable advantages in competing with newer, private operators because of high start-up costs and other impediments to market entry; such would require, in return, some official "affirmative action" in order to ensure a reasonably level playing field and to minimize built-in discrimination against newcomers. These and other problems led Stig Larsson, head of Swedish rail, to speculate that bold moves to privatize rail systems would produce chaos in services and rider uncertainty, and could even lead re-nationalization of services as a means of reintroducing stability and predictability (1993: 68). The very nature of rail operations seems to preclude competition among more than a handful of operators and to ensure the heavy regulation of any future system, whether private, public, or mixed.

On the other hand, these domestic-oriented concerns may be less pressing at the international level, where there does seem to be more scope for private cross-border services. Two such trends are likely. One is greater international freight competition, which could maximize rail's inbuilt competitive advantages over road on long-distance routes. The other is the possibility of treating high-speed passenger routes as wholly separate undertakings, and selling them off as (generally) profitable enterprises. Insofar as EU advocacy of HST is predicated on the belief that rapid rail can promote international rail mobility, this could help marry the privatization trend with that of harmonization of different national networks and services. Whether such a development would free up more resources for maintaining and upgrading regular rail services, or lead to their further neglect, remains an open question and source of concern, likely to defy blanket European solutions.

The still-piecemeal nature of rail reform, including efforts to promote widespread modal switching, has led many analysts to call for the creation of some type of centralized railway authority for Europe. Such an authority would serve several purposes: to coordinate much-needed technical standardization as one path toward more harmonized systems; to promote planning of future international routes; to oversee and coordinate public-private partnerships in rail investment; to prevent excessive consolidation of the industry leading to renewed monopolistic practices; and to provide seed money for new international rail (especially HST) ventures. Two problems, however, immediately arise. One is the political opposition of states and national rail authorities, notably SNCF. The other, more technical problem is that rail itself is not divisible from other modes; most freight and much passenger movement between two points involves road and/or sea as well as rail use, in which case any such authority would presumably have to be multi- rather than unimodal in orientation (Button 1994: 115). This problem of European transport governance will be taken up further in Chapter 8.

In sum, real competition on international rail services is far from imminent; on domestic services throughout Europe's states, it is further off; and widespread privatization of rail infrastructures is highly unlikely in the less-than-distant future. At the very least, the railways must be modernized and put on a potentially profitable footing (thus validating early EC concerns about the railways' financial condition), before extensive introduction of market conditions could have any reasonable chance of success—a tall order indeed, particularly in an era of EMU-mandated government budget cuts and consequent difficulties in making major new investments in costly technologies. Here, much depends on EU action to reduce cost discrepancies between rail and its chief competitor, road transport, which is discussed in the following chapter.

NOTES

1. In Clinton's pre-convention whistle-stop tour in summer 1996, nostalgic use of antiquated rolling stock unwittingly created an odd counterpoint to a campaign theme dwelling on America's future.

2. Silvio Berlusconi's *Forza Italia*-led governing coalition in 1994 included, as Transport Minister, a member of the far-right National Alliance who pointedly had praised Mussolini's rail policies.

3. Japan's accumulated rail debt reportedly grew to a record 27.6 trillion yen ([$250 bn] by 1996 [IHT, 31 May 1996: 19]). Unpalatable options to reduce it include new taxes, reduced transport spending, and issuing government bonds. Two others, selling rail property or listing shares in the seven operating companies, were shelved due to the prolonged slump in property prices and equity markets.

4. For 1995, losses at SNCF were estimated at FF 11 bn (over $2 bn), a rise of FF 3 bn in just a year. Total debts of FF 175 bn, or $35 bn (offset by FF 50 bn of annual public subsidies) accrue interest charges totaling over FF 14 bn annually, while turnover has improved only marginally (FT, 20 Nov. 1995: 2).

5. These earlier measures had included Decision 65/27/EEC of 1965, on the harmonization of certain provisions pertaining to the equal competition between the three inland modes; Decision 75/27/EEC of 1975, on the harmonization of

rules governing relations between rail companies and public authorities; Decision 82/529/EEC of 1982, on the fixing of rates for the international carriage of goods by rail (and its passenger equivalent by Decision 83/418/EEC the following year) (Coopers and Lybrand 1994: 3).

6. The European Parliament was even more emphatic, calling HST a "driving element in the comprehensive recovery of rail services within the Community"; EP 1987: 73.

7. In December 1990 the Council decided (CE 1990a) to expand its transport-related R&D promotional efforts (euret), based on a pilot program dating from 1987. A key focus was improving Europe's rail traffic management to promote efficiency and competitiveness, although the small sums involved (just ecu 25 m for 1990–1993) were indicative of the limited EC role in new technology investments.

8. These (EU-promoted) links include TGV-est, to link Paris with Germany and central Europe; TGV Languedoc-Roussillon, linking the Avignon-Nimes-Montpélier tri-city area with Barcelona in northeast Spain; and Lyon-Torino, a Rhine-Rhône connection serving also Swiss and German catchment areas. See Mathieu 1995.

9. Lille's hosting of the 1995 Eurailspeed exhibition and its (abortive) bid for the 2004 Olympiad, and the G-7 meeting in spring 1996 in Lyon, where a former French premier, Raymond Barre, serves as mayor, indicate the growing visibility of regional centers.

10. The knock-on economic effects in France include: growth in tourism markets, growth in business travel, and exchange of services; industrial relocations to TGV catchment areas; commercial development near main stations (e.g., Paris Montparnasse; Lyon Port-Dien; EuraLille business quarter). Arguments for TGV Mediteranée development include 19,000 jobs created or retained.

11. The CER report emphasized seven facets: (1) Europe's ideal location for HST development; (2) national progress enabling an overall EC policy framework; (3) concentration on Europe's "missing links" would better connect national networks; (4) gradualist development over 20–25 years; (5) technical harmonization and cost savings; (6) the public benefit of common financing terms; and (7) its overall importance to Europe's integration. See CEC 1990: 24.

12. In mid-1996 Adtranz unveiled plans to modernize older carriages by using lighter aluminum bodies with multiple safety features (crumple zones, electric doors), at around a third of the average price ($1 m) of new carriages. This may become the preferred solution for cost-pressed operating companies, especially in Britain (FT, 3 July 1996: 7).

13. Prior to the 1988 structural policy reforms, 43 percent of all infrastructure expenditure by the Regional Development Fund (ERDF) went to transport projects. For more see Vickerman 1991.

14. In contrast to Japan's experimental system, which relies on magnetic repulsion and large magnetic fields, Germany's Transrapid uses electrically generated magnetic propulsion to create a "wandering magnetic field" attracted by levitation magnets beneath the train itself. Speed increases in proportion to strength of electrical current, allowing the train to glide about 10 mm above a concrete "guideway" (as opposed to parallel tracks). Attention generated by mag-lev (NYT, 25 Sept. 1994: 6; FT, 15 Dec. 1994: 18, and 28 Jan. 1994: 11) has outstripped its commercial development, limited thus far to the Berlin-Hamburg corridor.

15. Heinze and Kill 1994. Blum (1991) estimates that the volume of East-West traffic in Germany will multiply sevenfold from 1985 to 2010, with a rise from 6 m to 43 m trips by rail.

16. Berlin's self-advertisement as "the transport metropolis of the future" is backed by infusion of technological development aid, Transrapid mag-lev development, TENs focus on improving Lehrter station, new regional rail systems, and a mooted new airport.

17. GEC-Alsthom has sold more than twice as many sets to France alone (well over 600) as Siemens has in total (267 sets by 1995, all to the German government for ICE services), and has sold to Spain (for the Madrid-Seville AVE line), the four-city PBKA system, and the Channel Tunnel Eurostar trains (FT, 26 July 1995: 9). It also beat out ABB for a $1 bn contract to supply 100 new train sets for London Underground's aging Northern Line (FT, 9 Dec. 1994: 7). Accurately if predictably, GEC-Alsthom boasts of having produced "the only HST to be exported."

18. GM recently contracted to supply British freight rail operators with 250 diesel-electric locomotives at a cost of $400 m. U.S. freight locomotive manufacturers, such as General Electric, benefit from natural scale economies deriving from a large domestic market, and less reliance on the latest technology (FT, 13 June 1996: 7).

19. As a result of the damaging South Korean episode, Siemens and Alcatel-Alsthom contracted in March 1996 to market, but not manufacture, high-speed trains jointly, mainly in Asia. The move was prompted by heavy corporate losses, mainly at the French company, totaling FF 25.6 bn in 1995 (FT, 29 March 1996: 17).

20. Roadways and motorways take up about 1.3 percent of Europe's land space, compared with just .03 percent for rail infrastructure.

21. For example, the inaugural ICE line from Hannover to Würzburg, a total of 328 km, contains some 62 tunnels with a combined length of well over a third of the overall route (ECMT 1990).

22. Efforts to link east Europe's rail systems with the EU are complicated both by lengthier distances (e.g., Berlin-Moscow, 1885 km) and the problem of aligning standard with wider continental (eastern) rail gauges.

23. *The Economist* (29 Oct. 1994: 23) estimates a cost savings of around 20 percent since Sweden's rail decentralization. Larsson (1993) notes a 1987–92 decrease in SJ employment from 29,000 to 18,000, though clearly, claims that such downsizing is also a success in macro-economic terms are open to question.

24. The sale of the three companies (Angel Train Contractors, Eversholt Leasing and Porterbrook Leasing), involving the transfer of BR's 11,000 locomotives and carriages to be leased to a total of 25 train operators, brought a price (1.8 billion pounds, or about $3 bn), much higher than expected (*The Times*, 10 Nov. 1995: 13).

25. Despite some notable successes (the QE2 bridge at Dartford; London Underground's Northern Line upgrade), other PFI projects have lagged, including Network Southeast rail, where bidders failed to materialize due to overstringent government conditions; the east London Docklands light railway extension; and an upgrade of the west coast line, added late to the EU's list of priority TENs projects (see Table 7.1), but now apparently to be funded by Railtrack itself (FT, 10 Nov.

1995: 27). Upcoming projects, especially the $4.5 bn Channel Tunnel rapid rail link, will be far sterner tests of PFI's ultimate viability.

26. For example, heavily discounted shares (at 190 p) were offered to private investors prior to the public flotation on 20 May. The government also withheld 69 m pounds for dividend payments in the first year regardless of Railtrack's actual performance (WSJE, 17 April 1996: 1; FT, 15 April 1996: 7). It is estimated that hidden government subsidies to the privatized rail system will amount to 1 bn pounds ($1.5 bn) annually for the next decade (*The Economist,* 3 Feb. 1996: 31). Most passenger fares were also "capped" for an initial three-year period.

27. For example, FT 2 Dec. 1994: 14; 10 Nov. 1995: 27; 1 Feb. 1995: 11; WSJE, 17 April 1996: 11. The public campaign for BR's selloff lurched from crisis to crisis; BR's own outgoing chairman, Sir Bob Reid, publicly questioned the wisdom of the methods chosen, while a junior transport minister stirred controversy with an unfortunate off-hand reference to rail commuters as "dreadful human beings" (FT, 9 Feb. 1995: 10), suggesting a perpetuation of two-tiered thinking, between communal (rail) and individual (car) transport and the social class implications of those using each.

28. In one memorable outburst, Short attacked Railtrack managers as "disreputable and incompetent . . . a bad bunch of people" (FT, 15 April 1996: 7).

Chapter Four

Insolent Chariots: The Road Sector

Countless millions of people, devoid of any public
or social constraints . . . have thrown themselves
into a dependence on this vehicle [the automobile]
that has assumed the dimensions of an extremely
serious and not readily curable mass addiction.
—GEORGE F. KENNAN
Around the Cragged Hill

While European transport discussions often commence with the railways,
they inevitably become dominated by developments in the road sector.
This is so because of its relentless postwar growth throughout the developed world, and its increasing predominance as a carrier of both passengers and freight. For all the European rhetorical focus on rail policy, the
facts tell of a basic, and worsening, modal imbalance caused by a massive
shift toward road use, based on a potent combination of cost and convenience factors for both individuals and enterprises. In turn, this usage pattern reflects and sustains the clout of powerful road-based interests which
have successfully pushed for expansion of the motor industry as the most
feasible means of moving people and goods within, and between, developed economies, in which flexibility and network reach, rather than
weight and volume capacity, become crucial criteria affecting modal
choice.

Because of this constellation of interests and the nature of the mode
itself, road use increasingly has dwarfed other land modes in every sense:
in numbers of trips taken and passengers carried; in volume of freight
goods hauled; in numbers of vehicles; in length of infrastructure; in num-

bers of jobs directly and indirectly related to it; in amounts of pollution produced; and in numbers of deaths and injuries caused. The automobile itself has truly emerged as both an individual blessing and a collective curse in modern society. While the "car culture" epitomizes a free and mobile society, the manifestations of overuse (externalities such as congestion, blighted landscapes, smog and noise) all make it a source of stress and even social isolation in modern life.[1] What has long been seen as a reflection of prosperity has emerged as a key impediment to a balanced CTP.

Europe's single most daunting transport challenge arguably lies in restricting this hitherto unchecked growth of road use, for at least six reasons:

1. The motor industry's establishment as the predominant mode has had the added if dubious virtue of being associated, or having associated itself, with the wider success of the European economy: restrict road use, it is claimed, and economic prosperity will suffer.

2. Europe's entire manufacturing industry has been shaped by vehicular access to roads and motorways, shifting heavy industry out of cities but contributing to urban sprawl.

3. Powerful motor interests are deeply entrenched via car and truck manufacturers, transport unions and road-dependent, oil-based industry and service interests, who are able to translate their currently favorable position into one of influence regarding the shaping of future road policy, a privilege they will not easily relinquish.

4. Excessive road use generates highly negative (environmental) externalities, increasing efficiency/equity tensions in transport policymaking.

5. Many road-based problems are local and regional, hence beyond the CTP's scope. Thus any wide-ranging policy changes will depend on the convergence of local, regional, national, and international interests (and thus on the evolution of the subsidiarity debate).

6. Finally, the explosion of road usage in southern and eastern Europe will severely challenge EU-led attempts to apply uniform limitations on unrestricted road use, even if they can somehow be agreed upon by the EU15.

This chapter will first briefly discuss the European historical and societal context behind the inexorable growth in road use. Then it will examine the national and EU policy environment, focusing particularly on recent liberalization and harmonization initiatives in the sector. Finally, it will examine the changing nature of the motor industry itself in response to pressures both internal to Europe, especially Single Market-led rationalization and environmental imperatives, and external to it, via the growing foreign challenge to European car manufacturers.

HISTORICAL ELEMENTS

Societies are frequently characterized by their principal means of movement, which reflect spatial realities but also shape the way they function internally and interact externally. This truism has been no less relevant in modern times than in the ancient world; the main difference lies in the design and function(s) of the prevailing transport systems. One of the elements distinguishing the Roman empire from the Greek city-state system was the centralization of rule, which was reinforced in a physical sense by a determined road-building effort; this contrasted with heavy Greek (Athenian) reliance on sea power as a way to mitigate the natural divisions of a scattered archipelago. The expansion of the Roman road system was characteristically systematic and centered on the Forum itself, first connecting areas of Latium via the via Appia, later extended south and east; the via Latina (inland, Rome to Capua); and the via Flaminia, north across the Appenines to Rimini. Later, in 2d century A.D., the system was extended further afield, to Spain via the via Domitia and eastward across the Balkans via the via Egnatia (De Burgh 1953: 246 n.1).

The function of these roads, which were paved solidly in layers of sand, gravel, and sometimes concrete, was primarily military and strategic, and a means of shifting legions between garrisoned towns and helping to control disparate populations. The road system was equally important for spreading intelligence, creating in Gibbon's words a "great chain of communications" extending for nearly 4000 miles from northwest to southeast. Part of the system's uniqueness was the regular stationing of outposts roughly every five miles to allow rapid relaying of communications via imperial fiat to remote territories (Gibbon 1981: 74–75). Historian George Trevelyan (1959) noted that the Roman road system in Britain even had a delayed nation-building effect, by aiding later Saxon and Norman efforts to subjugate the native peoples under a single rule.

Overland routes long have been associated with international and intraregional movement, which after the collapse of the Roman empire in the west developed primarily commercial applications. Iran's emergence as a trading center, for example, derived from its position as a central Asian crossroads—a legacy that even now is being reflected in new road/rail projects to exploit its proximity to the Arab states and the former USSR southern republics. The spread of merchandise went hand in hand with the spread of culture, such as between medieval Europe and the far east via the Silk Road and by the singular (though now, alas, increasingly doubted) 13th century forays into China by the Venetian Marco Polo. Spiritual pilgrimages produced a new kind of road use, with its own commercial applications, in the pre-Renaissance era.

Even so, in the late Middle Ages and early modern period road and trade routes were as often barriers to travel as facilitators of societal development. This was due to the very slow nature of transport by carriages and to the primitive state of most of Europe's roads, particularly in Germany, choked with dust in summer and mired in mud for much of the rest of the year. The German society and polity remained fragmented partly as a result of poor road communications in the pre-rail period. France, in contrast, enjoyed better connections due to a superior road system in place by the Napoleonic era. Access to east-west trade routes was a key determinant of the peculiar nature of Swiss modernization, affecting both its federal structure, through the existence of a "polycephalous city network" of urban centers (Basel, Zürich, Schaffhausen, St. Gallen) all competing for trade business, and its overall levels of wealth.[2] It was indeed partly because of the backwardness of European roads that the 18th century emergence of the Grand Tour assumed value as a kind of finishing school for young English gentlemen, in which the means were just as important as the ends; nobly facing the hazards of the road (bad weather, bandits, breakdowns) was considered no less a builder of character than was the cultural enrichment of looking at great art in Rome.

In modern times the quality of transport systems has become a more direct measurement of national economic health. Whereas in the 18th century the ability of states to construct inland waterways went hand-in-hand with the expansion of trade just before the onset of industrialization, and in the 19th century the building of the railways was closely associated with national economic strength and prestige, the 20th century has been the era of the road and the motorcar. Road growth on a national scale once lagged because asphalting techniques have been refined only relatively recently, enabled by the industrial shift from coal to oil and stimulated by the emergence and widespread application of the internal combustion engine.

Intermodal rivalries also played a part in the emergence of road transport. In mid-19th century Britain, turnpike trusts (and canal companies) had waged a furious but futile rearguard action against the encroaching railroads (Thompson 1950: 47). In 1920s Germany, aggressive pricing strategies by the railways, aimed at consolidating their control over the haulage industry, seriously backfired and brought about reforms such as the 1931 introduction of a road licensing requirement that established a policy basis for a new (road) growth industry. A reversal of strategy in more recent decades has been aimed at maintaining rail freight and thus a semblance of a modal balance in Germany.[3]

Thus like rail, the road sector has been a measurement of economic power, but with a different focus. Whereas rail symbolized collective, societal strength, based primarily on the length and breadth of the national infrastructure, the motor car has become a universally recognized symbol of individual wealth and status. Vehicle ownership replaced network infrastructure as the yardstick, coupled with the car's emergence as "the defining technological artifact of the 20th century" (Field and Clark 1997). Unrestricted car ownership and operating rights accordingly have become metaphors for individual freedom itself. Aside from its obvious relevance in the American context, such perceptions now prevail in eastern Europe, where mobility is considered a "cornerstone of emancipation," a symbol of personal and familial territoriality and even an "extension of home on wheels" (Transport 1990: 10).

Accordingly, road transport policymaking is a veritable political minefield because any meaningful reform implies an attempt to use public policy mechanisms to alter entrenched personal behavioral patterns. Indeed draconian attempts to restrict access to and usage of cars would be tantamount to political suicide for politicians of all stripes. Road politics involve special bottom-up pressures unlike any other mode, because of wide individual dependence on regular use; or as Lord Stokes, a former car executive, is said to have lamented, "everyone is an expert on the motor industry" (quoted in Owen 1983: 47). For these reasons, the road sector has been the most demand-driven of all the travel modes, as well as the most obvious target for criticism based on the consequences of overuse.

This factor alone helps explain much of the success of the road industry in 20th century transport prioritizing in western Europe (and indeed, in the western world); wider social concerns have remained secondary to those affecting individual priorities, which has made the road lobby, by combining industry muscle with consumer interests, a formidable actor in shaping transport policy. While no politician has dared echo President Calvin Coolidge in equating European interests with those of the motor industry, motor interests successfully have sold the notion that cost-effective road use is also broadly valuable for the overall European economy. The reverse argument, of course, is that attempts to raise the aggregate relative price of road transport via e.g. fiscal (tax) measures or peak-use charges, will produce a drag on future growth.

Less often recognized is the convergence of union and industry interests, in awkward defiance of Marxist logic, in maintaining the predominance of the sector. This has been particularly true in Britain, where the joint intransigence of the car industry and road unions was as a key element frustrating governmental road initiatives in the 1970s (Healey 1990: 408). Such interest group expression has also led to suboptimal decision making because of the self-serving nature of many of the arguments; it is all too common to decry traffic-related pollution and congestion while being quite blind to the fact that, by driving, the haulier or consumer directly contributes to these same negative externalities.

MODERN ROAD GROWTH:
INEXORABLE EXPANSION AND ITS PROBLEMS

The justification for relentless expansion of road systems in the late 20th century is a direct extrapolation of the earlier elements discussed above. While rail systems were being nationalized, they were burdened with public service obligations but without sufficient economic resources to maximize rail's natural advantages, namely a wide infrastructure and large capacity. In contrast, road building has proceeded apace because it facilitated commercial prospects for industrial economies as a whole, and also for individual firms. States have been more inclined to lavish road interests with expanding infrastructure because it has served many interests in a growing economic pie, whereas rail has been subsidized in spite, rather than because, of its declining competitiveness, i.e. for social rather than strictly financial considerations. Road-based interests have also benefited from perceptions that a strong motorway network is in the national interests of states as defined in security terms, though not to the extent as in the U.S. with the Cold War-related planning and building of the Interstate highway system begun in the 1950s under Eisenhower (Galbraith 1964). Apart from isolated modern examples, such as in northern Scandinavia,[4] road planning has been less a security than a commercial enterprise.

However, to many analysts this economic orientation of the road industry is richly symptomatic of everything that is wrong with European transport writ large. In a June 1995 address, the then-chairman of the European Conference of Ministers of Transport, Viktor Klima, excoriated European transport policies in recent decades for their "meek submission to demand" that has been overwhelmingly based on road building at the expense of other modes (Allen 1995). While much attention has focused on Britain, long notably parsimonious with aid to its rail network, other societies perceived as being more rail-oriented have also strongly favored road in relative terms. Even France, with its rapidly developing HST network, has devoted many times more resources to motorway building since the 1970s than it has for rail (.65 percent versus just .09 percent of GDP); and the investment imbalance is equally evident in the case of Germany (Holliday et al. 1991: 160).

Predictably, however, there is more agreement on the problems of growing road use than on the possible solutions to them. These problems include the following:

1. *Unrelenting traffic growth.* The road sector has grown massively in the postwar era, both in overall vehicle numbers and lengths of infrastructures. Overall transport activity in Europe has grown over 50 percent in the past twenty years, with road traffic accounting for most of that increase. As noted much earlier (Tables 1.2 and 1.3) road use now accounts for about 70 percent of all freight activity and nearly 80 percent of passen-

ger trips. In 1995 Eurostat reported an even greater imbalance in domestic freight transport, where a massive 86 percent was covered by road but just 5 percent by rail. Road traffic volumes have grown by 3.7 percent annually over the last twenty years (CEC 1993a: 10), far outstripping overall economic growth rates (averaging little over 2 percent during the same period). Table 4.1 illustrates a fifteen-fold rise in the number of cars per population since 1950; the increase in total cars owned is even greater, as it does not allow for demographic changes (growth in population).

Of all the reasons for these massive increases, flexibility is perhaps key; both car and lorry are mobile, with door-to-door delivery possibilities on tighter schedules, using "just in time" delivery methods, than anything possible on the railways. For this reason, road traffic is most advantageous over shorter distances; some two-thirds of all goods transported by road travel a distance of less than 50 km, while only 14 percent travel over 150 km (CEC 1993a). Very much the same is true with passenger traffic; in Germany, for example, of an average of a thousand trips by car yearly, more than half are for trips under 3 km, and those of over 50 km account for just 2.5 percent of the total (Holzapfel and Schallabock 1994: 200–201).

2. *Stagnant investment.* Booming demand and traffic growth has increased pressures greatly on existing resources and infrastructures. Yet these pressures, including overall and peak-period congestion, bottlenecks on key routes and deterioration of roadbeds, have not been met with like increases in spending. Up to the 1970s, road network expansion continued apace, partly for reasons of expediency by ribbon-cutting politicians anxious to demonstrate progress with new physical infrastructure. Since then, however, the trend has been in the opposite direction, given the overall decline in transport investment expenditures from around 1.5 percent in the 1970s to the current European level of little over 1 percent.

Aside from the problem of new road construction is the less glamorous but no less necessary task of maintaining existing road networks, now showing distinct signs of middle age wear and tear. Growth in traffic volume is actually a minor source of the problem. Mostly to blame is ever-

TABLE 4.1
Increases in European Road Use, 1950–1985

	1950	1960	1970	1980	1985
Motorways (1000s km)	2	4	13	26	30
Cars owned (millions)	6	20	58	96	114
Cars per 1000 population	22	72	194	300	353
Commercial vehicles (millions)	3	5	8	10	12

Source: Molle 1990.

growing truck sizes which have increased from 28 tons up to 44 tons, the maximum limit recommended by a recent EU proposal for intra-Union traffic.

3. *Feebleness of the policy response.* The EU has been attacked from many directions, including the abovementioned ECMT, because of the widely perceived inadequacy of its policy response to the growth in road traffic, marked by deference to individual state attempts to meet demand by increasing supply. But demand-driven policy has been inadequate, for three main reasons. First, it represents reactive rather than proactive response by public authorities continually attempting to keep abreast, rather than get ahead, of the problem. Second, the pressure for rapid expansion of European road and motorway systems has meant haphazard rather than carefully planned expansion.

Third, despite all efforts road-building has failed to keep up with the growth in demand. A chronic problem in European road-building has been that, as capacity has expanded, so too has traffic volume—filling even supposedly "final" solutions to localized problems, like London's M-25 orbital motorway system built in the 1970s—more quickly than was ever thought possible by planners. In the 1970s and 1980s, the proliferation of road networks and traffic came to be seen as a contributor to societal ills and a reflection, in the transport realm, of growing societal population pressures. This factor has major implications for the ambitious international motorway networks now envisioned for Europe (see Chapter 7), since better long-distance routes may generate further growth in long-haul traffic but without a corresponding reduction in short-distance, localized use. A schematic presentation of core-area crowding can be seen in Figure 4.1.

4. *Energy consumption.* Since the early 1970s, energy usage of road traffic has increased a full 3.8 percent on an annualized basis (up 103 percent overall) (CEC 1993a). Here the relentless growth in traffic volumes has more than offset gains in fuel efficiency in engine technologies. The severity of the problem is compounded by European dependency on foreign sources for fuel needs. Apart from individual oil producers such as Britain and Norway, most European economies and transporters are heavily dependent on Middle Eastern oil supplies, a factor keenly appreciated during the oil shocks of the 1970s but much less so at present, given the lack of immediate urgency about the problem. The increase in urban densities is also a contributing factor, since increased vehicle idling in slow-moving traffic decreases overall fuel efficiency.

5. *Environmental consequences.* The EU's focus on "sustainable mobility" in the transport sector has centered on controlling the emissions of harmful substances by road vehicles. According to the Commission, carbon dioxide (CO_2) emissions have grown 76 percent between 1971 and 1989; nitrogen oxide (NOx) by 68 percent; and hydrocarbons (HC) by 41 percent (CEC 1993a). As shown in Table 4.2, the road sector accounts for

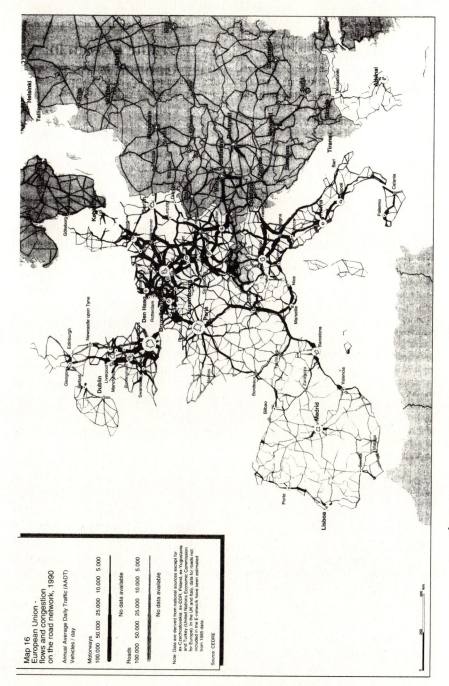

Source: CEDRE

Map 16
European Union -
flows and congestion
on the road network, 1990

Annual Average Daily Traffic (AADT)
Vehicles / day

Motorways

100.000 50.000 25.000 10.000 5.000

No data available

Roads

100.000 50.000 25.000 10.000 5.000

No data available

Note: Data are derived from national sources except for
ex-Czechoslovakia, ex-DDR, Poland, ex-Yugoslavia
and Turkey (United Nations Economic Commission
for Europe). In the UK and Italy, data for roads not
included in the E-network have been estimated
from 1985 data.

0   250   500 km

Figure 4.1   European Union Flows and Congestion on the Road Network.

TABLE 4.2
Modal Share of CO_2 Emissions

Transport Mode	Emissions share (percentage)
Road	79.7
Private car	55.4
Trucks	22.7
Buses, coaches	1.6
Aviation	10.9
Rail	3.9
Passengers	2.8
Goods	1.1
Inland waterways	0.7
Other	4.3

Source: CEC 1993a.

around 80 percent of all CO_2 emissions. There is ongoing scientific debate about the long-term effects of these increases, particularly as regards "greenhouse" gasses and the effect of hydrocarbons on ozone levels and ultimately on human health, though the cyclical, knock-on nature of these problems (as represented in Figure 4.2) means that the debate is primarily over the extent, not the existence, of the damage incurred. In addition, environmental pressures result from ever-growing land take on a crowded continent—both directly via eminent domain demands for land convertible to road use, and indirectly due to blighting of adjacent lands by traffic-related soil, air and noise pollution. Other problems, including aesthetic deterioration of rural and urban landmarks, all detract from quality of life in cities and along transit routes.

Responses to these problems range from the tendency to downplay them as wholly reversible to the positively apocalyptic, with references to "environmental infarction" as the environment's tolerance for the consequences of traffic is simply overwhelmed, as might be measured, for example, in increasing health maladies and declining life expectancies (Holzapfel and Schollabock 1994). All of these problems have been recognized by the EU as European problems, although the nonlocalized effects of many, such as global warming and ozone loss, mean that even stringent measures taken at national or even EU level will have an attenuated effect on the global environment. This is particularly the case as road usage, and dependence on less efficient vehicles, climbs even more precipitously in less developed regions of the world. The EU itself has recognized the impetus for traffic-related environmental awareness begun at the first UN environmental conference in Stockholm in 1972, and its follow-up at Rio, yet policy initiatives and follow-through have lagged.

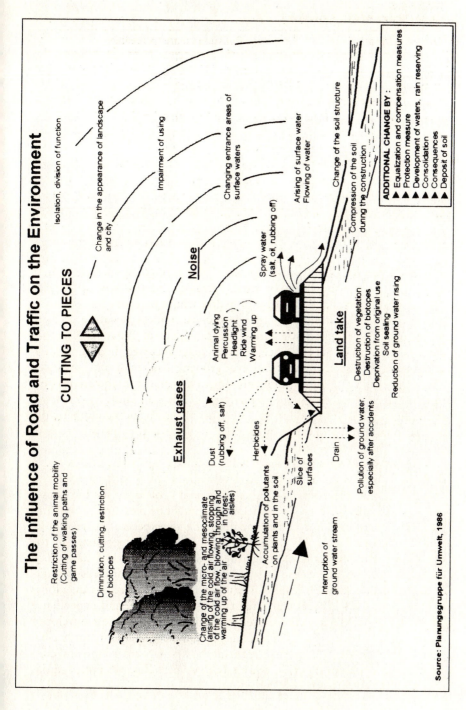

Figure 4.2 The Influence of Road and Traffic on the Environment

6. *Safety concerns.* In 1992, according to Eurostat, over 45,000 persons were killed on European roads and around 1.5 m injured—an annual carnage that approximates the total number of American lives lost during the whole of the Vietnam war. A contributing factor to safety concerns is the growing number and greater size of trucks on the road, which not only contributes to problems of crowding and visibility but are also responsible for up to 90 percent of all roadbed damage, and for increasing the severity of what road accidents do occur (Heinze and Kill 1994). The overall economic cost of such elements is again hard to quantify, but they percolate all through the economy and society at large.

7. *Insufficient costing.* Many hold that the huge growth in road traffic has been the natural result of advantageous pricing for road traffic in comparison with other modes. Whereas national rail systems have labored under public service obligations with often inadequate compensating public investment, road users have not had to cover fully the costs of operating their vehicles. In other words, the externalities of road use (energy consumption, pollution, congestion-related time lost) substantially are carried by society at large. The imbalance is even greater in the American context, where economic pressures and oil-based political considerations keep the domestic oil market, and gasoline taxes, far below world levels.

Costing is a major factor determining modal choice, though not the only one. Speed, reliability, and overall quality of service are equally, and in some cases even more, crucial considerations, especially in value-based freight movement. Even so, many now regard movement toward full internalization of all the associated costs of operating a vehicle, such as through higher carbon taxes or peak use charges, to be the necessary centerpiece of future European transport policy. Only then would operators be forced to consider alternative modes for the same trip, or to forgo the need for travel altogether, all with the broader aim of reducing, rather than controlling, overall levels of traffic. But despite the elegant simplicity of the "polluter pays" principle, it has proved neither marketable nor politically feasible as a public policy solution even in Europe; and its capability of forcing substantial modal shifting is widely doubted.

A factor in the predominance of the road sector has been the aggressive promoting of road use by the lobbying of auto interests in national capitals and, increasingly, in Brussels. In their discussion of the growth of lobbying at European level ("lobbyfication" in the new if awkward vernacular), Andersen and Eliassen (1993: 41) note that the car industry is particularly well-entrenched at the European level, where the main industry organization includes some twenty different technical groups to influence specific regulatory aspects of EU legislation. These interests are union- as well as industry-based; in Britain, for example, the single largest and most powerful union has long been the road-based Transport and General Workers' Union (TGWU), once the springboard for Ernest Bevin's political career; in 1980, before the Thatcher trade union reforms, the TGWU counted over 2 million members (Sampson 1984a).

THE EUROPEAN POLICY RESPONSE

The Common Transport Policy has tended to focus primarily on freight transport (road haulage) rather than passenger transport (Lee 1994). In part, this prioritization reflected earlier (pre-1970s) emphasis on enhancing intra-European trade and maximizing the Common Market's potential, as opposed to the longer term aim of freer movement of people. It also reflected the intra-regional and national, rather than international, nature of most individual coach and car trips, and the consequent lack of urgency in tackling the passenger market's international dimension.

Within this context, the EU has approached the road and rail transport questions from an altogether different perspective because of divergent operational and ownership patterns. Whereas the longstanding "fusion" of rail infrastructure and operations means that decoupling efforts remain in their early stages, the road sector has always been based on largely private, individual usage of public infrastructure. The relative size and number of freight operators has also differed greatly. Whereas rail operations tend toward the monopolistic (and government-run) for reasons of economies of scale, the road haulage industry has encouraged numerous small operators, with consolidation into large conglomerates restricted to the larger states.

Thus a small firm capable of operating a fleet of trucks, either as a separate business or on an "own-account" basis, would be simply shut out in a market structure such as rail. Even so, there is a parallel between the EU's treatment of the two modes (as well as with the airlines), insofar as a truly single market would require the ending of distortions created by restrictions on cabotage (the right for operators, whether public or private, to conduct business wholly within the borders of another country). The difference is that the greater mobility of road vehicles should make full cabotage rights easier to achieve, on a practical basis, once introduced in 1998.

From the outset the EEC was empowered to promote a common road policy in at least three ways. The CTP itself (Rome Treaty Articles 74–84) targeted the road sector, along with rail and inland waterways, as its core area of competence. Equally applicable were general competition provisions (Article 3), calling for "the institution of a system ensuring that competition in the common market is not distorted." The treaty also called for "the elimination of quantitative restrictions on the import and export of goods," thereby associating road transport also with the free movement principles of the single market (Treaties 1979). Subsequent practice, however, was to allow the continuation of restrictions on the operations of foreign road transporters within the territory of Community countries.

Traditionally, the movement of goods across EC territory has been restricted by different national regulations regarding overall pricing and capacity policies that favored domestic users of national road infrastructures. Foreign hauliers have been restricted by quota systems, hammered out directly via binational negotiation, in which hauliers had to apply to other countries' DOTs for a restricted number of licenses to operate within their territory.[5] The quota system was reinforced by general restrictions on cabotage that denied nonresident carriers the right to pick up and deliver goods wholly within another member state. Because of such restrictions, road haulage, though a lucrative business, has been hampered by the prevalence (estimated at anything from 30 to 50 percent of all trips) of "empty runs" on return trips by carriers to their home base. Such restrictions on road haulage were estimated by the Cecchini report on the costs of non-Europe to add a cost of about 2 percent to the value of each consignment (Lodge 1989).

As in many other policy areas, one of the main problems in addressing discrepancies in the road haulage business was the divergence of national priorities. In countries like the Netherlands, Belgium, and especially Britain, a relatively liberalized (and competitive) market has existed. Britain opened up its road system to foreign hauliers by eliminating quantitative restrictions as early as 1968 and deregulated its bus and coach services in the 1980s. Many other countries, including France, Italy, and especially West Germany, bowed to national interests in protecting their domestic hauliers, thus thwarting efforts toward European liberalization. Indeed, lack of progress in road haulage was a central factor leading to the pivotal 1985 Court ruling on the CTP (see Chapter 2).

German foot-dragging on road liberalization reflected two broad concerns of the Transport Ministry and the government at large. One was the perceived need to maintain a significant role for rail freight and thus for a competing industry in the national railway company. The other was in protecting the interests of some 200,000 truckers (*Guterverkehr*), aligned through the BDF association—an almost exclusively middle class grouping which, unsurprisingly, is an important source of political support for Chancellor Kohl's ruling Christian Democratic Union. The truckers were slow to realize the significance of the 1985 ECJ ruling on transport which, according to Kammerer, "unleashed panic" in the German transport ministry (1990: 32–33), leading to reactive road policies that for a time defied European attempts at coordination. All this provided an awkward counterpoint to Kohl's championing of the European federal model during the same period.

Nonetheless, progress toward low-level European road harmonization—or at least toward minimum "Community rules"—was evident by the late 1960s in e.g. social questions (minimum driver hours and ages; mandated rest periods). The member states also pursued two other strands, regarding minimum harmonization in technical matters (brakes, lighting, axle sizes, maximum truck weights) and, more recently, in fiscal matters as well (vehicle and fuel taxes), though progress in this latter area has been slower in coming.

The efforts to complete the Single Market in the 1980s had an inevitable chilling effect on the quantitative road quota system, since the abolition of intra-EC frontier posts has meant the ending of road checks for safety standards and other authorizations (CEC 1985). The 1985 White Paper optimistically asserted that common road policy measures should be taken by the Council by the end of 1986, aiming at the phasing out of quotas and the establishment of conditions for non-residents to operate in other states by the end of 1988, and for complete freedom to provide services for road passengers by 1989 (CEC 1985).

Though delayed well beyond this putative deadline, these reforms have been implemented gradually since the late 1980s. Significantly, most of the changes have come in the form of generally applicable regulations, rather than directives needing to be transformed into national legislation. After years of British pressure and under renewed Commission threats due to non-action, a breakthrough of sorts was achieved at the Luxembourg Transport Council in June 1988, in which West Germany finally conceded the abolition of quota restrictions by January 1993 (Owen and Dynes 1989).

In turn, the abolition of quantitative restrictions (quotas) has been replaced by an EU licensing arrangement based on qualitative criteria, to which hauliers must comply in order to have access to road networks on a Community-wide basis. A 1988 regulation (no. 1841/88) reorganized the quota system, while another four years later (no. 881/92) aimed to replace the quota system altogether by five-year general authorizations to companies, contingent on their meeting certain requirements regarding professional competence and financial worthiness. Additionally, from 1990 pricing of international road operations has been freely negotiable.

Steps have also been taken to eliminate restrictions on road cabotage, though more slowly, and the process will be completed only in July 1998. This delay has partly resulted from greater ECJ scrutiny of EU legislation. For example, a 1989 Council regulation (no. 4059/89), laying down conditions under which non-resident carriers could operate road haulage services within a member state and states to introduce road-use charges for lorry traffic, later met with opposition, and eventually this provision was annulled by a European Court ruling. A subsequent regulation (no. 3118/93) amended these conditions. Other important initiatives have included a harmonization of procedures for checks on the transport of dangerous goods by road (CE 1994a).[6]

The passenger road market has also been liberalized, especially via two regulations in 1992; one (no. 648/92) set down common rules for the international carriage of coach and bus passengers, and the other (no. 2454/92) established the conditions under which non-resident carriers could operate in other countries (cabotage). Road-based initiatives have also proliferated in the area of increasing use of information technologies (telematics), such as in road traffic information and early warning devices, to ease traffic flows. Here the Council has requested the Commission to set up a working party for the strategic study of telematics deployment.

But even with the EU's recent steps to sweep away the former restrictive practices, a number of key issues have not been fully addressed, including road haulage of EU companies within nonmember countries, the problems of own-account operators, and the variances in road pricing in different EU countries. On this latter point, progress is as elusive as ever; as of 1996, foreign hauliers using the roads of some north European countries (Belgium, Luxembourg, the Netherlands, Denmark, and Germany) will be required to pay an annual motorway tax of 1000 pounds per vehicle, while domestic users will be granted rebates. This measure will help offset the worst effects of liberalization—competitive advantages accruing to more efficient competitors—while also maintaining rail systems, both being political aims with domestic consequences. Other countries charge tolls for motorway use (Spain, Italy, and France), while others (Britain) are at a relative disadvantage because of free access by outsiders to its motorway system. The EU road haulage market has become freer but not yet free, and still falls short of complete harmonization.

As with rail, EU-initiated reform of antiquated national restrictions has reflected a rapidly changing marketplace. Haulage by road continues to dominate, but with the Single Market reforms the international sector is now growing much more rapidly than is the domestic haulage market; for example, between 1984 and 1989, a period of overall rapid economic growth after the severe recession of the early 1980s, domestic road haulage increased by 50 percent, whereas international road freight (within the EC) increased a full 84.4 percent ("Poor Response" 1995). This increase is due mainly to the growing cross-border nature of European business, although individual runs have also lengthened.

By the same token, the abolition of many border controls in Europe via the Schengen accord paradoxically has increased the problem of collecting information on traffic flows, which traditionally has been provided by national authorities. For this reason, the ECMT's 1995 report on European transport infrastructure calls strongly for the establishment of a Europe-wide database to monitor international traffic flows, in order to help with future infrastructure planning. The need will be particularly acute for eastern Europe, where the modal shift from rail to road is creating pressing concerns for the EU's external dimension as well as its internal market reforms.

Much of the problem lies in controlling the worst excesses of car overuse at the most localized level. Over the past fifteen years alone, the energy consumption of urban transport has increased four times more quickly than that of intercity transport and now accounts for nearly 40 percent of all energy usage in transport (Molina 1995). In Germany, an estimated 80 percent of all motorized individual transport (MIT) occurs within a 15 km (10 mile) radius, which in local areas makes this the main competitor with public transport (Heinze and Kill 1994). Most of the research focus, however, has been on solutions for road use (e.g., development of "smart" roads and virtual infrastructure), which is primarily a matter of traffic management rather than inducements to modal switching, use of public transport or encouraging urban nonmotorized traffic.

The reductions in public transport investment represent a clear prioritization of economic over environmental considerations, since "it is generally recognized that measures aimed at transferring people from private cars to energy-efficient public transport provide the greatest opportunity for energy savings and environmental gains" (Molina 1995). And although the EU Commission has emphasized savings in urban energy usage, via such programs as Thermie, its range of options remains restricted by a number of factors. A key problem remains one of measurement of the true costs of road travel, including the mixing of quantitative with qualitative criteria and the inherent difficulties of valuing obtuse elements as clean air and safety, much less the value of a human life or the costs of an injury. Other difficulties result from differences between states in traffic conditions and pricing policies; varying local conditions; and prevailing policies already in practice.

Recently the Commission has addressed directly the two important and interrelated questions of encouraging public transport via a Citizen's Network in Europe (CEC 1996a) and more efficient costing of road transport vis-à-vis other modes (CEC 1996b). While the Commission readily admits its limited scope for action in either sphere, its interest remains vital to encourage and sustain cross-national research efforts and for setting the tone of the overall debate. The cost question is crucial in market-oriented economies, and many observers believe that the imbalance favoring road use can only be tackled via widespread adjustments in pricing policies to require users to cover both infrastructure (capital) and operating and maintenance costs of road use, including the costs of accidents, environmental damage and congestion.

The pricing Green Paper (CEC 1996b) underscores the need to emphasize policy shifts to enable equitable costs of transport, while rejecting taxation-based instruments as the way forward. The demise of the long-touted carbon tax for road vehicles no doubt dampened enthusiasm for fiscal solutions. Part of the problem is the frequency with which charges are levied; in contrast to normal transport services, by which passengers are charged on a per-trip basis, automobile charges are partially hidden by their periodic nature, as with annual licenses or need-based refueling stops (Button 1994). Hence the growing interest in using electronic road-use charging systems, pioneered in Singapore and soon to be introduced in Austria, Germany, and the Netherlands. Another, more radical solution would be a move toward private road management as was recently tested in the American states of Virginia and California, although developments in Britain, where private tolling systems have been tested, may offer some limited scope under optimal conditions.

In general, however, attempts to introduce costing shifts will be painstaking and general efforts to paint policy with a broad brush, especially since costing is not always the main consideration in mode choice of either hauliers or individuals. Lack of EU authority in making fiscal policy in Europe is another significant limitation. And the potential for political fallout of such reforms is great. It would not only raise the ire of entrenched road-based interests, but would inevitably work against hauliers from eastern Europe. A major problem could be brewing, with the combination of rapidly growing dependence on road transport to the east, combined with the increasing resistance of EU countries "to be flooded with clapped out, polluting lorries, driven by drivers of doubtful competence" (CEC 1995b: 19). Greater harmonization of road standards for hauliers remains one of the critical areas of transport policy reform in the years immediately ahead, and requires action not only from the Commission but from the Council and eastern European governments whose domestic political credibility will be measured in terms of how quickly they can secure full EU membership.

LIBERALIZATION AND RATIONALIZATION
IN THE AUTO INDUSTRY

The creation of the Single European Market has also had a transformative effect on the European automotive industry itself, though the changes have been far from uniform. Since the war, many car manufacturers in Europe have enjoyed relatively privileged positions, protected as industrial national champions by governments eager to maintain a manufacturing capacity in automobiles and trucks. Again however, there have been differences between market-oriented states such as Britain, where a traditionally robust, domestically owned car manufacturing sector has all but succumbed to foreign (mostly nonEuropean) predators, as opposed to others (Italy, France) which have promoted or allowed virtually a monopolistic or duopolistic domestic position for one or two companies (Fiat; Renault and Peugeot). Still others, notably Portugal, have benefitted from a shift toward lower-cost production areas in Europe.

All states, however, have actively or passively provided protectionist measures such as favorable fiscal policies at the national level, and bailouts of troubled industries (even in Britain, with its rescue of Rolls Royce in the 1970s) have been the rule rather than the exception. Even today, there are wide European discrepancies in car taxation, import regulations, and the like, which have a dampening effect at the individual level when it comes to transferring one's car to another country. The notoriously slow removal of national restrictions on car transferrals is a prime example of passive resistance at national level to CTP implementation (via dilatory implementation of directives).

In contrast to the haulage industry, however, the auto manufacturing industry has greeted the coming of the Single Market with considerable apprehension. Though the Single Market project was largely predicated on the belief that it would promote European competitiveness by promoting cross-border mergers and cooperative agreements—in Mrs. Thatcher's words, to make Europe "open for business"—it has challenged a key, protected national industrial sector by inviting unwelcome international competition. Much of this competition has come not from the U.S., where the travails of the motor industry in Detroit became symptomatic of America's declining competitiveness in the early 1980s, but from Japan with its traditionally powerful market presence in the more efficient smaller cars favored in Europe. The Japanese "threat," in fact, has itself hindered completion of a single European car market, as it has divided the smaller, non-producer states (Belgium, the Netherlands) from large states with a vested car manufacturing interest (France, Germany, Italy, Spain), which therefore aimed to limit the influx of foreign-made vehicles (Owen 1983). The EU has maintained a common external tariff against Japanese imports of around 10 percent (Smith 1990).

Most international attention on the car industry as an instrument of external trade policy has focused on high-level brinksmanship between the American and Japanese governments over access to domestic car markets.[7] However, the difficulties faced by European auto manufacturers from a resurgent Detroit and in a more open industrial environment are vividly symptomized by the bitter legal case between General Motors and Volkswagen concerning alleged industrial espionage involving Jose Ignacio Lopez, who defected to Volkswagen in 1993. The Lopez case became additionally problematic because of alleged support from the Lower Saxony government headed by a prominent Socialist politician, Gerhard Schröder.

More generally, the threat to Europe's car manufacturers has taken two forms: one is Commission pressure to end heavy state subsidizing of manufacturers, which had allowed mid-size "national champion" firms to continue to function in spite of noncompetitive positions; the other is the gradual lifting of restrictions on imports from non-EU states. These restrictions, the so-called voluntary export restraints long imposed nationally by Britain, France, Germany and others on Japan's share of their overall market,[8] were replaced by a Community-wide ceiling of 1 million cars until 1992. There has been, however, fierce opposition to the abolition of ceilings altogether as a threat to their viability as auto manufacturing countries.

Another major problem in this sector has been inadequacies in the car distribution system in Europe, by which car manufacturers have maintained considerable control over dealers' operations. Since 1985 the sale and servicing of new cars has been covered by a block exemption from EU competition law, allowing manufacturers to choose their dealers and areas to serve, and to limit each dealer's supply. Dealers have also been prevented from access to spare parts from independent suppliers, allowing manufacturers virtually a monopoly over the spare parts market. Consumer groups have understandably railed against this system as contrary to free choice and competitive pricing and as inconsistent with prevailing practices in other manufacturing sectors; on one view, this system is tantamount to a collusion between the Commission and Europe's car markets and is inconsistent both with logic and with its own commitments fully to liberalize the car market by 2000 (FT, 30 May 1995: 13).

Current Commission intentions, stated in a mid-1995 draft regulation, involve a partial liberalization of the dealer market without lifting the block exemption altogether.[9] This case represents a clear trade-off between industry liberalization to help consumers and a continuation of managed trade and thereby keep Japanese imports at limited levels for the rest of the decade in order to give European manufacturers more time to adjust. Such adjustment is the more vital considering the major retrenchment in sales in the early 1990s; in 1993 alone, car sales in Europe fell 15 percent, while increasing production of Japanese "transplant factories" in Europe, and a surge in better-quality, cheap dollar-aided vehicles from Detroit, have put unprecedented pressure on European manufacturers.

European efforts to promote cooperation leading to a more competitive European car industry, championed by Industry Commissioner Martin Bangemann, continue to be challenged by more focused Japanese and (more recently) U.S. competitors which have gone one better in their globalization of operations, utilizing the ultimate economies of scale. Both General Motors and Ford (Chrysler to a lesser extent) are established major players in Europe, the former in fact emerging in the 1990s as the most profitable volume carmaker in Europe, with over $1.3 bn in operating profits in 1994 from its European operations alone.[10] Ford is well on its way to realizing its aim of becoming the first truly global car manufacturer, based on the success of its highly touted "world car," the Mondeo, introduced in 1993, which cost some $6 bn to develop. The impending full liberalization of Europe's car industry by 1999 thus makes western Europe a "key battleground in creating the motor industry's new world order" (*The Economist*, 29 Oct. 1994: 73). Major Japanese producers such as Toyota, Honda and Nissan are hardly less well placed, despite a punishingly high yen for much of the 1990s, to expand further internationally, including Europe, in coming years. Still other producers, such as South Korea's Daiwoo (which recently beat out General Motors for rights to build a car plant in post-civil war Bosnia) are expanding the scope for international competition.

In turn, the economic threat to Europe's carmakers is being seconded by growing attention to the road-based environmental fallout, increasing tensions among different interest groups over the viability of road use. The debate has been acute in Germany since the 1970s oil crisis, focusing on ecological issues such as the "dying forests" of Bavaria due to increased acid rain levels. Even in Britain there is growing attention to such questions in influential circles. In an October 1994 report, the Royal Commission on Environmental Pollution roundly criticized the government and its DOT (Department of Transport) for failing to implement a sound and effective national transport policy and for caving in to the road lobby by its continual emphasis on road building. The Royal Commission proposed a host of quite radical changes including a doubling of fuel taxes within five years, a massive shift in investment priorities from roads to rail and public transport, and new road-pricing measures (Transport 1995).

The European Commission's environmental emphasis has elicited wider recognition of similar problems in Europe (CEC 1993a). Environment-based interests have found a more sympathetic ear in Brussels, particularly through the Parliament and secondarily through the Commission, with a vocally supportive Environment Commissioner in Ritt Bjerregaard (and Kinnock himself), but less so with the Council. Its efforts to restrict road use, however, remain fragmented due to political differences and are hence weaker than otherwise might be the case (Andersen and Eliassen 1993).

On the other hand, industry groups like the Confederation of British Industry (CBI) and Germany's DIHT (the German Industrial and Trade Association) have argued that by choosing the opposite course in following environmental solutions, governments and the EU would wind up defeating their own efforts to enhance competitiveness through industry liberalization and by the elimination of internal barriers. What all this represents is no less than a battle for the heart and soul of European road policy as such; and the policy response has been one of increasing attention to the environmental aspects while falling far short of achieving a balance between the two perspectives. Europe's motor industry, so long dominant in transport planning, seems set to maintain its strong position relative to the other inland modes for the time being, especially given its slow return to profitability in 1993–1994 after several years of steep losses. This reality can be seen in European R&D priorities. The Prometheus research program,[11] which has produced rapid advances in transport telematics (the pooling of information technologies to provide new systems and services such as variable message display, collision warning systems, and electronic toll gate tags) is clearly designed to ensure that existing transport problems are approached through better road and vehicle systems, as opposed to induced switching to other transport modes.

It is likely, however, that this continued predominance of road interests will be accompanied by an industry trend toward greater consolidation. This has particularly been the case with the truck industry, traditionally vulnerable to the business cycle's fluctuations in demand. Over the past twenty years the industry has shrunk greatly; whereas in 1975 there were 52 truck makers in Europe, the figure in 1995 was just 11 (FT Survey, 16 Dec. 1994). The same holds true for the auto parts industry. In the car industry the trend so far has been more mixed due to the diversity of the pressures on it, ranging from heavy Commission pressure on governments to reduce subsidies to companies like Seat (the Spanish subsidiary of Volkswagen) and Fiat (Italy), to relentless foreign competition and even outright takeovers (Britain's leading car manufacturers are now all foreign-controlled), to punitively high exchange rates and wage costs in Europe (causing auto manufacturers like Mercedes, a subsidiary of Daimler-Benz, to increase manufacturing in lower-cost areas such as east Asia and the American south).

The European car industry, dominated by middle-sized companies with smaller firms filling niche markets for high-performance cars,[12] may now be similarly poised for further merger attempts, with Italy's Fiat and Germany's Volkswagen considered prime targets for takeover after years of indifferent results. The decision by Gianni Agnelli to stand down as CEO in 1996 has fueled speculation about the future of Fiat in particular, long a family-run concern. Even Volvo, despite an unexpectedly positive performance and high share price following the Renault debâcle (see below), remains vulnerable now that Sweden is a full EU member. Even so, the incipient globalization of the auto industry means that such mergers or cooperative agreements are almost as likely to be with outsiders as with other European companies; Rover (a British car manufacturer), for example, in 1994 switched allegiance from Honda to BMW, which bought a controlling stake. Such decisions are based on cold commercial interests with little concern for loftier principles of closer European integration.

There is also evidence of retrenchment among Europe's transport manufacturers, once firmly modal-based but which expanded as multipurpose conglomerates along with the belief, prevalent in the 1960s and 1970s, in inherent synergies between particularly the airlines/aerospace and road sectors. The heady business climate of the 1980s encouraged relentless expansion; for example, Daimler-Benz, Germany's largest company and Europe's largest manufacturer, extended to other modes like aerospace and even to nontransport functions such as microelectronics and white goods. However, shareholder pressure[13] is now forcing a slow retrenchment to the core car business (Mercedes-Benz, the world's largest truck and bus maker, has always provided around two-thirds of Daimler's total sales) (*The Economist,* 18 Nov. 1995: 79). The reverse development is also evident, as companies that once expanded into the auto sector from other modes, like British Aerospace (BAe) which took a large stake in Rover, an auto company, have gradually pulled back to their original areas of expertise.

A similar development affected Sweden's Saab-Scania, which recently broke up after a 25 year union, allowing greater emphasis on Scania's more lucrative, core truck-manufacturing business, which was largely overshadowed by Saab's troubled aerospace operations (FT, 16 May 1995: 22). But even cross-border mergers of more targeted modal-based industries have proved problematic. The long-touted merger of two key, mid-sized carmakers, Sweden's Volvo and France's Renault, foundered in 1994 because of a Volvo shareholder revolt over fears of continued control of Renault by the French state, which would have put the (private) Volvo subsidiary at a clear disadvantage in the partnership. There were also conflicting national interests at stake, with evidence that (Swedish governmental) political intrusion helped bring about the deal's collapse.[14] It is clear that national-based differences in thinking, combined with an EU political structure which, perversely, promotes industry consolidation even while strictly limiting merger activity, continue to hinder European attempts to be a third major actor in the global struggle for dominance of the car manufacturing industry. Even Europe's hard-won technological lead in telematics may be jeopardized by the greater ability of larger, non-European companies to absorb the new technologies on a high-volume (hence lower cost) basis.

CONCLUSIONS

In the end, the EU remains limited in terms of how active a role it can truly play in the increasingly international car market, or how effective it can be in encouraging a more equitable balance between social and economic considerations in (road) transport. It is important not to overstate the EU's power to change the shape of the industry itself or to make policy changes sufficiently far-reaching to bring about major changes in the behavior of consumers or enterprises, such as altering the pricing structure. Indeed, many continue to question the very viability of changing policy priorities (especially involving fiscal measures) likely to be perceived as punitive to the road sector, since market considerations clearly have favored road over all other modes as a means of movement. A more effective determinant of future modal choice may well be the deterioration of the sector itself, with evergrowing congestion on roadways giving renewed emphasis to rail, on the basis of time saved.

Even short of bringing about wholesale modal switching, however, the EU can play a positive role in combatting the worst excesses of road use. It has already taken steps to promote further research into road information systems, spurred by the success of the industry-led Prometheus program. The promise of full rights of cabotage, even if long delayed (until 1998), eventually will reduce greatly the number of wasted empty runs by hauliers. Its emphasis on combined transport, encouraging connections between roads, ports, and rail terminals in long-range freight movement, will also add to the efficiency of the movement industry, particularly given the trend toward somewhat longer-distance movement resulting from the borderless market.

Indeed an insistence on maintaining rail capacity alongside road is far from being an idealistic distributional aim, since there would also be clear financial costs to allowing the deterioration of an existing rail infrastructure. And future steps toward more equitable pricing of road use may raise unit costs for shippers and consumers, but these costs would be largely offset by gains in other areas. Increased revenues from road use could not only help pay for infrastructure by new means, but could well aid ongoing research efforts to increase the efficiency of road traffic, to the ultimate benefit of users. And a more even pricing structure could well have some impact on modal choice in the intercity passenger market, leading to greater use of rail systems. The trade-off is somewhat less relevant, however, in the two modes to be discussed in the following two chapters, namely air and sea respectively.

NOTES

1. For an elegant but devastating indictment of the isolating social effects of auto use, one could do far worse than see George Kennan's exposé (1993: 159–167).

2. Several writers (Daalder 1973; Deutsch and Weilenmann 1965) have linked Switzerland's proximity to key trade routes (and the centrifugal forces it generated) with consociational domestic political practices, designed to combat the fragmentary tendencies of a divided polity via elite consensus. Such was a political necessity for the maintenance of sovereignty in a so-called "pass-state" with primarily locational relevance. The impact on Swiss foreign policy was no less strong (Ross 1989).

3. Kammerer (1990) maintains that one of Germany's aims in protecting its

freight market from unwelcome competition from foreign (particularly Dutch) hauliers has been to help the federal rail system to maintain a foothold in the freight market.

4. In northern Sweden the long distances between air bases led military strategists to build roads with wide roadbeds unencumbered by exposed telephone lines, so that military jets can use straight road stretches as landing spots in an emergency.

5. For example, in 1986 West Germany provided 91,000 licenses for Italian hauliers to operate on German soil, while Italy provided 145,000 reciprocal licences (Owen and Dynes 1989: 152).

6. This Council directive (94/55) subjects a representative proportion of dangerous goods carried by road to checks along much of the road network (CE 1994a). The apparent aim is to meet safety needs without compromising the free flow of traffic.

7. American negotiators have long argued that Japan discriminates against auto imports, and they have pushed for opening it up via quantitative agreements. In early 1995 the U.S. upped the ante by threatening punitive sanctions against Japanese car imports (via a 100 percent luxury tax). The Japanese regarded this as unjustified unilateralism in contravention of GATT and WTO rules.

8. Restrictions on Japanese car imports have varied widely; from Britain's 11 percent share of the overall market, to the Franco-Japanese agreement (1977) limiting Japan's share to just 3 percent. Italy's restriction (just 2300 units sold directly per year, excluding indirect imports from other European countries) virtually amounted to a prohibition (Smith 1990: 81–82).

9. Under the proposal dealers would be free to offer more than one car model, and manufacturers would not be able unilaterally to terminate dealer contracts nor control their prices; this would allow greater cost-cutting and thus potentially lower consumer prices (FT, 26 May 1995: 1).

10. GM's European operations include the Opel/Vauxhall group, with a market-leading 12.6 percent share (1.5 million vehicles sold in 1994), and a 50 percent holding in Saab Automobile. It also has a joint venture (60:40) with Isuzu in Britain in IBC Vehicles (FT, 1 Feb. 1995: 16), and a new mini-car venture with Mitsubishi.

11. The Prometheus ("Program for a European Traffic with Highest Efficiency and Unprecedented Safety") initiative brought together a panoply of Europe's car, truck, electronics and defense systems makers in an eight-year effort costing nearly ecu 1 bn, and has been heralded as a pathbreaking EU R&D effort despite being an industry initiative. The program has focused on three areas: safer driving through on-board systems; cooperative driving involving interaction with road systems and other vehicles; and traffic management. The European road telematics market is estimated at ecu 6 bn over the next decade, with much greater knock-on effects via savings in congestion, accidents, and environmental damage.

12. Europe's "big six" auto manufacturers added a seventh volume producer with the BMW-Rover merger early in 1994. Others, niche producers of high-performance cars like Alfa Romeo and Porsche, found it impossible to maintain independence due to high unit costs that cannot be offset by volume production; as Owen (1983: 51) has trenchantly observed, "history is not on the side of the specialist producer or of the smaller volume producer."

13. Daimler-Benz set a precedent in 1993 by becoming the first German com-

pany to take a New York Stock Exchange listing. While opening up new sources of financing, it also put more of a premium on financial performance. Not surprisingly, Daimler's chairman, Jürgen Schrempp, has led the growing European chorus for attention to "shareholder value," partly as a means of softening harsh cost-cutting at the company since 1995.

14. Media reports abounded of behind-the-scenes governmental influence at both ends, though the French government's stake was the more obvious since the merger was to foreshadow Renault's privatization. In Stockholm, there were indications that the government, while publicly favoring the deal, in fact put pressure on Volvo to scupper it, partly to prevent Volvo from coming under French state control even temporarily, and partly to force the resignation of Volvo's ambitious chairman, Pehr Gyllenhammar.

Chapter Five

Birds of Prey: The Airlines

> Flight would make men near-angels, it was
> believed; and a peaceful world one.
> —GORE VIDAL, *At Home*

Comparative to rail as the mode associated with early industrialization and road use as the most ubiquitous in modern society, air travel stakes its claim as the most high growth and high cost of the transport sectors. Its topical attractiveness in recent years partly reflects the major restructuring that the European air industry, after a lengthy period of stability, has been undergoing in the 1990s. All carriers, whether private or state-run, find themselves under relentless competitive pressure associated with the fully liberalized European air market that took effect in April 1997, forcing them to pare costs and form cross-border alliances in order to maximize their survival prospects as independents.

The burgeoning number of new niche operators and exogenous challenges from non-European carriers have further shaped the European air market both from without and from within. These pressures have changed all three segments of the European air market, namely: (1) the external dimension, via growing access to European routes and gateways by non-European operators; (2) the intra-Community dimension, via the opening up of the cross-border EU market to all European operators; (3) the domestic dimension, via the ending of cabotage restrictions to allow European airlines to operate domestic services within other EU states.

In turn, these steps have ushered in a contentious series of political issues, including the following:

1. The application of EU competition rules to a traditionally

cartelized industry, characterized by market dominance of single, usually state-owned, national airlines, sparking differences over the pace (and even desirability) of applying market principles;

2. Occasional intra-Commission disagreements over air policy (state aids to national airlines; mergers and acquisitions), between the transport and competition directorates;

3. Commission-member state struggles over issues with external ramifications, such as negotiating competency for Europe vis-à-vis foreign governments;

4. Widespread labor unrest (France, Belgium, Italy) due to government and EU-mandated cutbacks in airlines subsidies;

5. Transatlantic disputes, both bilaterally and within trade fora (GATT, now WTO), over subsidies to aircraft manufacturers (Airbus Industrie) and over anticompetitive mergers (Boeing-McDonnell Douglas);

6. Intramodal disputes between private and state-run airlines and between large and small carriers over the establishment of a more level playing field and the continuation of governmental advocacy roles for mainstream operators;

7. Intermodal disputes over EU prioritization of different transport modes, especially rail vs. air interests;

8. Government vulnerability to consumer group pressures over environmental concerns about airlines traffic, noise, airport expansion, pollutants and ozone depletion, as well as safety.

Despite its emergence as an intensely politicized transport mode and a CTP focal point, the air sector's overall importance as a carrier of peoples and goods remains quite modest. Table 1.2 indicated earlier that the airlines' share of overall passenger traffic in Europe remains well in the single digits; in 1990 it accounted for under 6 percent of all EU passenger traffic; and its role in intra-European goods movement is so limited on a volume (though not value) basis that comparative EU freight transport statistics tend to exclude it. This factor has not, however, prevented damaging political disputes over air freight from arising.[1] The sector's overall economic importance is increased by a number of other factors, especially its persistence as the transport industry's strongest growth sector, given the dramatic and continuing upsurge in demand, amounting to some 7 percent annually since 1970. Despite increasing congestion and declining profit margins, the industry's growth (upward of 5 percent) by far still outstrips overall economic growth levels. Its impact on issues of free trade in services and in high-tech manufacturing subsidies amplifies its politico-economic impact still further.

This chapter begins by tracing the emergence of the airlines industry and the ramifications of its close ties to national interests. Then it examines the evolution of EC/EU air policy, concentrating on the series of air liberalization packages commencing in 1987. The impact of these policy initiatives on the European air market is considered next, followed by a final section examining the extent of change within the intensely competitive airframe manufacturing industry, highlighted by the emergence of Europe's Airbus consortium as a rival to America's Boeing.

BACKGROUND AND CHARACTERISTICS OF THE AIR SECTOR

In contrast to the two land-based (road and rail) sectors, the air sector, together with its maritime counterpart, is virtually a class apart, in terms of both its industry structure and governing regime. Both air and sea transport are inherently more global operations offering longer-distance services unmatchable by the terrestrial modes. The global reach of airlines in turn affects the industry's regulatory regime, which is based on intergovernmental cooperation both bilaterally and organizationally (within the International Civil Aviation Organization, or ICAO), a specialized UN agency. Cooperative efforts via the European Civil Aviation Conference (ECAC), dating from 1954, provide a similar regional function along the same (technical, intergovernmental) lines. The primacy of the external dimension affected early European treatment, by causing the EEC framers to leave the airlines (and shipping) sectors outside the immediate ambit of initial CTP guidelines (Article 84).

Other modal contrasts also emerge. For example, the air and road sectors stand apart as the two main transport growth industries, but also as political targets for being relatively more wasteful modes, responsible for more than their share of emissions (notably, nitrogen oxide and carbon dioxide) and noise; heavy (fossil) fuel requirements; and growing safety concerns related to overcrowding. There are also parallels in governmental targeting of both industries as strategic, spawning national champion strategies by the 1960s that went virtually unchallenged until recent years.

On the other hand, the airlines have resembled the railroads in their strong resistance, as monopoly domestic operators, to application of EU competition principles. Patterns of cooperation between national airlines also bear similarity to those linking national rail companies: both are characterized by extensive networks of arms-length agreements with other states, permitting cross-border travel without actually challenging the separate authority or independent corporate structure of national companies themselves.[2] In addition, high-speed rail services provide the main competitive challenge to the airlines' dominance of the crucial middle-distance, intercity sector of the European transport market.

The historical parallels with the rail sector also shed light on the developmental characteristics of the much newer air industry. Like 19th century rail development, postwar civil air industries quickly overcame chaotic beginnings to emerge as national concerns closely identified with advanced industrial power and political prestige. The persistence of national air carriers in even the smallest European states (e.g., Ireland, Portugal, Iceland), and indeed use of the very term "flag carrier," shows continuing belief in the air industry's strategic nature. The close government-industry ties that developed early on were a boon to the nascent air industry in terms of technological innovation, yet they were also a major drawback in terms of consumer services, by maintaining artificially high prices.

In the larger European states, a secondary assumption grew concerning the perceived need to maintain an aircraft manufacturing base, again paralleling the auto sector. The creation of the Airbus consortium linking major state manufacturers, each bearing responsibility for building separate parts, is a prime example; the strenuous effort to keep the heavily loss-making Dutch air manufacturer, Fokker, afloat in the 1990s has been another.[3] In turn, a third technical focus, jet engines, has further narrowed the scope of European involvement, and Britain's longrunning efforts to sustain a market position for Rolls Royce aircraft engines vis-à-vis the competition (e.g., General Electric; Pratt & Whitney) speaks to similar pressures at the high-technology end.

There is also considerable parallel irony in the privileged (monopolistic) treatment of rail and air within states. Just as rail's postwar decline was a sad denouement to a once-great representative industry, so too have continued perceptions regarding the prestige value of airlines diverged increasingly from the mundane realities of modern air travel, characterized by features (chronic delays, harried services, surly customs officials on arrival) that any seasoned traveler would be hard pressed to accept as even remotely glamorous. It is indeed paradoxical, but also a telling indication of the power of airlines companies to shape wider public perceptions, that the industry has maintained an upmarket profile despite the proletarianization of the air travel market itself. The reality of a still ruthlessly anticompetitive European air cartel also sits uneasily with lingering romantic notions about air travel or the industry that provides it.

Despite such similarities, there are a number of crucial if subtle distinctions between the rail and air sectors with direct impact on industry management and governance. One difference lies in the underlying (politico-economic) conditions under which they respectively became incorporated and monopolized as public enterprises. Early rail development was based largely on commercial enterprise relying on the speculative application of the 19th-century equivalent of venture capital. State network planning emerged early in some states (notably Belgium) yet nationalization as such generally proceeded slowly and in stages up to World War I. A crucial factor was timing; rail development took off in the post-Napoleonic era of European restoration and early industrialization, and could proceed apace in a generally stable political environment overseen by the Concert of Europe. There was no pressing need to transform rail networks into the public domain until the late 19th century, when nationalist pressures and colonial ambitions led to governmental marshaling of industry assets.

In contrast, the air sector had little time for consolidation before the First World War led governments to press fledgling air operators into national military service. The first heavier-than-air flight, in 1903, preceded the war by little more than a decade, and the first international air convention, at Paris in 1910, by a mere four years. Many early independent aviators, responsible for first-ever point-to-point feats in Europe (e.g., Baron Carl von Silverström, first to fly across the Öresund from Copenhagen to Malmö) subsequently became war casualties. Thus, whereas expanding rail networks helped solidify state-building processes in many countries, air industries were themselves beneficiaries of an established foundation of government-industry ties, first as extensions of military power and later as flagship civilian industries but still having distinctly strategic overlaps. And despite basic similarities as monopoly industries, state treatment has differed. Rail systems (apart from HST) have been regarded as public service-oriented, downmarket industries, whereas airlines have been championed as modern transport standard-setters in new technologies, and highly visible indicators at home and abroad of national strength. One of the first political acts of new states is very often the creation of a national air carrier, often quite oblivious to the inordinate costs involved. The emergence of civil air services in the 1920s and 1930s reinforced government-industry linkages because it coincided with the intense nationalism characteristic of the era in Europe. The critical importance of the air sector in the Second World War redoubled the linkage between national security needs and prowess in the air. Churchillian rhetoric highlighted the key role of the airborne Battle of Britain, but few could doubt the tremendous political and psychological impact of air-based saturation bombing against Germany (especially Dresden), or the capability for joint air-sea operations enabling the first truly global war.

Similarly, the airlines' emergence in the 1950s as mass passenger carriers with overseas reach overlapped with the Cold War. East-west political pressures funnelled generous government subsidies to air/defense industries, enabling rapid technological advances, especially in sub- and supersonic jet engines. The numerous civilian-military spillovers helped nurture and sustain industrial enterprises such as Lockheed, Boeing, and Rolls Royce in their crucial formative years. In turn, the market dominance they achieved by the 1960s gave them a sustained boost in a sector where high costs, the imperatives of scale economies, and long development lead times all hinder would-be market entrants.

The early pathbreaking air service agreements, namely the (post-Bretton Woods) Chicago Convention of December 1944 and the Anglo-American Bermuda accord of 1946, established a loose system of international governance of the civil air industry based strictly on sovereign rights and bilateral reciprocity—essentially the same two principles prevailing up to the present. Certain (mainly technical) aspects of this regime were to be regulated by the intergovernmental ICAO, established in April 1947 under the Chicago Convention.[4] A UN specialized agency, the ICAO superseded two earlier agreements, the 1919 Paris Convention on Aerial Navigation and the Havana commercial aviation convention of 1928.

More specifically, the Chicago conference produced a compromise agreement based on a minimal set of multilateral principles regarding minimum technical standards and including overflight and landing rights for refueling or maintenance stops. The other three of the five "freedoms" were set via bilateral accords. Two developments subsequent to Chicago set the tone for industry governance. First, the airlines established the International Air Transport Association (IATA, now with over two hundred members) to promote the industry and set ticketing procedures, schedules, landing rights, and the like, with some aspects (e.g., fares) subject to governmental approval. IATA's clout, and a persistent if understandable emphasis on operating profits, enhanced the Bermuda precedent, based on opening air transport routes on a strictly bilateral, government-controlled basis, thus limiting access to the third and fourth freedoms (the right to carry traffic from home to a foreign state, and vice versa). On the back of a regime characterized by bilateralism on substantive practical questions within a loose multilateral regulatory framework, governments tended to limit foreign landing rights to a single carrier in return for reciprocal landing rights in the cooperating country. This market division also implied coordinated schedules and identical ticket prices on shared routes, which essentially split revenues from international flights equally between the two countries. For decades this system sustained high prices and hence airline (and indirectly, tax) revenues, particularly as the market relied heavily on lucrative business, as opposed to leisure travel.[5] It also effectively shut out all competition from established intercity routes. The distortions in such a rigged market were clear; and Europeans' protection of home markets often gave preference to non-European international airlines, such as the American pair up to the 1980s (Pan Am and TWA) and to far eastern airways (e.g., Singapore Airlines) even over competing European carriers. Transatlantic fares long have been far lower, per passenger km, than intra-European flights.

Postwar airlines growth was little short of spectacular. From 1960 to 1985, overall travel (in passenger kilometers) grew by a factor of nine, and individual carriers recorded still greater growth. Germany's Lufthansa increased from just 1.3 bn passenger kms in 1960 to 24.5 bn in 1985 (Molle 1990). Table 5.1 documents the corresponding rise in total passengers after

TABLE 5.1
European Airline Passenger Movements, 1970–1990 (in thousands)

Country	1970	1975	1980	1985	1990
Belgium	3,186	4,272	5,270	6,027	7,485[1]
Denmark	6,791	8,492	9,404	10,182	7,882
Germany (West)	32 079	38,170	49,003	55,580	83,112
Greece	5,550	7,299	16,433	23,079	22,974
Spain	N/A	N/A	45,560	50,541	73,143
France	20,788	31,269	45,985	N/A	N/A
Ireland	2,921	3,471	3,812	4,119	7,846
Italy	17,237	23,330	26,176	32,802	48,535
Luxembourg	477	637	670	824	1,037
Netherlands	5,755	8,374	10,123	12,271	16,515
Portugal	N/A	N/A	5,450	6,985	10,811
Britain	32,025	43,006	58,942	71,812	104,143

[1]1989 figure.

Source: Eurostat: Transport Annual Statistics 1970–1990 (1993).

1970, with most countries showing two- or three-fold increases in two decades.

This growth of new markets and the evolution of the business traveler as a major new species was, however, a poor advertisement for industry reform. Indeed, along with burgeoning growth, the other characteristic industry element from the 1950s until the 1990s was a remarkable degree of stability. During the quarter-century from 1960, only two European airline mergers were recorded, both prior to 1970; and from 1970 to 1985, there were no major new market entrants or departures. British Airways' takeover of British Caledonian following BA's privatization was the sole merger in Europe during the latter half of the 1980s, despite progress toward the Single Market in general.

No less remarkable was the stability in airlines' ranking in terms of size. The "big four" in 1985 (BA, Air France, Lufthansa, and KLM) were among the top five even in 1960, with only the Scandinavian Airlines System (SAS) slipping down the list. This stability was noteworthy partly because it described large and small states alike; nearly all retained single trunk carriers on international routes, which also controlled domestic markets directly or via subsidiaries (e.g., Alitalia and ATI; Air France and Air Inter). Britain's two main carriers prior to 1988 allowed but a semblance of competition even there. Only two small exceptions emerged; Greece's Olympic Airways initially was private (developed by the Onassis group) and was nationalized only in the 1960s; while only one international consortium was formed (SAS), a trilateral venture between Denmark, Norway, and Sweden based at Copenhagen (with Finland retaining its own system, Finnair).

CRACKS IN THE NATIONAL EDIFICE

As long as the EEC remained primarily a customs union with aspirations as a single economic unit, the stubborn defense of nationalism in the air industry was tolerated in Brussels. Nearly all Europe's national airlines were either created or revamped and taken into the public domain in the decade prior to the EEC's establishment—an additional reason, perhaps, for leaving the sector off to one side of the initial CTP provisions, since these companies were both new and in the first flush of expansion. The rapid market growth of a lucrative, high-visibility industry warded off political challenges to the prevailing industry structure, even though the market-sharing, price-fixing arrangements clearly contravened the Rome Treaty's commercial principles, especially Article 85,[6] quite apart from making a mockery of notions of competition as such. Loose CTP provisions pertaining to the air sector provided a further excuse for inaction. Even the emergence and rapid growth of two related, secondary operator markets, the charter and commuter industries, were unable directly to challenge the ascendancy of the large carriers servicing major cities.

The expansion of charter airline companies from the 1960s was facilitated by increasing disposable household incomes, greater leisure time, and state-mandated minimum holiday periods (reaching, in the case of France, five full weeks by the 1980s). In addition, the availability of planes for leasing on the secondary market at discounted prices fueled the rapid growth of the tourist industry to areas, notably the Mediterranean, previously off-limits as a short holiday destination. It has even been argued in Britain that the growth of the package holiday to Europe in the 1960s directly affected political attitudes, by ameliorating British skepticism toward the idea of EEC membership. For a time the charter industry remained primarily a niche market, relying on a different clientele, peripheral rather than central destinations, flight times at unsociable off-peak hours, and restricted services (e.g., low weight allowances, set return dates). The introduction of flexible fares, however, did have broad industry reverberations, and by the early 1990s one of every two European air travelers was taking advantage of fare discounts (Expanding Horizons 1994). Meanwhile, the air commuter industry also grew in order to meet travel demand from regional airports, though these have continued to be regarded mainly as feeder services to the major airlines.

A more decisive impetus for change came via a series of ECJ rulings that brought the air industry into the CTP's direct gamut and provided the legal basis for partial market liberalization. In 1974 the court ruled that the general EC competition principles also covered civil aviation (and sea transport), in essence chipping away at earlier assumptions, based on Article 84 of the Rome Treaty,[7] that airlines policy lay outside the EC's competence. The Commission subsequently concluded, on the basis of a separate (nontransport-related) court opinion (1/1978), that the Community has exclusive competence to conclude bilateral or multilateral agreements on services, as part of the common commercial policy under Article 113 (CEC 1993a: 56); in doing so, however, it merely opened two decades of acrimony over translating principle to practice. EC action was bolstered further by the court's *Nouvelle Frontières* ruling (1986) that the Rome Treaty's competition principles clearly applied to the airlines as well.

Just as bilateralism had restricted consumer choice, so too did changes at the national level, instigated by Britain, ultimately reverberate widely within the European air industry. In the mid-1970s the British attempted to stem growing American access to its market by renegotiating the original Anglo-American Bermuda accords; the Bermuda II agreement of 1977 restricted the expansion of nonstop services and new routes from the U.S., which concentrated business further in Britain's southeastern quadrant, putting growth pressures on London airports, particularly Heathrow, that have since intensified further.

The Bermuda II agreement in turn highlighted the importance of the transatlantic (London-U.S. east coast) link, as a reliable volume market and also a potential impetus for market liberalization. In the late 1970s, the comfortable market division between two American and two British carriers[8] was broken by the inaugural Skytrain service of Laker Airways, offering skeletal services but cut-rate prices on the busy New York-London route. Margaret Thatcher's championing of the Laker enterprise even as opposition leader tied in with her early advocacy of BA's privatization, especially after 1982 when Laker went bankrupt (though BA's selloff came only in 1987). Another effect of the Laker initiative was to open up alternative airports (Newark, Gatwick) as transatlantic gateways.

The Bermuda II accord also geared up the pace of industry reform within the U.S. Displeasure with high set fares, maintained with IATA's blessing, led the Carter administration and its airlines czar, Alfred Kahn, to set about liberalizing the American domestic air market and simultaneously to export its "open skies" initiative to Europe.[9] There is little question that this external impetus, centering on the 1978 Airlines Deregulation Act, was a major stimulus for EC steps, beginning in the late 1970s, to address prevailing distortions of the air services market (McGowan and Seabright 1989). Within the EC itself, a bilateral Anglo-Dutch initiative produced a pathbreaking agreement in 1984 to open both markets to competition and allow more rate flexibility, helping to focus Commission attention on applying Single Market principles to the air sector. Other small states, especially Portugal and Ireland, also helped open markets by pioneering regional services outside their home territories.

EUROPEAN AIR LIBERALIZATION: THREE STAGES

The Delors-Cockfield 1985 White Paper challenged both the existing air industry structure and, more than in other modes, also directly confronted state-controlled market conditions. It called for changes in the tariffs system and for measures "limit[ing] the rights of Governments to restrict capacity and access to the market" (CEC 1985: 30), via a series of (unspecified) measures to take effect by 1987. The result was a three-stage, decade-long liberalization trend culminating, in April 1997, in nearly full cabotage rights for all European-based carriers.

The first airlines package, delayed by six months until December 1987 (after an Anglo-Spanish dispute over Gibraltar airport), was modest, calling for relaxation of bilateral agreements that maintained the market-sharing, 50–50 deals, slowly reducing flag-carriers' capacity "take" to 45 percent over the first two years, and to 40 percent in the third. Other initiatives included opening up international routes to alternative carriers (fifth freedom or "beyond" rights); expanding services to regional airports; and most importantly, increasing the scope for fare discounting on scheduled services. Four key 1988 regulations solidified the initiative.[10] The gradualist emphasis of the package was predicated on the need for a period of adjustment of market structures and standing government-industry ties. These measures scarcely represented full liberalization based on open-skies principles, given the lack of provisions for cabotage rights and its continuation of the bilateral structure of the market itself. Even by 1989, according to a Community transport report (CEC 1989b), European countries were connected by some 200 bilateral agreements (providing 400 routes), only 22 of which even tolerated fifth freedom rights.

The second liberalization package, of 1990, was prompted by a preliminary ECJ ruling of April 1989 (the so-called Saeed ruling), calling into question the legality of price-fixing air agreements (Coopers and Lybrand 1994: 9.1). It called for a phasing out of capacity-sharing agreements altogether over three years, and for relaxing the exclusion of foreign-owned airlines from fifth freedom rights within the EC. It also called for greater fare flexibility and provided for mutual recognition of pilot and air traffic controllers' licenses and other technical elements (e.g., airline airworthiness certificates).

The third and most ambitious package, four measures set out in July 1992, opened market access widely, by amending prior regulations to allow freer competition also on domestic routes and by allowing, after 1996, "Community air carriers freely [to] set air fares" (Regulation 2409/92/EEC, Art. 5). The associated regulations (2407–2411/92/EEC), which purport to open all European air routes to qualified Community carriers, are nonetheless littered with exceptions to the general principle of free access. Certain areas (the Greek islands; the Azores) were granted delays (until at least July 1998) on grounds of protecting regional services. States also have leeway to restrict services for safety or environmental reasons, or to distribute air traffic more evenly; they can also take measures to "prevent unjustifiable economic effects on air carriers" (CE 1992b), which has stimulated some decidedly creative arguments for continuing state aids to loss-making carriers.

The prospect of a fully liberalized European airlines market after April 1997 promises or threatens—depending on one's perspective—to alter Europe's air industry in profound and possibly unforeseeable ways. While fares are expected to decline modestly, especially on routes with three or more competitors, it is unlikely that Europe will suffer the upheavals that followed American air deregulation. Indeed the combined industry power of the major operators, backed by proprietary governments, will no doubt ensure that they themselves are best positioned to dominate that market; the rapid demise of Europe's air cartel is by no means assured. The phased implementation of a liberal air regime has given the major carriers ample time to adjust strategies, and the abovementioned exceptions suggest ample scope for individualistic national interpretations of public service needs, congestion problems and the like, to the detriment of newer European carriers attempting to establish themselves in foreign markets. Their ability, by virtue of their wide route network, to undercut competitors' fares on single routes (i.e., predatory pricing) is but one method, as Virgin Express Europe found in attempting to establish routes servicing Amsterdam and Scandinavian destinations. Thus one clear danger is that states, while allowing token landing and take-off rights for nonnational carriers (such as Lufthansa's inaugural Nice-Marseilles service in early 1997) will nonetheless ensure that overall market conditions favor their own.

Along with its aim of minimizing market distortions, the EC Commission developed two other policy priorities: harmonization and liberalization of auxiliary elements including infrastructure, air space, traffic control, landing slot allocation, and ground services; and state aid policy for carriers themselves. The air space problem stems from the longstanding principle of territorial sovereignty above as well as on the ground, dating from earlier (e.g., 1919; 1944) multilateral air conventions, and by the substantial military use of airspace which restricts scope for civilian use. Even so, creation of a common airspace seemed to devolve naturally from the very idea of a single market, quite apart from the need to facilitate coordination of traffic movement in what had become the world's most saturated airspace. Both the Association of European Airlines (AEA) and, more recently, the EU's advisory *Comité des Sages* have called urgently for the creation of a new, merged European traffic control system, to transform the current loose network of air control coordination (based on 52 different control centers via the Netherlands-based Eurocontrol system, established back in 1963 (Expanding Horizons 1994). Transport Commissioner Kinnock has continued to downplay hopes for a single bureaucratic agency for this purpose (Neil Kinnock 1995), and the enviable safety record of European airlines ironically has worked to hinder such proposals. Even so, air traffic control remains a huge and unresolved problem-area.

Competitive Pressures and the Problem of State Aid

The second major Commission focus has been the gradual termination of state aids to airline companies. Direct or hidden subsidies have long figured in the airlines market, private as well as public. There is little doubt, for example, that existing guidelines and circumstances (e.g. Britain's Bermuda II accord with the U.S.; acute capacity problems at British Airways' home base at Heathrow airport) have effectively enabled British governments to continue to favor BA even after its 1987 privatization, at the expense of competing operators. Both Freddie Laker and (more recently) Virgin's chairman, Richard Branson, have won legal settlements against BA for conspiring to deprive them of business[11]—their actions emboldened by perceptions of the government's enabling, if not advocacy, role for BA.

Abuse of market dominance has been alleged in numerous other instances as well, sufficient to involve DG IV in an investigatory role. For example, it fined Aer Lingus, the Irish national carrier, for taking undue advantage of its stranglehold on the lucrative Dublin-London route, and EU investigators even raided Aer Lingus offices in February 1994 after complaints from Ryanair and British Midland about alleged price-fixing. Still another small company, Stelios Hadjioannou's EasyJet, echoed Branson's Virgin Express in charging KLM and SAS with attempting to drive it out of the Amsterdam and Copenhagen markets.

High overheads and rising labor costs became a major problem for European operators by the mid-1980s, though independent analysts have mainly blamed low productivity for European airlines' lack of competitiveness. Table 5.2 indicates total labor costs in Europe in 1992 were over a third (37 percent) higher than U.S. carriers. As long as markets were restricted, these costs could be hidden, covered by cross-subsidies or relieved by periodic government bailouts. However, the impact of lower-cost American competition (e.g., Delta, United), having significantly greater access to European airports than was the reverse case, brought about a new and decidedly awkward competitive situation which pits various European airlines against private American carriers (with U.S. governmental backing in their efforts to gain greater landing rights in Europe), as well as, increasingly, against each other.

A separate (intermodal) competitive threat also emerged in the form of home-grown rapid rail services, which have captured significant portions of markets long considered captive of the airlines. Martin Staniland (1995) argues that this double competitive thrust has effectively boxed in

TABLE 5.2
European vs. U.S. Airline Labor Costs (1992)

Measurement	U.S. Costs	European Costs	Percentage Difference
Gross salaries	$40,534	$44,493	10.26
Total labor costs	$52,256	$55,066	5.38
Total labor costs per ATK (US cents)	15.55	21.27	36.76
Productivity (ATK/employee)	336,019	258,908	–22.95

Note: ATK = Available ton kilometer.
Source: Expanding Horizons 1994.

the European air carriers and forced defensive corporate strategies. While the primarily domestic nature of HST services so far in Europe has cut mainly into domestic air services (for example, affecting Air France's domestic arm, Air Inter, much more than its international services), the cross-border implications of expanding intercity HST services will no doubt increasingly challenge international air links as well.[12] And third, EMU-mandated budget cuts "Europeanized" the problem of budget imbalances, compelling governments to rethink proprietary attitudes and financial largesse toward flag carriers.

Thus after years of inexorable growth in a favorable operating environment, deteriorating conditions came as a rude awakening for European carriers. Arguably the biggest jolt, however, was the economic crisis which beset the industry in the late 1980s, a result of general recession and of more specific shocks, especially the Gulf War and its major, though temporary, inflationary impact on the world oil market in 1990–1991. The half-decade from 1989 to 1994 was the single worst postwar period financially for European carriers. Collectively, IATA member airlines lost a total of $15.6 bn in the years 1990–1993 inclusive ($4.1 bn in 1993 alone); European airlines (the then-24 AEA members) alone accounted for nearly half the total losses. Worldwide, the industry came back into the black in 1994, though with total profits (under $2 bn) accounting for a mere 1.6 percent of total revenues (FT, 20 April 1995: 1). Tellingly, European airlines collectively did no better than breakeven in 1994 (earning just $120 m on sales of around $52 bn), after losing around $2.4 bn in 1993. And despite a substantial recovery in 1994–1995 (with world airlines collectively recording a record $5.2 bn in profits), 1996 saw yet another cumulative loss for AEA members, despite record high passenger loads.

The industry's difficulties in the early 1990s also sharply differentiated Europe's north and south. The former has undergone substantial costcutting and, in most cases, outright privatization; as a result, four of the largest north European carriers—SAS, KLM, Lufthansa and, spectacularly,

BA—all made substantial recoveries.[13] In distinct contrast, airlines along Europe's southern tier, most still state-owned, have been slower to reform and have continued to lose money.

Even so, the era of generous governmental coverage of air operating deficits appears to be at an end. The EU's DG IV (Competition directorate) has taken an increasingly stern, though less than draconian, approach to the question of state aids. A second Commission aim, with equally mixed results, has been to end political intrusion in airlines management. On the advice of the advisory *Comité des Sages,* convened to give impartial advice on air policy,[14] the EU adopted a "one time-last time" approach to state bailout plans for a number of carriers, contingent on restructuring, without actually refusing to sanction any single package. By early 1996, some $14.2 bn in EU-sanctioned aid had been funneled to operators.

The smallest such plan, a $97 m package by the Irish government to Aer Lingus, received Commission approval only as part of a three-year major restructuring plan including costcutting and job reductions. Greece's Olympic is in the midst of a larger EU-initiated corporate downsizing, involving three phases of share capital increases totaling $231.4 million by early 1997, contingent on deep operating cuts.[15] In 1995 Olympic eeked out its first profit ($27 m) in no less than seventeen years—an achievement for which, in a blatant demonstration of political intrusion, its interim chairman, Rigis Doganis, was summarily dismissed from his post. A strikingly similar fate befell Alitalia's cost-cutting chairman, Robert Schisano, dismissed at the same time (March 1996) in response to union pressure. Parallels between the two countries extend to their political leaders, both previously associated with transport restructurings.[16]

Three other European rescue efforts, involving state-owned Sabena, Iberia, and Air France, have attracted more controversy because of their much larger size and market share; together the trio has received an estimated $7 m in subsidies per day. Sabena's troubles date back to the 1980s, due to Belgium's high social security costs coupled with years of profligacy and alleged company mismanagement.[17] After a series of abortive efforts to boost profitability, including a substantial minority stake by Air France, the airline was propped up by a $200 m infusion of aid from Swissair, as part of their bilateral agreement giving the (privatized) Swiss company a 49.5 percent stake in the Belgian carrier, replacing Air France. This agreement finally provided Swissair direct market access to the EU, considered vital since the Swiss opted out of the EEA agreement.[18]

The Iberia rescue package, totaling Psta 87 bn ($700 m), drew criticism because it breached the Commission's one-time-only rule; it followed an earlier "final" rescue attempt in 1992, when the company received Psta 246 bn from the Spanish government. The bailout also raised questions of conflict of interest because it was supported by two consecutive EU transport commissioners from Spain, Marcelino Oreja and Abel

Matutes, prompting a public intra-Commission clash with the Competition Commissioner, Karel Van Miert.[19] It also suggested good money being poured after bad, in light of Iberia's disastrous expansion into the Argentinian market in the late 1980s, just before the market's downturn. Vulnerable to criticism of bending its own rules, the Commission took months before allowing the package to proceed in early 1996; it also insisted on a reduced aid figure (originally Ptsa 130 bn), and on changes in Iberia's corporate practices (obliging it to sell its 84 percent stake in Aerolineas Argentinas).

The widest controversy has been generated by the Air France package of 1994, which at nearly $4 bn (FF 20 bn) is easily the largest single European air rescue plan ever. Criticism of the plan has opened a new cleavage in the European airlines industry— economic in nature but with distinctly political overtones— between companies that operate on market principles and those that continue to enjoy direct governmental support with EU approval. The Air France package is the subject of a European Court case brought about by the British government and six north European (all private) airlines,[20] citing unfair subsidization in contravention of EU competition rules. That such a package could be offered to France, a key integrationist state and (at least at the time) an advocate of tight money policies for EMU, was a further source of irritation to the litigants. The ECJ also compelled the French government to open up its air routes and airports (Toulouse, Marseilles, Paris Orly) to non-French operators, which it had long resisted.

The Air France package has, however, stimulated a wide-ranging reversal of strategy, and Air France has emerged, not unlike SNCF in the rail sector and Renault in auto manufacturing, as a test case of reforming state-owned transport industries. Financial difficulties, and a net loss of FF 470 m (nearly $100 m) in 1994, led to a three-year restructuring package involving not only the usual costcutting (e.g., early retirements) but also a merging of the company with its loss-making domestic arm, Air France Europe (formerly Air Inter). Air France earned a small ($80 m) profit for the year ending in March 1996 (its first since 1989), though offset by a one-time restructuring charge of FF 2 bn (IHT, 27 June 1996: 13). The government is now aiming for a 1998 privatization, and despite union opposition may have little choice as a survival move.

More broadly, the opening of European skies promises to add pressure on governments to loosen their close relationships with national-based airlines, and on the carriers themselves to seek new coping strategies. Carriers themselves have responded to these new pressures in two ways: internal restructuring and external links. Apart from downsizing and costcutting, companies are increasingly being divided into separate carriers for long- and short-haul routes; such is the mooted plan for Alitalia, dourly presented as "the only alternative to bankruptcy" (WSJE, 17–18 May 1996: 3).

Changing Corporate Practices

The search for viable cross-border alliances, aimed at giving middling-sized carriers sufficient access to foreign markets and a decent chance of survival as independents, has spawned a multitude of corporate linkages. One, now seemingly permanent feature of the industry is code-sharing, involving co-ordinated schedules, reservations, and prices, which has proliferated in the transatlantic market despite occasionally vigorous criticisms from within the industry itself;[21] the U.S. DOT approved 39 such agreements between 1987 and 1993, and 50 more the following year (FT, 20 April 1995). KLM-Northwest and Delta-Virgin[22] are but two recent transatlantic examples, but the recent severance of the latter, and BA's decision to drop USAir for American Airlines (AA), have underscored the often transitory nature of such alliances.

A second practice involves joint marketing campaigns designed to link cooperating carriers in the public consciousness. Use of print advertising in in-flight magazines, joint fuselage logos, and linking frequent-flier programs are but some of the methods favored by the smaller airlines by virtue of their low cost. A third method involves coordination of schedules and use of joint onboard personnel; here Virgin's undertaking with Malaysia Airlines to offer joint flights with mixed crews is a notable example. A fourth and potentially the most risky method involves actual equity stakes, a route chosen by BA in its global expansion, both to the U.S. (via its 24.6 percent stake in USAir) and to Australia (via its 25 percent share in Qantas), in addition to its large stakes in both Germany (Deutsche BA) and France (TAT and Air Liberté). But financial difficulties at USAir caused BA to write off part of its investment (even before USAir's suit against BA in connection with its mooted AA agreement), highlighting the potential risks of such corporate strategies. Swissair's large minority stake in lossmaking Sabena raised eyebrows for similar reasons.

The proliferation of air alliances in the 1990s has had wideranging political as well as economic consequences. Such tactics enable airlines to blur the distinction between joint and separate corporate practices; while keeping their corporate identities and thus avoiding governmental interference, their operating methods presuppose joint decision making with foreign airlines. A second problem has been with American regulators, who have uncomfortably linked governmental air policy with corporate practices, reinforcing old patterns of exceptionalism in the industry and casting doubt on American claims to strict separation of markets and governments. The main European-U.S. links, starting with KLM and Northwest in 1993, have been granted antitrust immunity by American regulators (Justice and DOT). The U.S. "big 3" have all sought similar treatment, United vis-à-vis both Lufthansa and SAS (the two themselves linked), and Delta with the European trio of Swissair, Austrian, and Sabena (WSJE, 3 May 1996: 3).

U.S. authorities themselves have played an effective linkage strategy in immunity proceedings, withholding such antitrust exemptions until the countries in question agreed to bilateral open-skies agreements (see below).

The mooted BA-AA alliance in spring 1996 raised greater concerns because approval would give the two predominant transatlantic carriers a 60 percent dominance of the transatlantic route.[23] In response to industry pressure, the European Commission announced in June 1996 a joint DG VII and DG IV (Transport/Competition) investigation of six transatlantic agreements,[24] citing past insufficient European vetting of clearly uncompetitive practices. The investigation marked a new departure for greater EU involvement in industry regulation, and as of spring 1997 approval remained in the balance. Nonetheless the EU remains poorly positioned to halt an ongoing tide within the industry.

Despite the Single Market and the advantages of consolidation, the formula for successful alliance-building within the European market has proved more elusive. One reason may be lack of incentive, insofar as airlines' main revenue source is long-haul routes chiefly serving non-European destinations. Air France has seen two separate ventures, with CSA (Czech Airways) and Sabena, both come to naught; Dutch KLM has been unable to find the right links either bilaterally (with BA), trilaterally (with BA and Sabena in the abortive effort to create a new Sabena World Airlines), or even multilaterally (through the four-country Alcazar project with SAS, Swissair, and Austrian Airlines, which collapsed late in 1993).[25] More recent ventures have fared better; Swissair's profitable 10 percent stake in Austrian Airlines has been followed in 1995 by SAS's market-sharing agreement with Lufthansa and the Swissair-Sabena venture (French 1995). Other companies with poor balance sheets, particularly Alitalia, face similar pressures to secure non-national markets. Endemic financial pressures are forcing carriers into other retrenchment measures such as selling off non-core businesses (property, travel groups) and reducing travel agents' fees; some airlines (e.g., Easyjet) have dispensed altogether with agents by relying on direct sales, which some analysts suggest is a forerunner of a new, no-frills segment of the European market. Yet another attempted solution has been a tendency by governments to levy high airport departure taxes (sometimes up to 10 percent of fares) and en route charges to pay for various undertakings, often completely unrelated to transport, such as reducing overall budget deficits.

The relentless growth of air travel has created acute capacity shortages, and the advisory *Comité* has argued for a removal of infrastructure bottlenecks "as a matter of utmost urgency" (Expanding Horizons 1994). In response, a number of airport authorities are emerging as chief competitors for the possibly dubious title of Europe's main air hub. Four in particular—London Heathrow, Schiphol in Amsterdam, Roissy-Charles de Gaulle outside Paris, and Frankfurt—are all in varying stages of major expansion. Particular controversy surrounds plans, put forth by the privatized British Airports Authority (BAA), to build a fifth terminal at Heathrow, already Europe's largest (and the world's busiest for international passengers), which would expand overall capacity from its current level of 52 m passengers yearly up to 80 m.

The political debate over Heathrow expansion is also a prime example of the increasing environmental component of air service-related disputes at subnational level. Whereas BAA's expansion plan is backed both by BA and by union groups, as a means to boost local business and employment and (it is argued) maintain the City of London's preeminent financial position, regional political bodies have allied with local environmental groups fiercely to oppose the plan.[26] This opposition has already had some success; in February 1995, even before the public inquiry was underway, the transport secretary, Brian Mawhinney, ruled out all possibility of building a third Heathrow runway (or even a second one at London Gatwick) (FT, 7 March 1995: 8). The environmental impact on the existing two-runway structure will be much greater as a result, since the current practice, rotating traffic twice a day to give local residents a quiet period, will likely be terminated as air traffic demands (reinforced by a perverse regulatory regime capping landing fees at artificially low levels) mount. Mooted expansion at Dusseldorf's airport has drawn similar opposition from local residents. And in Berlin, plans to challenge Frankfurt's dominant position as an air hub with a new airport have raised a series of local and regional political disputes in which the federal government is little more than a spectator (FT, 23 Feb. 1995: 2).

REALITIES AND FALLACIES IN AIR PRIVATIZATION

While all European airlines have undergone reorganization in recent years, there is considerable variance in the extent to which flag-carriers have shifted from public to private orientations. Not surprisingly, the countries with the two traditionally most liberal approaches, Britain and the Netherlands,[27] were also the first to privatize their flagship companies, BA and KLM. Others sold off include Swissair, SAS, Finnair, and, as of January 1995, Germany's Lufthansa, Europe's second largest, all in northern Europe. Lufthansa's restructuring plan, announced in fall 1994, included separation of its freight, technical, and systems divisions; a new rights issue to raise DM 1.2 bn; and a selloff by the government of its own holdings in order to reduce its stake in the company from 51 to 39 percent (WSJE, 16–17 Sept. 1994: 12). The stated intention of Air France's chairman, Christian Blanc, is to follow current, stringent costcutting with eventual privatization, an approach at odds with the new Jospin government.

This growing trend toward selling off debt-burdened airlines, however, has prolonged a number of misconceptions about the nature of air privatization itself, and about the tripartite corporate-governmental-EU relationship. For example, mistaken perceptions persist concerning the EU's (virtually nonexistent) power to compel governmental selloffs. It can and does shape the politico-economic climate by challenging state subsidies and by promoting conditions of competition, but it has no treaty-based power to force a state to sell off its majority stake in companies.

Another such (potential) misconception concerns the linkage between private ownership and profitability. So far, there is a striking parallel between the two; north European airlines, in Britain, Holland, Scandinavia, Switzerland, and now Germany, have all reduced governmental stakes in their national airlines and have, simultaneously, been the happy recipients of increasing tax revenues with the return to profitability by their main carriers. For proponents of privatization elsewhere, the message is inescapable: eliminate public ownership and companies will thrive. The comparison is almost too easy, insofar as the top four north European carriers enjoyed profits of $2 bn in 1995, neatly matching cumulative losses for the state-owned airlines in the south.

As usual, however, the reality is more complex. One point is that the return to profitability of all the above (except BA) is both very recent and, in historical terms, anemic. It has also reflected post-recession return to overall sectoral growth, in which a rising tide (to mix a metaphor) has lifted all the carriers together. Another more serious concern is that such presumptions tend to confuse profitability with control. The former is directly a question of market share and attention to consumer needs, but only indirectly of management structure and governmental influence. State-run airlines have periodically made money, as have other state-sponsored transport undertakings (e.g. French TGV lines).

Thirdly, the linkage between the above companies' success and their status as private companies may, in fact, be reversed. It may be more accurate to say that they are profitable because they have paid more attention, all along, to commercial considerations than have the state-dominated monoliths in southern Europe, and that those privatized first were also, fundamentally, those most likely to succeed anyway. Furthermore, privatization was preceded by careful preparatory restructuring efforts. BA's financial turnaround in the 1980s was predicated on massive downsizing and new corporate strategies introduced by (now) Lord King, a Thatcher ally brought in as chairman in 1981. And Lufthansa's privatization came only after two years of painful cost-reductions (including 7000 jobs cut); it also benefited from a responsible labor-management relationship that minimized damaging industrial action.

Still other prevailing assumptions are open to question. One is that privatization—the placing of majority ownership of a company into private hands—is a means of solving a political problem of excessive governmental interference into corporate governance. It is possible, for example, for a public corporation dependent on governmental aid to maintain operational autonomy (as is the case with the British Broadcasting Corporation). Conversely, the ending of outright government ownership is no guarantee that governments will not act to perpetuate imperfect market conditions in order to help their privatized firms. Some of these ways are as follows:

1. *Substantial minority government stakes in privatized companies.* It is easy to overstate the significance of the shift from majority to minority ownership by governments from, say, 51 to 49 percent. During transitional phases, substantial government involvement can be a crucial means of ensuring a successful market launch, as a reassurance to new investors that exposure to market pressures will nonetheless be both gradual and sheltered. Initial public share offerings themselves are often undervalued in order to guarantee oversubscribed demand, a common (and justified) Labour criticism of the Thatcherite selloffs of the mid-1980s. Even after the process is completed, governments tend to remain substantial minority owners (BA's complete selloff being the exception proving the rule). In the Lufthansa case, touted as a revolution in airlines ownership, the German government continued to hold around 35 percent of outstanding shares. The Dutch government has retained a fraction more of privatized KLM (Kassim 1996: 123), and by early 1997 was touting a "major" reduction in its ownership from 38 to 35 percent. Domestic shareholders inevitably far outnumber foreign ones, often deliberately by means of "golden shares" that ensure national, even if private, dominance, and give governments an easier watchdog role.

2. *Issues apart from operator ownership.* With most attention gravitating to airborne operations, auxiliary elements including baggage handling, ground services and airport management have received much less attention as candidates for privatization;[28] as yet, few countries apart from Britain have private airport authorities. Governments also have a hand in safety regulation, national airspace, air traffic control systems, and airport takeoff and landing slots. As Europe's air markets and airports grow ever more crowded, these issues become more crucial, which can even solidify, in new forms, the symbiosis between governments and their main carriers, public or private.[29] This point, in turn, calls into question the widely assumed linkage between privatization and increased competition; indeed, a private company with market dominance may do no more to promote competition than its state-owned counterparts. Britain's selloff of BAA (the airports authority) merely created a regulated private monopoly out of a public one, and further, one enjoying a premium share price and higher-than-average P/E ratio on the London bourse because of favorable regulatory practices.

3. *The market power of large companies.* Even as private companies,

airlines exert major influence over national political economies. Companies like KLM, Lufthansa, and BA not only dominate the air sectors of their respective countries; their huge capitalizations give them commanding economic-cum-political presence in national markets. British governments have left little doubt that the continued financial strength of BA is regarded as coincidental with broader British interests,[30] even though such attitudes thwart the very competitive pressures that in liberal economic theory produce better performance (quite apart, of course, from doing little to help competing British carriers). The Dutch government's determination to expand KLM's base at Schiphol airport, despite strong environmental protests, attests to similar merging of governmental and corporate interests that are increasingly coming to the fore in the airlines debate (Staniland 1995). It may be that governments treat newly privatized major companies even more favorably than before, both in terms of a more subtle advocacy relationship rather than overt meddling, and in terms of a desire to show that a major governmental initiative (selling off a major public asset) was in fact well considered and even visionary.

4. *Established relationship patterns.* One final cautionary note is that the long and symbiotic relationship between governments and national firms involves numerous informal relationship patterns that continue irrespective of the question of ownership. Formal incomes policies and corporatist practices can be abandoned even while their influence, via elite intermingling, bureaucratic favoritism, and the like, persists. A recent French case is instructive; Louis Gaullois, a journeyman in French administrative circles, was shifted from heading Aérospatiale to run SNCF in the wake of the le Floche-Prigent scandal. Also, long-established public service assumptions for transport companies can be maintained in practice even if they are restricted in law.

In fact, the U.S. case shows clearly that the two questions of public service obligations and private ownership can be altogether unrelated. As European negotiators never tire of pointing out, the supposedly open American air market is nonetheless characterized by sharp restrictions on foreign ownership of American air operators (under 25 percent, and even then subject to government approval), and by de facto public service obligations, extending even to official travel to foreign destinations, for its (private) airlines.[31] Loopholes in U.S. bankruptcy laws under Chapter 11 are another source of contention, since they allow American operators (such as TWA) to continue operations, often for years, even while technically bankrupt.

On the other hand, privatization could reduce the scope for the labor unrest that has plagued state-owned carriers, especially in Italy, Belgium, and France (where a bitter strike forced the resignation of Air France's CEO, Bernard Attali, in 1993). Repeated air crew strikes by Alitalia personnel, and two (apparently insider) sabotage attempts prompted the company to make an unusual public apology in early 1995. Lengthy delays at

Athens Hellenicon the same year, caused by air traffic controller slow-downs, prompted Olympic to do likewise. The 1997 open skies regime, coupled with the market recovery that began in 1994, may well provide a window of opportunity for such countries to seek alternatives to existing patterns in the form of private investors and/or foreign partners. Even so, the narrowly averted BA pilots strike in summer 1996 demonstrated that no company is immune from industrial action.

Despite the pressures of a global market and Europe's newly open regime, few outright European air mergers had taken place even by early 1997. It may well be that existing carriers' hopes of remaining independent after 1997 are altogether misplaced; many now believe that the European air market, like its auto sector, cannot sustain more than six or seven major operators, and that the smaller or weak larger carriers, apart from isolated examples with special market conditions (e.g., Finnair) will eventually be bought out—whether or not such takeovers can be effectively disguised as mergers, as occurred with the engineering conglomerate ABB.[32] Codesharing practices notwithstanding, European airlines so far have resisted the trend toward true corporate globalization (Hayward 1995; Kassim 1995). Even BA, with the most aggressively internationalist strategy, relies on Heathrow operations for fully half of its profits; and its former chairman, Lord King, revealed much when he admitted that "the catchment area for BA is this little island" (quoted in Grant 1995: 90).

THE PROBLEMS OF EUROPEAN COLLECTIVE ACTION

The increasing responsiveness of the European air industry to international competitive pressures touches on two further issues relating to collective European action. One is the question of ending the bilateral air services regime established by the Chicago Convention, and its replacement by a multilateral approach shaped and led at the European level by the EU, and specifically the Commission and its Transport directorate. A second issue concerns the problems and challenges facing Europe's main aircraft manufacturer, Airbus Industrie, in establishing a European competitive presence in a civil airframe manufacturing industry long dominated by an American company (Boeing). In both areas, the American challenge is a critical exogenous factor because of its overall market size (accounting for nearly half the world's total passenger market) and its predominant position as a high-volume aircraft manufacturer.

European Open Skies and the Kinnock Campaign

The traditional European approach to air service agreements, based on the tenacious unilateral pursuit of sovereign interests by governments in one-on-one intergovernmental negotiations, has been increasingly anomalous in light of the near-completion of the European Single Market. The failure of governments even to attempt a common European negotiating position led to a new political impetus by Transport Commissioner Neil Kinnock, in the form of an April 1995 draft proposal to member states that they cede external negotiating powers to the EU and to the Commission.

The Kinnock campaign had several facets. One was the logic of the Single Market itself, from which a single European external aviation policy, in his view, should devolve naturally. A second, more contentious, view was based on the Transport Commissioner's reading of past European Court rulings, which he interpreted as giving the Commission legal authority to negotiate on the Community's behalf. The reverse point was also cited, that individual states were contravening their EU undertakings by supposedly breaking ranks and negotiating (mainly with the U.S.) individually. It was especially galling that three of the accused (Austria, Sweden and Finland) had just joined the EU, and it prompted an (unsuccessful) Kinnock attempt to forestall these negotiations by referring to the ECJ. A third motivation was to strengthen Europe's traditionally weak negotiating hand, and prevent "a policy that is not just America first, but America first, last, both ways across the Atlantic and within and beyond Europe" (FT, 27 April 1995: 3).

Understandably, Kinnock's high profile initiative, launched soon after his taking office in January 1995, was widely dismissed as not only a crude power play by an overenthusiastic new commissioner, but as an altogether poor choice of weapon, since under prevailing circumstances (strong member state opposition; lack of clear treaty guidelines; an unfinished single European air market) it seemed condemned to fail. Even so, he proceeded with unanimous Commission backing, particularly from its president, Jacques Santer (FT, 27 April 1995: 3). In addition, the initiative had a precedent; at the time of the third liberalization package in 1992, the Commission proposed that it replace governments in negotiating fares with non-EC countries, though this had been rejected by the Transport Council (*Economist*, 27 June 1992: 72–74).

The Kinnock initiative was also a response to a deliberate American strategy of playing off European states against one another by negotiating individual open skies agreements, in a step-by-step process of forcing greater access to European airports for American carriers. The dual American strategy was to negotiate, not only with governments one-to-one, but commencing with the smaller European states as a means of pressuring the larger ones by precedent. In 1995 alone, this produced no less than nine different (U.S.-European) open skies agreements.[33] Another clear element was an American strategy of overt linkage; in each succeeding case of proposed transatlantic air alliances, U.S. authorities withheld approval pending the conclusion of an open-skies deal with the country in question. Thus it was that the (pending) KLM-Northwest alliance produced an American-Dutch open skies pact in 1992; and the pattern was reinforced in 1996 when American approval of the United-Lufthansa alliance followed the two countries' conclusion of an open-skies arrangement. Similarly, its approval of Delta's linkup with three small European airlines followed, rather than preceded, open-skies pacts of 1995. The promise of immunity from antitrust investigations was another incentive on the part of the individual European states, even if it opened up the U.S. to accusations of allowing, even encouraging, inherently anti-competitive agreements on the part of its own, private, carriers.

The overriding American aim was to force changes in the US-UK relationship, still nominally based on the 1977 Bermuda II accord but subsequently revolutionized by huge volume growth, more carriers and increasing demand on Heathrow access. Drawn out and inconclusive bilateral negotiations continued in 1995–1996 over a new aviation agreement, producing only an interim arrangement. The talks were complicated by the fact that neither side appeared to be aiming at the kind of open-skies arrangement (based on mutually unrestricted access to each others' airspace and facilities) that the U.S. was in the process of concluding with the other governments. Britain argued for much greater access for British carriers to U.S. regional airports, including rights to pick up new travelers within the US for onward destinations (consecutive cabotage). It also held out for more flexibility in US restrictions on contracts to carry government personnel and mail so that British operators could compete for this business.

The Americans, in contrast, wanted greater landing access at Heathrow (then restricted to just two American airlines),[34] and more freedom for cargo operators such as Federal Express to use Britain as a link to the Far East. The failure of these two erstwhile exponents of free trade to conclude a worthwhile agreement even prompted the normally skeptical *Economist* to propose (9 Dec. 1995: 13–14) that Brussels be allowed, after all, to push for a multilateral liberal agreement in lieu of governments. And by spring 1996, the Transport Council finally assented to the Commission request by granting negotiating powers in this area, though with relevance mainly to eastern Europe.

The BA-AA air alliance, announced in June 1996, thus produced a timely test of both the bilateral relationship and the Commission's newly expanded role. Many regarded the alliance as foreshadowing a familiar development: antitrust immunity in the U.S. in exchange for an open-skies agreement with Britain. But industry pressure forced three separate public investigations into the deal (by the U.S. Justice Department, the UK Monopolies and Mergers Commission, and the European Commission), the final result of which remained uncertain even well into 1997. Regardless of the outcome, the issue has demonstrated growing Commission awareness of its own investigatory role; not only did its decision preempt Britain's own investigation, but it was based on a previously little-used provision (Art. 89), effectively setting a new investigatory precedent in this area.[35]

It remains to be seen whether the Commission's enhanced role will appreciably strengthen its regulatory hand in the air industry, much less overcome the imbalance of the two markets in favor of American carriers. There is little doubt, however, that it has been a response to growing concerns about anti-competitive practices and governmental advocacy of large carriers' interests even in a liberal air market. If nothing else, the controversy surrounding the BA-AA alliance, including some eye-opening episodes of mudslinging between BA CEO Robert Ayling and Competition Commissioner Van Miert, may demonstrate the upper limit for such industry practices.

Airbus Industrie and Europe's Airframe Challenge to Boeing

If public-private interests are occasionally muddled in international air alliances, then the distinction all but disappears in the associated airframe manufacturing industry, for which governmental largesse has been a critical factor from the outset. As rapid rail technologies have been advanced commercially by Europeans and auto manufacturing shaped by Japanese innovations, the airframe industry has been dominated throughout the jet age by American companies enjoying government support. Despite free trade rhetoric from Washington, advanced plane technological development has benefited greatly from government contracts and subsidies both direct and hidden. These efforts were long sustained by Cold War pressures, and they enabled technological spillovers from separate developmental programs in nuclear missile technologies and from the Space Race following the 1957 Sputnik launch.

Three different American companies emerged as giants in the field: Lockheed, McDonnell Douglas, and Boeing, the last of which has proven by far the most successful in the transition from military to civil emphasis, largely on the back of the huge undertaking to develop the large capacity B-747, which first flew commercially in 1970. Given the diversity and size of the American economy, it is a remarkable fact that an industry long dominated by a single company (Seattle-based Boeing) and relying substantially on sales of a single product (the 747), could become the country's largest industrial exporter, accounting for a net surplus of nearly $18 bn in 1991 (Tyson 1992).

The European response to the American ascendancy was to rethink traditional approaches prevailing until the mid-1960s, which had allowed industry fragmentation, even within individual states. From that point there occurred a dual shift toward national centralization and a market system of reference in manufacturing (Muller 1995: 164–165). The creation of France's Aérospatiale and British Aerospace (BAe) in this period typified the consolidation phase. In turn, this promoted multilateral efforts to promote cooperation in aircraft building. The cooperative route was largely forced by circumstance, in which single European countries, facing steep fixed costs, found it difficult to compete with the directed American approach to development and the easier economies of scale achievable in a fully integrated market. Although European defense cooperation was off the EC agenda, fears of U.S. domination technologically as well as politically within NATO—hence straightforward national security considerations—maintained pressures to develop new high performance European aircraft; in a thorough analysis of the industry, Keith Hayward holds that Airbus represented a "strategic challenge to the U.S." (1986: 201), though primarily a defensive one. In both contexts, the potential military applications merited (and helped justify) governmental involvement in what is essentially a "dual-use" industry (Tyson 1992).

Bilateral European developmental efforts proved disappointing. The Concorde supersonic aircraft project, a joint Anglo-French effort launched in the early 1960s, quickly overran its budget and was the source of much acrimony between the two governments. Britain's Prime Minister Harold Wilson blamed the problem on a bilateral contract without escape clauses (negotiated, naturally, by his predecessor), which locked them into the arrangement even after hopes for the project's commercial viability had long vanished. This has sometimes been interpreted as grudging British acquiescence in a French-inspired *grand projet;* however, another close participant at the time, Denis Healey (1990) has indicated that the French side was also very close to cancellation for similar reasons of excessive costs.

Notably, advanced U.S. research in the supersonic sector (via the SST venture) was ultimately abandoned as commercially nonviable (losing in the Senate by a single vote), after an Office of Technology Assessment estimate that total expenditures would exceed $1 bn. Only 13 Concorde planes were built, and the program was finally abandoned in 1979 (after initial interest by U.S. carriers dried up in the two oil crises), leaving BA and Air France as the sole purchasers. Creative marketing in recent years has enabled modest profits, though excluding depreciation from its original $1.2 bn development costs,[36] leaving a painfully split legacy between an economically unviable project and one whose technical superiority has only been consolidated by two decades of death- and injury-free service.

It was partly due to the chastening Concorde experience that the British opted out, in 1969, from participating in the subsonic Airbus venture after showing initial enthusiasm. Airbus Industrie instead relied on Franco-German ties to get production off the ground in the early 1970s. Both France's state-owned Aérospatiale and Germany's Daimler-Benz Aerospace (DASA) hold a 37.9 percent stake; Britain, after reentering the project in 1978, holds a 20 percent stake via British Aerospace (BAe), responsible for the high-technology wing sections of the aircraft; and Spain's

Casa holds the remaining 4.2 percent. Final assembly takes place at Toulouse in France, although only 4 percent of value is added there. Other countries with industry potential have not been involved, either for economic reasons (Italy), or because of concentration in a different sector of the market (e.g. Holland's Fokker, which until its bankruptcy built smaller craft). Still others, like Sweden, have had to concentrate, at great expense, on unilateral development of high performance aircraft with strategic applications determined by neutrality policies; and its nonmembership in the EU (prior to 1995), while not a de facto point of exclusion from Airbus itself, nonetheless militated against such cooperation in a European enterprise with distinctly political overtones.

From the start, four considerations distinguished Airbus from its American counterpart industry. First, it was a cooperative rather than a single-country venture, with all the accompanying challenges of equitable sharing of costs and responsibilities. Second, it entered the market with the commercially guided aim of building marketable aircraft for mass use (hence the name), rather than as an offshoot of military contracting. Third, Airbus itself was a consortium rather than a profit-oriented corporate entity, as a *Groupement d'Interét Economique* combining multiple national ownership with just enough autonomy to enable it to be marketed to potential buyers (however deceptively) as variously French, German, or even British. And fourth, it long benefited from direct governmental aid as opposed to the indirect (but still substantial) U.S. support for Boeing via research grants.

Airbus output grew steadily once aircraft delivery commenced in 1979. Initial production was in narrow-body jets and in the wider-body A300 and A310 models; the current series of longer-range wide bodies, namely the A330 and A340, were phased in starting in 1987. Overall Airbus deliveries rose from barely a fifth of Boeing's level in 1979 to close to half (1038 deliveries versus Boeing's 2433) by 1990. In the early 1990s recession, Airbus overtook McDonnell Douglas, which fell to below 10 percent of market share. Airbus then stunned market observers early in 1995 by claiming to have overtaken Boeing in total aircraft orders (though not deliveries) for 1994, with a 48 percent share of all orders.[37]

Subsequent orders and deliveries failed to keep this heady pace, however, and Airbus seems to have settled into a market share of around a third. It has, however, both stimulated and benefited from several trends: for carriers to split orders to Boeing and Airbus, thus playing the market more effectively to secure the best deal and influence airplane development at earlier stages; for attention to expanding Far East markets; and for purely political considerations (e.g., China's decision to bypass Boeing for Airbus in a major order; FT, 11 June 1996: 6). Despite its growing market share, there remains little likelihood of Airbus overtaking Boeing as the world's premier manufacturer, particularly as Boeing's new 777 model is proving a popular draw; Singapore Airlines, for example, opted for the 777 over the Airbus equivalents in a late 1995 order worth over $12 bn.[38] The mooted merger between Boeing and McDonnell Douglas, worth over $14 bn, if approved by U.S. and European regulators, would of course reshape the entire face of the industry.

The emergence of direct European-American competition in such a highly visible industrial sector has been so compelling to industry observers[39] that it masks a number of other developments that are of far greater import. One major effect, reinforced by the recent recession, has been a major costcutting and downsizing effort in the airframe industry along with the carriers themselves. Production costs at Boeing have been cut by around 25 percent over the last few years, and delivery time of its larger wide bodies (the 747 and 767) has been reduced from 18 months to 10; it aims for a further 20 percent time reduction. Over 30,000 jobs have been lost at Boeing since 1990, some 7000 of them announced, rather injudiciously, just as the first 777s were being delivered in mid-1995. The emergence of a leaner Boeing is bound to put further pressure on Airbus, particularly as Boeing, with its dominance of the U.S. market, is also competitive in selling aircraft to European airlines anxious to demonstrate their independence, especially BA. One clear disadvantage of Airbus is that European airlines are under no obligation, legal or otherwise, to buy its aircraft. Airlines privatization could worsen the problem by reducing governments' ability to argue persuasively for the Airbus option as part of a "buy European" strategy. Further, Airbus has been increasingly handicapped by its ungainly ownership pattern; and the problem of strategic direction has worsened since two of the subsidiaries (BAe and DASA) are now private companies while their two other partners remain state-owned.

In light of these disadvantages, there is movement afoot to expand Airbus's potential via a major restructuring. In June 1996 DASA's head, Manfred Bischoff, proposed a wide-ranging change including privatization of the French and Spanish partners and creation of a limited company, which would give it a distinct corporate identity with more targetable market aims. This proposal also reflected a shift in DASA's own strategy of focusing on larger craft while pulling out of two regional aircraft makers, Fokker and Dornier, early in 1996. The growing belief is that Airbus must better position itself to take advantage of the huge growth expected in the air industry over the next twenty years.[40]

Ever-growing air demand, especially in Far East markets where distances are greater, is already creating pressures for new types of craft with faster speeds and greater capacities. It has been long expected that the inordinate development costs of new generations of aircraft will force a joint collaboration with firm governmental and/or EU support. There are already signs of increasing EU involvement in Airbus, nominally an intergovernmental venture. For example, U.S. complaints forced the EU into a negotiating position on behalf of Airbus regarding so-called "refundable advances" by governments to the consortium, which were reduced to 25 percent in a 1992 European-American agreement. The EU is also directing increasing amounts of R&D support, via its Fourth and (later) Fifth Framework Programs, for developing quieter and more efficient aircraft for future use.

Two particular possibilities have emerged. One proposal is for some form of subsonic mass carrier, long unimaginatively referred to as the Very Large Commercial Transport, designed to seat up to 800 passengers in two decks. This would effectively double the capacity of the currently largest craft, the 747 and A340. Both Airbus and Boeing publicly floated (and apparently, actively pursued) ideas for a joint venture, though it now appears that they will pursue divergent approaches; Boeing first opted for a stretched version of the 777 (the 777–300) for carrying up to 550 passengers, but later demurred, citing uncertain demand. Airbus, on the other hand, has unveiled plans for an entirely new model, the A3XX, at much higher cost ($8 bn vs. $3 bn for Boeing).

A second alternative, proposed by Aérospatiale's then-chairman Louis Gallois, is for a new supersonic jet with larger capacity than the 100-seat Concorde, which would greatly reduce travel times from Europe to the Far East and Australia. The so-called High-Speed Commercial Transport project has generated American enthusiasm as well, including from NASA (Rosen and Williams 1993). For the moment, however, such dreams of mass supersonic travel are outstripped by more prosaic commercial realities.

CONCLUSIONS

After a tentative beginning, the European Union has succeeded in laying down the elements of a bona fide common aviation policy for Europe. Progress is most evident in the area of liberalization, the third phase of which is in the process of being implemented. A climate of competition now pervades the industry, leaving no carrier—whether large or small, state-run or private—unaffected. Gradually, the bilateral Chicago regime is being replaced by an unofficial multilateral one, characterized by growing numbers of carriers, falling fares, company restructurings, new routes on offer, and a bewildering array of alliances that blur national boundaries.

The European Commission in particular has expanded greatly its regulatory involvement in the air industry. Goaded on by the *Comité des Sages*, it increasingly has utilized its investigatory powers in the BA-AA and Boeing-McDonnell Douglas cases. Its application of state aids policy, while uneven and criticized, nonetheless has kept more or less on course and has helped stem the most blatant linkages between national carriers and supportive governments. And the decision by the Transport Council to cede it negotiating powers on behalf of the EU in spring 1996 was another major advance, even though its practical application remains to be seen. Its harmonization proposals and other measures such as the 1993 regulation relaxing "grandfather rights"[41] are other steps toward a comprehensive approach.

By the same token, the globalization of the world air industry itself paradoxically makes it increasingly difficult to isolate a specifically European dimension. Endemic code-sharing practices have given European airlines significantly greater access to routes far beyond Europe. New corporate strategies being unveiled at BA and Lufthansa suggest a hiving off of long-haul, extra-European routes from domestic ones and widespread outcontracting. Even identifying Airbus as a specifically European endeavor is becoming more problematic, as cost imperatives are increasing the scope for extra-European subcontracting and joint aircraft development. Restrictions on state aids, privatizations, and more competition are all chipping away at the once impregnable position of traditional market leaders.

On the other hand, the demise of the European flag-carrier is not yet at hand. State management of airlines is being replaced by advocacy relationships by which governments continue to favor their own by indirect means (e.g., control of landing slots, expansion of central airports rather than regional ones). Public national champions are being replaced by private ones, and retrograde pressures continue to slow restructurings of the remaining state carriers, mainly in southern Europe. Privatized airlines continue to be important generators of national revenue, and even the largest of them—BA and Lufthansa—continue to maintain distinctly national bases despite their claims as Europe's main carriers with global strategies. Paradoxically, their very success suggests that national orientations are a useful selling point that is unlikely to disappear. On the other hand, it may be that other airlines with internationalist ambitions, such as Brussels-based Virgin Express, could emerge as more distinctly nonnational, pan-European companies (akin to ABB in engineering and rail systems) precisely because of a frustrating lack of progress at home.

These ongoing industry changes have also increased the nature and scope of political contention, in a field in which separation of political from economic concerns, and public from private interests, remains problematic. A whole hierarchy of political disputes has arisen: between privatized, newly profitable carriers (BA, SAS, KLM, Lufthansa) and still state-owned, heavily subsidized ones (Alitalia, Iberia, Air France, Olympic), accused of undercutting their business with governmental acquiescence; between the EU's smaller and larger states, the former being much more aggressive in pursuing open-skies agreements with the U.S.; and between large carriers and smaller insurgents seeking to challenge their traditional supremacy. Virgin's longrunning accusations of a BA "dirty tricks" campaign, and Easyjet's cases against SAS and KLM, may be just the beginning of a series of struggles within an industry, once a cartel of near-equals, that faces massive change.

Despite the open regime, it seems likely that the European air market will approximate, rather than replicate, the post-liberalization pattern in the U.S. That development was characterized by the rapid growth of new airlines, challenging and ultimately displacing the traditional market leaders,[42] followed eventually by consolidation to a relatively small number of major carriers. It is true that the emergence of numerous new small carriers in Europe (Maersk, Transwede, Crossair, Air UK, Air Europa, Easyjet, Virgin Express) has already shown great scope for expansion of participant carriers, and the niche markets and underused regional airports still to be exploited. But many other factors seem likely to help avert the sort of ruinous, "Texas-style" competition that long unsettled the U.S. air industry.

A key factor is overcrowding, especially at central airports, where there simply is little room for infrastructure expansion. Indeed the expected tripling of passenger volume in the next two decades creates a huge new factor that remains largely unaddressed. Vigilance against market excesses is, in Europe, two-pronged, with a more assertive European Commission complementing efforts of national governments. There remains, however, a thin line between excessive and insufficient competition, and the Commission faces a difficult task in ensuring that the need to regulate further growth (via its mergers and acquisitions policy) does not translate into new, quasi-cartel conditions that would continue to frustrate consumer advocates of substantially lower European air fares.

For all its progress, the EU has been a tempting and common target for criticism. Its three-phase program was characterized widely as excessively slow and timid. Its reliance on the *Comité des Sages* for advice on industry reform has been interpreted as a lack of political will directly to challenge airlines' and states' supremacy; the *Comité* itself has criticized the EU for inconsistent application of its own state aid rules. Even its investigation of air alliances has been roundly criticised by states wary of encroaching EU regulations and by consumer groups accusing it of tokenism. Other crucial policy areas, especially safety and air traffic control and environmental issues (noise, emissions) require greater attention. Both issues are growing in urgency as a direct, if ironic, result of EU liberalization measures, with its implications for even faster future market growth coupled with a more turbulent industry environment.

Even so, it would be churlish to deny that the Commission has endeavored earnestly to learn from the American deregulatory experience, emulating where necessary while attempting a smoother transition; there may be, after all, useful scope for managed, gradualist deregulation as opposed to "big-bang" measures. Criticism from both ends may even be a sign of admirable even-handedness. Further, the Commission is compelled to operate within the twin structural impediments of a long tradition of air sovereignty, and an increasingly globalized industry. Particularly in its worldwide scope, the air sector has similarities with the maritime sector, which is discussed next.

NOTES

1. On behalf of American freight carriers (Federal Express and UPS), the U.S. has been locked in disputes with both the British and Japanese governments. A damaging tit-for-tat developed after Japan refused to grant "beyond" rights for U.S. carriers to points outside Japan. The U.S. DOT threatened retaliatory sanctions against cargo flights by Japan Airlines (JAL), prompting immediate Japanese counterthreats to ban US cargo flights altogether to five key Asian destinations (IHT, 19 July 1996, p. 17). The dispute involved changing interpretations of bilateral agreements (Japan's dating back to 1952); and in the British case it disrupted open-skies negotiations between Washington and London.

2. Even in the 1995 Swissair-Sabena agreement in which the former took a 49.5 percent stake and provided a large cash infusion, neither carrier's corporate identity was altered.

3. Fokker was controlled by Daimler-Benz's aerospace division (DASA) from 1993. Conflicts arose between DASA and the Dutch government, a minority shareholder, over responsibility for needed capital injections, leading to a stunning decision in early 1996 by DASA to pull out after Daimler's huge, DM 6 bn loss in 1995, due in part to the Fokker venture. The year 1996 saw suitors come and go, though a potential Russian buyout—one of the few in any European industry—was being actively mooted.

4. The ICAO's main functions include: (1) establishing international standards and recommending practices and procedures; (2) promoting simpler formalities at international borders; (3) developing regional plans for ground facilities and services; (4) collecting and publishing air transport statistics; (5) studying the economic aspects of aviation; and (6) fostering the development of commercial air law through conventions (Schiavone 1983: 139).

5. The traditional division between business/first and economy classes has been repeated under various guises (e.g., BA's Club Class). Business travelers have long suffered from restrictions requiring a Saturday stayover to avoid paying premium fares.

6. Article 85 (rules on competition) prohibits "agreements . . .which directly or indirectly fix purchase or selling prices or any other trading conditions [or] . . . share markets or sources of supply." (*Treaties* 1979).

7. Under Art. 84 "the Council may [unanimously] decide whether, to what extent and by what procedure appropriate provisions may be laid down for sea and air transport" (*Treaties* 1979).

8. Namely, TWA and Pan Am; British Airways and British Caledonian.

9. American deregulation led to rapid growth of new market entrants, huge discounts, and ruinous if temporary fare wars. The new boom-and-bust environment led to a thorough reshuffling of industry leadership, with the replacement of

traditionally dominant carriers (Pan Am, TWA, Eastern) by others (United, Delta, American, USAir), relying on dominance at regional hub airports, many of which attempted to couple domestic growth with internationalist pretensions based on skeletal services to European cities.

10. Through Council regulations 2671-73/88 and 4261/88, the Council applied competition principles respectively to capacity sharing, computer reservation systems, ground handling services, and complaints and hearings procedures (CEC 1989b).

11. Branson's litigation against BA has taken several turns. The first action was a libel suit, claiming that BA had defrauded him by dismissing his accusations against BA's anti-competitive practices as mere attention-getting tactics. In a surprise result, BA agreed to pay $940,000 in damages (Jackson 1995). In early 1995 U.S. courts agreed to hear Branson's much larger ($1 bn) antitrust action against BA, claiming BA attempts to monopolize transatlantic services—an argument that resurfaced in Branson's strenuous objections to the mooted BA-American Airlines linkup in 1996–1997.

12. For example, falling demand after the Channel Tunnel opened caused British Midland to cancel its thrice-daily flights to Paris's Orly airport.

13. In 1994, BA netted close to $900 m, becoming the world's most profitable airline, a feat it duplicated in 1995. Lufthansa took pre-tax profits of nearly $300 m in 1994, while KLM and SAS also posted substantial profits, the latter for the second year running.

14. The "committee of wise men" made some 100 recommendations in its report to the Commission, *Expanding Horizons* (1994). However, continuing problems (lack of a single air control system; alleged EU bias toward rail; inconsistency in state aids policy; no common aviation policy) led to a committee split, with five members meeting separately to follow up their initial report and to criticize the EU's lack of progress (Odell 1995).

15. The Olympic bailout program required official commitments for deep spending cuts, a two-year wage freeze, early retirements, and the termination of two loss-making routes, Athens-Tokyo and Athens-Chicago. Due to these measures, Olympic's operating loss for the first half of 1995 was cut to $23 m, mainly due to a 15 percent drop in total expenses and lower wages (AN, 11 Nov. 1995, p. 10).

16. Italy's Prime Minister, Romano Prodi, was formerly head of IRI (Instituto por la Riconstruzione Industriale SpA), the government-owned holding company with a 90 percent stake in Alitalia. Premier Costas Simitis of Greece was, as industry minister in 1995, involved in efforts to sell off loss-making Greek shipyards, which caused his dismissal from the Papandreou government of the day.

17. Sabena's chairman, Pierre Godfroid, stirred controversy with his plans to shift the company's pilots' base across the border to Luxembourg, where employer payroll contributions are two-thirds lower. His typically defiant response to critics was that "I won't take any lessons from anyone. . .I inherited a company in a shambles, on the verge of bankruptcy and with a balance sheet that did not reflect reality" (FT, 2 Feb. 1995: 2).

18. Swiss progress toward EU membership was halted by an unexpected referendum defeat, in December 1992, of the EEA agreement, delaying treaty implementation because of the need to renegotiate part of it. The Swissair-Sabena ac-

cord's viability has been questioned because of Swissair's large payout in a meager profits environment, and by its minority rather than majority stake.

19. FT, 17 Nov. 1994: 1. The transport and competition directorates have also diverged on the question of air mergers policy, which led to a perfunctory Commission attempt in 1990 to bridge the differences by cautiously endorsing a relaxation of competition rules to help Europe's airlines compete worldwide, while also arguing against an oligopolistic situation of giant carriers (Coopers and Lybrand 1994: 9.1).

20. The six airlines are BA, KLM, Air UK, Maersk Air of Denmark, SAS, and the French domestic carrier, TAT. The action is primarily a British one, as BA also holds a 49 percent stake in TAT.

21. A typical code-sharing agreement allows two airlines to share a computer reservation number, giving each one direct access to the other's (often restricted) air market and allowing easier transfers, without actually merging their operations or requiring heavy investments. American Airlines' CEO Bob Crandall has been a sharp critic of code-sharing, arguing that it is deceptive because customers are generally not told when purchasing tickets that they will, in fact, be flying on a different airline for part of the route. His attempted deal with BA in spring 1996 naturally attracted allegations of a double standard.

22. The Delta-Virgin agreement was particularly significant because it allowed Delta, the third major American carrier, indirect access to coveted Heathrow landing slots, denied to Delta on a direct basis by the current British-American air agreement.

23. The BA-AA code-sharing alliance would combine 36,000 routes and 1300 planes, linking the world's largest and third-largest international carriers. Fears of market dominance led competitors, mainly Delta, Continental, and Virgin, to conduct a massive public relations campaign (including a lively exchange in the *Financial Times* letters page) to stop it; see WSJE, 13 June 1996: 8; *Economist,* 1 June 1996: 68; FT, 25 May 1996: 8, and 5 July 1996: 4.

24. The six being investigated were KLM-Northwest; United-Lufthansa; Delta-Swissair/Austrian/Sabena; United-SAS; BA-USAir; and BA-American Airlines. Despite Commission denials, the timing left little doubt that the attempted BA-AA alliance was the trigger. Also, some agreements (e.g., Virgin-Delta) were left out.

25. The Alcazar project collapsed because KLM refused to drop its market-sharing agreement with Northwest for Delta (which the other three subsequently joined in a separate pact). Among the reverberations was the immediate resignation of SAS's CEO, Jan Carlzon, who had staked his company's future to the effort.

26. Among the most vocal opponents of Heathrow expansion is the Airports Policy Consortium, representing thirty local authorities, arguing that nearby communities will suffer with the additional traffic generated by more flights and need for ground access; and the Heathrow Association for the Control of Aircraft Noise, an environmental pressure group (FT, 19 Dec. 1994: 12).

27. Privatization of BA and KLM was stimulated by parallel bilateral developments involving the two countries, specifically the pathbreaking Anglo-Dutch air liberalization accord of 1984.

28. The problematic groundhandling question causing two members of the *Comité des Sages* to dissent on the majority call to privatize ground services (*Ex-*

panding Horizons 1994). A 1994 Commission proposal for a Council directive (COM (94) 590 final) advocated freer access for providers of such services without calling outright for their privatization.

29. Dominant airlines benefit by the practice of "grandfather rights" that give carriers with slots in one year first option on the same slots the next year. BA thus still has precedence (40 percent) in Heathrow landing slots, despite a more open system in place since 1991. A BA competitor, Virgin, has long clamored for a better foothold at Heathrow, though less to increase its number of slots than to force a change of rules in allotment (e.g., by auctioning them off to the highest bidder).

30. Assessing British government-BA links, *The Economist* (9 Dec. 1995: 14) held that "rarely has there been such a perfect example of . . . government and business working together in passenger-defying harmony."

31. Note, for example, the requirement for all US civil service personnel, and others on governmental contract, to fly with U.S. carriers when abroad on official business. This requirement (partly relaxed in mid-1995 with the air services agreement with Britain) has been awkward, as the author discovered when taking up a Fulbright fellowship in Finland in 1993, since Helsinki is poorly serviced by American operators.

32. The takeover of Switzerland's Brown-Boveri by Sweden's Asea, both long-standing independent firms, is frequently misinterpreted as a merger of equals, due to deliberately nonnational corporate strategies and the relocation of company headquarters to Zürich.

33. Six of these states were EU members: Belgium, Luxembourg, Austria, Finland, Sweden, and Denmark. Three other, nonmember states (Iceland, Norway, and Switzerland) also concluded agreements with the U.S., unencumbered by pressures for collective action.

34. Restrictions on Heathrow access can be overstated; even in 1991 no less than 87 airlines had landing rights there (Grant 1995), though most were token rather than extensive.

35. Article 89 states that "the Commission shall . . . ensure the application of principles laid down in Articles 85 and 86 . . . [and] shall investigate cases of suspected infringement of these principles." *Treaties* 1979; FT, 4 July 1996: 1.

36. With a seating capacity of just 100, Concorde's profit-making potential is virtually nil, even at high fares and full loads. Another problem is that its main technical accomplishment, use of supersonic speeds (up to mach 2), is rendered useless in the European sector, where environmental restrictions keep the craft at subsonic speeds to eliminate sonic boom noises.

37. Airbus claimed 125 firm orders worth $9.1 bn in 1994. Boeing of course dismissed this as a misleading anomaly, since orders can be cancelled; in actual deliveries Boeing outdistanced Airbus with 270 total aircraft compared to 123 (FT, 10 Jan. 1995: 5).

38. Overall, Boeing retained a 70 percent market share, with $31.2 bn in total 1995 orders, over three-quarters coming from non-U.S. airlines. Airbus orders totaled around $7 bn, though its annual turnover again set a company record (FT, 5 Jan. 1996: 14).

39. The head-to-head competition extends also to claims for the longest flight range. Airbus believes its A340-200 is the leader, with a range of 7450 nautical

miles, while Boeing claims its 777–100x will fly 8600 miles without refueling when launched in 1999.

40. Airbus estimates that worldwide demand, based on an annualized growth rate of 5.1 percent, will produce aircraft orders worth some $1000 bn over the next two decades, which would effectively triple present traffic volumes. With most of this demand from East Asia, the Airbus-Chinese production agreement in early 1996 assumes potentially great importance. Boeing's estimate (some 10,000 new aircraft worth $780 bn over the same two-decade period) is lower (FT, 22 March 1995: 1; 5 Jan. 1996: 14).

41. This regulation created a pool of airport landing slots, half of which must be available to new market entrants. However, many, including Britain's Civil Aviation Authority, argue that competition at major airports has not risen (FT, 11/12 Feb. 1995: 22).

42. The problems of three of the main U.S. market leaders of the 1970s (Eastern, Pan Am and TWA) in Chapter 11 proceedings, and the demise of the first two by the 1990s, in turn had negative consequences for airport development at New York's JFK, since all three had guided its expansion in the 1960s.

Chapter Six

Ships of Fortune: Maritime Transport

> Roll on, thou deep and dark blue Ocean—roll!
> Ten thousand fleets sweep over thee in vain;
> Man marks the earth with ruin—his control
> Stops with the shore.
> —George Gordon, Lord Byron
> *Childe Harold's Pilgrimage*

In a field (transport) already characterized by lack of attention in the EU literature, the maritime subsector carries the dubious distinction of being possibly the least considered of the four major modes. While in keeping with its small share of European passenger traffic, this paucity of treatment belies its role as the oldest form of long-distance mobility as well as its continuing predominance in the extra-European dimension of goods movement. The EU, now the world's largest trade bloc (accounting for 38 percent of all foreign commerce), relies on maritime shipping for over nine-tenths of this commerce.

After a slow beginning, the EU has succeeded in carving out the basis of common shipping guidelines that partly make up for past neglect. Even so, its efforts have been complicated by unusual elements of the sector, including the following:

1. A natural division into numerous sub-markets. The Rome Treaty itself recognized this factor in incorporating inland waterway systems into the original CTP while leaving high seas shipping (a complicated sector in its own right) to the side, the latter, as with air policy, being addressed from the 1970s after key ECJ rulings and the accession of major shipping countries.

2. An unclear division between the European and global dimensions. Unlike operators in other modes, shipowners are able to skirt specific EU rules by flagging out practices that proliferate under a policy environment in which multilateral, not regional (EU) fora, take precedence in establishing maritime standards.

3. An unusual policy profile, due to the outsized influence of small and peripheral states. Unlike rail, primarily a concern to core regions, and road and air travel which concern all states, shipping is mainly an issue for states hindered by lengthy, poor, or nonexistent land links to the continent, especially along the Mediterranean littoral. In the maritime equivalent of the tail wagging the dog, two small states (Greece and Norway, the latter also an EU nonmember) dominate European shipping statistics, while a third (Britain), with its shipbroking and classification expertise, is hardly a fast-track integrationist.

4. Its recent emergence as a dark horse in the European search for alternative transport modes. Aside from underutilized cargo capacity, maritime operations are even emerging as a viable passenger mode via new engine technologies, double-hull ship designs, and large capacity superferries operating in the North, Irish and Adriatic seas and even in the English Channel.

5. The volatile nature of the industry. Belying its staid, leisurely image, the operational side of the shipping sector is characterized by sharp price and capacity swings, while the manufacturing side is increasingly littered with bankruptcies at some of Europe's largest shipbuilders in both northern and southern Europe. All this reflects the perilous nature of an industry threatened with lower-cost competitors worldwide.

6. Its strongly political component. Shipping has been and remains politically contentious, as a symbol of nationalism and union muscle (Poland's Solidarity movement was born at the Gdansk shipyards, now, alas, bankrupt). This element reflects the symbolic, national and even psychological boundaries set by territorial waters, which makes the ending of cabotage restrictions in maritime and insular states a sensitive political question.

After a brief discussion of the sector's overall characteristics, this chapter examines the development of European shipping legislation, including the landmark 1986 regulations and their aftermath. It concludes by discussing contemporary issues, dominated politically by two themes: economics, and environmental and safety concerns.

DEVELOPMENTAL CHARACTERISTICS OF THE SHIPPING SECTOR

The overwhelming maritime influence on major human endeavor—facilitating trade, fostering global exploration and later mass emigration, and shaping geopolitical strategies—has flowed from three elements peculiar to the sector, which together have produced a decidedly split sectoral milieu. One is its territorial and spatial function as both divider and unifier; a second is its inherently cosmopolitan nature, in awkward coexistence with the strongly national basis of maritime law; and a third is its dual strategic/commercial role for societies.

The *spatial function* of the maritime sector derives from the fact that shipping lanes and waterways, unlike rail tracks or motorways, obey neither boundary lines nor, as per the opening quote, human dictates. Indeed, Europe's waterways themselves delineate its boundaries: symbolically separating continental and offshore (insular or peninsular) territories, such as the English Channel or the Kattegat between Sweden and Denmark, and often defining national borders and even political blocs (e.g. the Oder-Neisse and all its Cold War implications for *Mitteleuropa* and German-Polish relations). In turn, waterways often emerge as shared political concerns and objects of political regime formation; the international conventions on the Rhine (ICPR) and Moselle have endeavored to establish pollution control regimes along those two rivers. As such, traffic on inland seas, lakes (Lake Constance bordering Austria, Switzerland, and Germany), and rivers is scarcely less "international" than is deep-sea traffic. The convening in December 1995 in Barcelona of a conference on protecting the Mediterranean is another recent manifestation, which in turn has been cited as a model for the Persian Gulf region.

A second basic maritime element is the *cosmopolitanism* which sea access created in those societies prescient enough to exploit the possibilities. The Mediterranean basin's importance and temperate climate made it a European developmental determinant of the first magnitude. To the ancient Greeks, the sea was a prime identifying feature of Cycladic cultures and focal point of geographical, political, and even literary (Homeric) and religious (Delian) reference, giving substance to the belief that "the land divides; the sea unites." Proximity to the sea facilitated exploitation of the eighth century B.C. equivalent of export markets, and enabled colonization as far as the Black Sea, North Africa, and Sicily— not only by Athens but by Corinth (De Burgh 1953). On the other hand, separation by water fostered independent city-state development and a political culture resistant to centralization.

Though not often regarded in terms of cultural enlightenment, the three Viking expansions in ca 900–1100—eastward from Sweden into Estonia and Russia; westward from Norway to Iceland, Scotland, Greenland, and even America's east coast; and southward from Denmark into southeastern England and Europe—in combination spread Nordic culture, as well as misery and violence, to areas as far afield as Constantinople (Istanbul). Unparalleled in both mobility and range (despite using open boats), Viking excursions had profound influence in conquered areas. In Britain, for example, their influence reintroduced largely lost maritime traditions, and even fostered political unification for Saxon law and culture (especially under Danish King Canute), in contrast to the subsequent Norman invasion (Trevelyan 1959). The sea-based link with Britain long dominated Scandinavian foreign policy concerns, and even into the 1970s Scandinavia's foreign trade policy (in EFTA, and later the EC) was influenced heavily by Britain, until recently its predominant trade partner.

In turn, this cosmopolitanism links to the third determinative element of the sector, the *linkage between commercial and strategic interests* for states in exploiting the sea's possibilities. Early Athenian interest was mainly with seaborne commercial and colonial enterprise, but Themistocles's naval defeat of the Persians at Salamis in 480 B.C. opened possibilities for Athenian domination of the Delian League based on the speed and finesse of the trireme. Defeat to Sparta in 404 B.C., however, indicated the limitations of sea as opposed to land-based power—especially if it depends on foreign imports (in this case, timber from Macedonia).

In ancient Rome the strategic balance shifted more decisively toward an emphasis on a systematic terrestrial (road) transport system (noted briefly in Chapter 4) which, unlike sea routes, could be maintained and fortified. Though the Mediterranean was a Roman sea for centuries, Rome's shipping interests (as with Byzantium's later on; see Runciman 1956) were primarily commercial in nature, partly because it lacked a natural port to match the Piraeus near Athens. Ostia, its main port, suffered silting problems, and it became mainly a transshipment point for smaller cargo vessels plying the Tiber to Rome itself; a second port, at Aquileia at the Adriatic's head, facilitated trade further north (Grant 1969: 291).

The Baltic Sea became the focal point of another strategic-commercial configuration, namely the Hanseatic League from the 12th century, a quasi-geographical pact linking the region's port towns to commercial interests in the German hinterland. The great German Hanseatic centers (Lübeck, Hamburg, Rostock) developed trade and cultural ties as far afield as London, Bruges, Bergen, Kalmar, and Novgorod. However, the awkward political linkage between far-flung port towns, and between these and larger inland regions (Mecklenburg, Pomerania), was racked with internal dissension before breaking up in the 16th century. Nonetheless, it reinforced the potential geopolitical significance of the sea as a common bond, in a way unmatched by proximity to inland road routes.

The great age of exploration in the late Middle Ages was pursued by those nations capable of a sustained shipbuilding and seafaring effort based on combined, high-level political and financial support. National self-interest, and the search for riches and new territorial claims, led to extraordinary official risk taking with long-range expeditions. Equally noteworthy was the internationalist nature of these explorative efforts. The westward voyages of Christopher Columbus himself—a non-Italian speaking Genoese inspired by a Venetian explorer (Marco Polo), based in Portugal, nearly gained sponsorship by France before being financed by the Spanish royal house—were indicative of the strength of old Mediterranean ties. The Spanish search for riches and glory later financed the voyages of Balboa, a Spaniard, but also of Magellan, a Portuguese, who shrewdly played off the Iberian rivalry in order to gain Spanish King Charles V's support for his search for the Spice Islands, in what ultimately became a three-year circumnavigation of the globe (Boorstin 1983). Portugal's use of another foreigner, Vespucci, to do its explorative bidding showed that this extranational trend was widespread.

Shipping also emerged as the first more or less mature transport industry in the late pre-industrial era. Like early road and rail development, canal-building began as a speculative commercial enterprise that transformed patterns of (goods) movement in the late 18th century (Europe) and early 19th (North America). In Britain, early rail development focused on connecting different inland canal systems for transshipment of coal (Trevelyan 1959). Symptoms included increasing specialization of building and operations, with ownership patterns based on small partnerships ("husbands") for refitting vessels and arranging their routes and contacts with merchants. The hazards of marine transit also helped create the first modern service enterprise; even by the 17th century, Lloyd's Coffee House (since, of course, renamed) developed as brokers and underwriters of shipping ventures. Marine insurance helped give the City of London an early reputation for financial probity and raised its profile as a transport and financial center to match Amsterdam, Genoa, and Venice (Ogg 1965: 75–77)—a reputation that went unsullied until the great crisis of the 1980s, when huge losses were suffered by the backers ("Names") in the unlimited liability world characterizing Lloyd's of London.

Britain's emergence as a seafaring nation was partly in response to Dutch supremacy in East Indies trade, facilitating strategic British ties with India as well as closer to home (Russia, the Baltic). Here marked the emergence of mercantilist, organized trade, based on large regulated companies like the Hudson Bay Company, underscoring the marriage of national and commercial interests behind colonialist ventures. The textile-based India link was crucial to Britain's emerging, dual sea and industrial predominance; its import-export trade more than doubled from 1834 to 1847 alone, and by mid-century some 60 percent of the world's sea-tonnage was British (Thompson 1966: 179). And just as harnessing mechanical engineering technology for the colonial aims of *pax Britannica* produced the Suez Canal, subsequent American sponsorship of the Panama Canal project facilitated its growing global ambitions. Shipping's significance for Britain led governments to treat it as a separate transport question, insofar as its transport and shipping ministries traditionally were separated; they merged only in 1941 and as a result of wartime pressures for centralized decision-making (Taylor 1965). The development of steamships in the mid-19th century further enabled new external migratory patterns for Europeans (Swedes, the Irish) making their way to the New World.

The strategic imperatives of the two world wars highlighted the pivotal importance of shipping. One primary cause of World War I was undoubtedly the Anglo-German naval arms race prior to 1914. The mutual German and British sea blockades of 1914–1918 affected the war's course no less than did the trench-based war of attrition on land. Violations of neutral shipping led eventually (1917) to U.S. entry into the war itself. The impact in 1939–1945 was hardly less dramatic: conduct of a global war effort required seaborne movement of troops and supplies on a massive scale. Portugal's controversial (and non-neutral) decision to grant Anglo-American use of the Azores provided a crucial transatlantic base which helped turn the Allied war effort. One authority (Taylor 1965: 613) has argued that the shipping war in the Atlantic was more critical than the Blitz in determining the war's ultimate course—even while sea losses, principally Germany's battleship *Bismarck*, "gave a disregarded warning that sea power in the old style was drawing to an end." Similarly, the traumatic evacuation of Allied troops from Dunkirk in 1940, even while underscoring the potential symbiosis of commercial and defense needs, was, equally, a reminder of the decline of British dominance of world shipping circles.

PROBLEMS OF MODERN EUROPEAN SHIPPING GOVERNANCE

General Issues

The historically powerful international dimension of the shipping industry has typified, in modern times, the twin characteristics of the international political economy of (a) increasing competitive pressures and (b) growing foreign direct investment and capital mobility, indeed as "the apotheosis of mobile capital" (Aspinwall 1995: 23). Both these factors, in turn, have enabled the switching of business in two senses, first to lower-cost builders in eastern Europe and the Far East, and second to national ship registrations offshore, to countries with laxer social and fiscal requirements. Though both trends indicate the global nature of the industry, the latter is made possible by the strongly national dimension of maritime law, by which ships must conform to the laws of the country under whose flag they fly, rather than those of the territorial waters in which they are physically based.

Despite the early codification of international maritime law under Grotius's formative influence, European shipping governance was long limited to inland rather than sea shipping. The oldest existing European transport agreement pertains to the inland maritime sector, namely the

Central Commission for the Navigation of the Rhine (CCR), established in 1868 under the Mannheim Convention. Of the signatory states (Belgium, the Netherlands, France, Germany, Britain, and Switzerland) all but the last became original EC members, which caused an awkward problem for the CTP provisions, since Rhine navigation must conform to CCR and not EC principles. Rhine cooperation since the 1963 Berne Convention has focused largely on pollution control.[1] A similar situation has affected the 1956 Convention on the Moselle, the three signatories of which (Germany, France and Luxembourg) all became original EEC members the following year (Abbati 1987: 23–24). With both (as with the UN's ECE), the EC has since established interinstitutional cooperative agreements, under Article 229 of the Rome Treaty.

And internationally, responsibility for laying down shipping rules, such as the Safety of Life at Sea (SOLAS) and Marine Pollution (MARPOL) conventions, centers on the London-based, 148-member International Maritime Organization (IMO), again making it difficult to establish a European, much less a specific EU, dimension for the mode. Further, the Geneva-based International Labor Organization (ILO) has taken a close interest in the special working conditions of shipboard employment, adding a degree of sensitivity to the needs of non-European developing nations.

Another problem hindering EC involvement in the maritime sector was the geographical reality of the original EEC6, all continental states, which prioritized terrestrial transport services and, to a lesser extent, inland waterways. Though all (except Luxembourg) also had direct sea access, and some (the Netherlands, Germany) have long maritime traditions and major port operations at Rotterdam and Hamburg, the deep-sea sector was, along with the airlines, left aside from the CTP. The opposite was true for the original "outer seven" of EFTA, five of which (excepting only Austria and Switzerland) were major seafaring nations with substantial national resources tied up in shipbuilding.

In Scandinavia, shipbuilding has accounted for around 10 percent of total exports; the figure for Norway has been much higher still (over 20 percent), even excluding its merchant fleet, fifth largest in the world.[2] Another Nordic strength has been its great diversity, spanning both goods and passenger traffic, shipbuilding, and professional expertise; the World Maritime University was established in 1983 in Malmö (Sweden), while Norwegian banks have long underwritten ship purchases and leasings in the Mediterranean. For Denmark, shipbuilding is the country's third largest export trade, with an emphasis on dry bulk, cargo, and container traffic. Finland, on the other hand, has maintained a strong competitive presence in passenger ferries and shipbuilding (producing the Viking and Silja Line ships servicing the Baltic lanes). Well over half (55 percent) of all exports from ECMT countries are accounted for by states that were not original

EC members, principally Ireland and Britain and the four Nordic countries (van de Voorde and Viegas 1995: 35–36). This Nordic role has had two other effects: first, from an industry standpoint, European shipowners have been anxious to involve Scandinavians in their activities, to the extent of admitting Norway, Sweden, and Finland into the EC Shipowner's Association (ECSA) in 1993, well before their countries' EU accessions. Second, it raised the political profile and legal significance of the EU-EFTA agreement, the EEA, which also took effect in 1993.

The entry of Britain, Ireland, and Denmark into the EC in 1973 and especially Greece in 1981 brought maritime issues to the fore without translating immediately into a common shipping policy. The main shipping nations all suffered serious problems of overcapacity, as a result of rapid expansion in the early 1970s, and the severe, recession-induced contraction of business which followed later in the decade. Thus the 1970s and 1980s have been characterized by growing public subsidies for fleet development and shipyards (Hart 1993), especially in Scandinavia, with the familiar aim of saving jobs in industries widely perceived as strategic. Another, more pernicious effect of the first and second EC expansions was that it brought in new states that, even if facing similar problems, also had entrenched traditions of go-it-alone shipping policies, reinforced through the loose framework of EFTA and its absence of common policy aims.

The EC-EFTA split hindered the search for common European shipping policies internally, and also development of a coordinated external policy, with all its implications for the EC as a trade bloc. Shipping is a vital element of European trade, though its relative importance varies enormously according to its function. Domestically, seaborne trade is insignificant, accounting for only about 2 to 3 percent of all EC traffic. However, it accounts for about one-third of cross-border, intra-EC freight traffic; and in overseas trade, shipping has been the overwhelmingly predominant mode, accounting for over 90 percent of the market in volume terms.

In terms of tonnage of goods carried (1986 figures), waterborne transport accounted for around 60 percent, divided about equally between sea (32 percent) and inland waterways (28 percent) (CEC 1989b). The inland waterways sector, like its maritime counterpart, has long suffered overcapacity problems, and more recent EC attention has focused on ways to encourage scrapping of old vessels, as well as on conventional harmonization measures (access to the occupation of goods carrier; mutual recognition of boatmasters' certificates).

The division between inland and high-seas shipping began eroding in 1974, as a result of an ECJ ruling (on the "French seamen case") that sea transport could not be excluded from the general Treaty provisions; thus it struck down French practices discriminating against non-Frenchmen on the basis that maritime traffic constituted a special case (Aspinwall 1994: 9). The impact of this case was reinforced by the Court's seminal 1985 ruling, obliging the Council to shape common Community transport legislation.

A more serious practical concern was the early 1980s recession, and its disastrous consequences for European shipyards and owners alike. Overall European employment in shipping fell by 45 percent between 1980 and 1986 alone (CEC 1989b), underscoring its boom-and-bust nature, along with its main supplier of building materials, the steel industry.[3] The recession greatly accentuated an ongoing trend away from European dominance of world shipping. While from 1970 to 1980 the EC's percentage of the world's cargo fleet held relatively steady (dropping from 31.9 percent to 28.7 percent), this figure was more than halved in the subsequent decade (falling to just 14 percent in 1990, or 18 percent for the EEA group) (Eurostat 1993). As of 1994, ship tonnage registered under foreign flags but beneficially owned by EC countries (83 m gross tons) had come to outweigh the fleet flying European flags, even if Norway is included (81 m gross tons) (ECSA 1994: 5). Even so, it is possible to overstate the magnitude of the flagging-out problem, since many other maritime activities with significant home value (e.g., port operations) are not transferable abroad.

This longrunning overall drop was due primarily to two factors. One was growing competition in both shipbuilding and services from outside, from the COMECON countries of eastern Europe and from the Far East (Korea, Japan), all able to undercut western European companies in price while maintaining standards. Indeed, market monitoring of unfair external practices was among the first common shipping steps introduced via Council decision, in 1978 (Moussis 1996: 400). Second, in terms of operations, obscure smaller states offering social and tax advantages encouraged transferrals of ship registration to so-called flags of convenience. Overall tonnage of the EC12 fell around 10 percent from 1970 to 1987; but COMECON countries doubled in capacity, while countries in the Far East rose ninefold (Bredima-Savopoulou and Tzoannos 1990: 19). This innocuous EC figure disguises large national variations, with states facing the highest labor and social costs also suffering the most flag transferrals, including Germany and Denmark. They soon followed the lead of Norway, which in 1987 created its International Ships Registry, Europe's first parallel registry, to stem the offshore flow. By far the most precipitous EC dropoff, however, was in the UK, which saw its huge predominance in 1970 (35.6 percent of the eventual EC12) fall to just 11.4 percent in two decades; and its total fleet fell from nearly 26,000 vessels to less than 7000.[4]

Because of this major decline, accentuated by the post-1973 recession, earlier Commission plans to end shipyard subsidies by 1975 were shelved in favor of an 11 percent subsidy ceiling by the mid-1980s (Hart 1993: 49). The falloff in business, however, has continued into the 1990s, hitting politically sensitive shipyard employment. Two recent announced closures have reinforced the negative trend and perceptions of overall crisis. First the Danish shipyard Burmeister & Wain (builders of the first diesel passenger ships) announced the termination of its operations by 1997, after 152 years in business. Even more traumatic was the collapse of Germany's largest shipbuilding group, Bremer Vulkan, which involved much larger financial losses and charges of breach of trust.[5]

Even among relatively healthy shipping companies, the cross-modal (and cross-industry) trend toward concentration on core activities is evident. Stena Line's decision to concentrate on high-speed, large volume passenger ferries; the Norwegian Kvaerner Group's sale (worth over $1.5 bn) of non-core assets; P&O's mooted disposal plans and its September 1996 decision (since challenged by the EU's Competition directorate) to consolidate its Channel routes with Stena; and the sale by Nedlloyd, a Dutch group, of $300 m of its offshore drilling subsidiary, are all recent manifestations of international pressures on the overall industry to consolidate.

The 1986 Shipping Reforms and Their Aftermath

The combination of crisis-induced pressures for shipping reform and the dearth of Community initiatives over previous years gave shipping a prominent place in the 1985 White Paper on completing the internal market. In terms of inland waterway transport, the White Paper called for the establishment of conditions for nonresident carriers to operate services in other states (cabotage), which was already a fixture in some states (Britain, Belgium, and the Netherlands) while others (mainly in southern Europe) fiercely opposed it. The White Paper also called for freedom of services for international inland transport, also by 1989. In sea transport, freedom to provide services between member states was to be phased in from the end of 1986. Thus the maritime sector was slated for more immediate action than were the airlines (by 1987) or road freight (1988) (CEC 1985).

In accordance with the White Paper, the EC adopted a series of four landmark shipping regulations in 1986, which formed the basis for the future establishment of a common shipping policy without actually establishing such a policy. The four regulations, adopted by the Council of Ministers as a set (Nos. 4055–4058/86 (EEC)), pertained to ocean trades, competition, tariffs, and freedom of services, all designed to increase the Community's overall competitiveness in the shipping sector. The first (4055) applies the principle of freedom of services on a nondiscriminatory basis, both between member states and between EC states and third countries (but not within states, i.e., cabotage). It also required the phasing out, by 1993, of unilateral cargo reservation and bans discriminatory bilateral cargo-sharing arrangements between Community-based ships and third countries.

Regulation 4056/86 applied EC competition principles (Rome Treaty Arts. 85 and 86) to international maritime transport services to or from

Community ports. However, in an attempt to strike a balance between shippers (consumers) and owners, it exempted so-called liner conferences from its provisions.[6] The third regulation (4057/86) deals with unfair pricing practices, applying a regressive duty against third country shipowners if they disrupt Community freight routes or cause injury to Community shipping interests. The fourth and final regulation (4058/86) concerns coordinated action to safeguard free access to ocean cargo trade. It provides for countermeasures against third countries that practice restrictive cargo reservation, including the possibilities of EC-imposed quotas or levies. Extraordinarily, its provisions have been used to justify subsequent EC Commission search-and-seizure actions against foreign shipping companies suspected of discriminating against EC flags. Thus the regulations apply to all ships, irrespective of nationality or flag, which transformed, at a stroke, a virtually nonexistent shipping policy to one that had, albeit with exceptions, extraterritorial applicability. It is striking that the final two (4057, 4058) provide the possibility for sanctioning foreign firms that breach the rules, the former needing Council approval and the latter possible even in lieu of a Council decision. These provisions have occasionally applied (in 1989, against Hyundai Marine Insurance).

Despite these changes, numerous other elements went unaddressed, including cabotage rights (freedom to provide shipping services within other member states), the introduction of a Community shipping fleet, harmonization of operating standards (such as tax and social security requirements for companies and seafarers; determining minimum percentage of EC nationals aboard ships), and state aid policies. Some of these gaps were subsequently addressed, and since 1989 a semblance of a "Stage 2" shipping policy has emerged. Greater harmonization of operating standards was introduced, but the longrunning attempt to establish a Community shipping fleet under a single flag has foundered.

In June 1989, the Commission proposed a Council regulation to establish a Community ship register (EUROS) providing for the flying of the Community flag by sea-going vessels, along with a proposed regulation to establish a common definition of a Community shipowner. The aim here was to create favorable, common European conditions that would offset the comparative economic disadvantage accruing to (higher-cost) European operators, and thereby to stem the outflow of registrations to non-EC flags,[7] in two directions: to open registry or flag of convenience (FOC) states such as Panama and Liberia; and to parallel registries in EU-affiliated territories (Isle of Man, Cayman Islands, Hong Kong, Netherlands Antilles). Common registry proposals met stiff resistance, even though the Community flag was to fly alongside national flags, was largely symbolic, and was practically limited by continuing restrictions on cabotage (up until 1993). By March 1996 it appeared that the European registry was off the agenda indefinitely, due to lack of member-state interest, with many opting for parallel registries with less stringent requirements and more favorable conditions for owners (e.g., repayment of seafarers' taxes).

This setback, however, has been partly counterbalanced by another step in the direction of imbuing the industry with some sense of common purpose, via the establishment of the Maritime Industries Forum (MIF) in 1992, a joint initiative of EU Commissioners Martin Bangemann and Karel Van Miert. The MIF has concentrated its efforts on promoting the overall industry and particularly in developing intra-EU shipping as a bona fide transport alternative.[8]

The important question of coastal cabotage has also been addressed, in 1992 (via Regulation EEC 3577/92), allowing European owners the freedom to provide maritime transport services within other member states, by which cabotage rights can be exercised by all EC shipowners with EC registration (but only for smaller ships, under 6000 grt). Extra-national passenger services are becoming a feature of European travel as a result, centering on the Irish and North Seas; for example, Greece's Strintzis Line now operates a ferry route between Wales and Ireland (Yannopoulos 1995), and Stena have followed with two further fast lines between Ireland and Britain, in a major strategic shift toward high-speed services (FT, 3 July 1996: 14). Despite the freeing of coastal cabotage, exceptions still apply in the case of mainland-island and interisland cabotage, to which the measure will apply only from 1999; and the Greek islands are exempted until 2004 (CEC 1989b). Inland waterway cabotage restrictions were removed along with entry into effect of the Single Market in January 1993.

Another pressure for reform has been the UN Code of Conduct for Liners (the so-called UNCTAD Liner Code), originating in the postcolonial North-South conflict. The Code aimed to give developing states greater say over sea transport operations, by guaranteeing them a minimum proportion of cargo originating in or bound for their territory. In effect, the Liner Code artificially divided the market and played into the hands of shipping cartels (liner conferences). Intra-EC conflicts over the Code's provisions produced the 1979 "Brussels package," by which EC states ratified the UN Code of Conduct; the so-called 40:40:20 formula was a compromise designed to satisfy free traders within the OECD, such as Britain and Denmark, and those (France, Belgium, Germany) supporting the Liner Code (and hence developing countries) for political reasons (Bredima-Savopoulou and Tzoannos 1990: 79–81). It was the gaps in coverage (in EC international commerce) that the 1986 regulations were meant to rectify (Aspinwall 1994).

The establishment of common European rules has also been hindered by the continuation of national registries of shipping at the expense of EUROS, on the one hand, and (paradoxically) on the other by tightening EC social standards for sea-related employment, which encouraged flagging-out practices by European shipowners anxious to dodge stringent Community regulations on safety, technical, or taxation matters. Another problem is the reluctance of coastal states to maintain standards for ships, via Port State Control, not policed by the flag states themselves; a December 1992 regulation extended to host states responsibility for ensuring that smaller ships and those operating interisland services comply with their cabotage requirements (Moussis 1996: 401).

The vexing problem of registrations is shown by the Greek-owned fleet, only around a third (36 percent) of which actually flies the Greek flag, while the Cypriot, Maltese and Panamanian flags together account for nearly half.[9] Beneficially owned European ships flying under FOCs now outstrip shipping tonnage under combined EU flags. Because of growing competition and industry over-capacity, however, and accompanying pressures on shipowners to provide quality services, the trend in offshore ship registrations appears to have leveled off since the late 1980s. Even so, the shipping industry is so internationalized that it is unlikely ever to be governed solely, or even mainly, by EU regulations.

This is is particularly the case because of the great predominance of one country, Greece, in the overall European context. Outside the former USSR, Greece has the largest number of short-sea vessels in Europe, with 12 percent of the total (van de Voorde and Viegas 1995). Far more impressively, the Greek-owned merchant fleet, including tankers, in 1994 accounted for well over half (53.3 percent) of total EU tonnage, which represents a dramatic upward shift since the 1980s (see Table 6.1).[10] Greece is now the world's largest shipowning country, with combined national and flag-of-convenience registration of around 16 percent of the world's total (McDonald 1994); even the Greek-flag component alone is largest in the

TABLE 6.1
EU Member States' Merchant Fleets (1994)

Country	Share of EU Total (percent)	Tonnage (thousands GRT)
Greece	53.3	30,161
Italy	12.1	6,818
Germany	10.1	5,696
Britain	7.8	4,430
Netherlands	5.9	3,349
France	3.8	2,132
Spain	2.8	1,554
Luxembourg	2.0	1,143
Denmark	1.0	0,573
Portugal	0.5	0,264
Belgium	0.4	0,233
Ireland	0.3	0,190

Source: Greek Business Review, October 1995.

EU and third worldwide. Sheer dead-weight tonnage gives it great influence in EU shipping policy, as does its currently very strong financial position after years of industry retrenchment;[11] and a Greek shipping executive, John Lyras, assumed the presidency of the European Community Shipowners' Association (ECSA), the main owners' pressure group, in 1995. In addition, the Union of Greek Shipowners diverges considerably from the other Mediterranean states in pursuing a much more liberal, free-market approach to shipping regulations—a striking confirmation of the adage that the powerful benefit the most from free trade. Its advocacy of freer markets has been the more forceful due to the once-exemplary safety record of Greek passenger vessels, although several notable mishaps in winter 1996–1997 dented this reputation.

Other characteristics of the Greek shipping community include its close-knit tradition of family ownership, of which the Niarchos and Onassis groups have been but the best known; an aversion to exchange listing due to financial disclosure rules; a transnational presence, often represented in three or more cities (generally Piraeus, New York, and London);[12] flexible entrepreneurship, ideal for meeting sudden shifts in market supply and demand; widespread use of secondhand vessels, adding to overall fleet age;[13] heavy concentration on transporting bulk commodities;[14] and a liberal independent proclivity to remain outside collusive liner conferences. The result has been a pronounced decentralization of the Greek shipping community itself, in which the Hellenic Registry of Shipping is unable to speak for the most important shipowners and remains unrecognized even by the EU or the International Association of [ship] Classification Societies. Because of this decentralization, only a tenuous link connects the Greek state and its shipowners, who enjoy an extraordinarily favorable, open-registry type tax regime, allowed to flag out to states charging only an annual tonnage fee, in exchange for generous state subsidies and loan guarantees. Shipping remains a major source of invisible earnings, estimated at $2 bn in 1993 (or 16 percent of Greece's trade deficit).

These liberal international practices, however, contrast uncomfortably with the fierce defense of national rights within Greek territorial waters. Greek ferry companies have long operated under state-imposed public service obligations, regulated by a strict licensing system, based on the need to offer year-round interisland services even to remote areas;[15] this need has only increased in light of ongoing disputes with neighboring Turkey over Aegean territorial rights, precipitated by the January 1996 Imia crisis.[16] For this reason, Greece was exempted from EU cabotage legislation until 2004; and recent industrial action has shown a fierce determination to defend this exemption to the letter.[17] A second set of such obligations, on the Italian Adriatic routes, has grown along with increasing shipping demand because of the Yugoslav conflict. Since the late 1980s, new government regulations have been established in order to cope with growing business.

For example, the six ferry companies operating Italian runs are obliged to cater to truck (thus goods) as well as passenger and car traffic, on strict timetables; and they must apply for a government permit to withdraw a ship from service even temporarily.

RECENT DEVELOPMENTS IN THE MARITIME INDUSTRY

Changing Economics

Shipping's awkwardness as a policy area stems partly from the great discrepancies in its relative significance for goods and passenger traffic. Its considerable role in moving goods between member states and its overwhelming dominance in overseas traffic is counterbalanced by its decline in passenger travel, reflecting the growing importance of speed and convenience as factors in passenger modal choice. Worldwide, seaborne trade has continued to grow, reaching a record 4.48 bn tons in 1994, reflecting the growth of cargo shipping and ever-larger tanker sizes. Approximately a third of this volume is in crude oil and oil products, with much of the rest accounted for by low-value, dry bulk shipments, such as raw goods shipments to the steel industry (e.g., iron ore) (FT, 2 Feb. 1995: 5). Much of this trade, however, is due to growth in non-EU markets, particularly East Asia. The goods shipping market, however, is subject to rapid changes in world market conditions, reflected in wide swings in rates.[18]

However, passenger services on long-distance (transatlantic) routes have all but disappeared because of frequent, faster, and cheaper air services, leaving individual companies such as Cunard (itself owned by the Norwegian group Kvaerner), which operates the *QE2,* as exceptions proving the rule.[19] Tourist-oriented cruise lines in fast-growing markets like the Caribbean have picked up much of the slack, though the Mediterranean market (wholly separate, as the aborted merger between Miami-based Carnival cruises and Greece's Epirotiki lines proved) was badly hit by the *Achille Lauro* hijacking, the Gulf War and the 1990s recession.[20] The luxury sector has in turn sustained a handful of specialist west European shipyards in business.[21] Other European shipyards, particularly in Scandinavia (Swedenship at Oskarhamns; Fosens in Norway; Seebeckwerft in Bremen), have also benefited from new demand for faster passenger ferries. Indeed, rather like Mark Twain, reports of the death of passenger shipping have been highly exaggerated, and the industry has fought tenaciously to maintain its share of the market on shorter routes, even in direct competition with speedier alternatives.

Many analysts now regard short-sea shipping as an especially promising growth market (van de Voorde and Viegas 1995). A Spanish transport minister, José Borrell, who also served as EU Transport Council president during 1995, emphasized the need to increase short-sea shipping because of its lower demands on the environment, lower costs and energy use, and flexibility, especially in smaller ports, though industry spokesmen likely overstate their case with claims that shipping is "environmentally friendly by nature" (ECSA 1993: 3). Traditionally, short-sea routes have only been used where alternative land routes are circuitous or nonexistent; and exploitation of this alternative often has been limited by poor handling facilities and slow transit times, and by the generally downmarket image of port operations in an industry (transport) that puts a premium on modernization and speed.

Despite these concerns, increasing congestion along land-based routes has diminished the special attractiveness of the road sector and given renewed emphasis to point-to-point ferry services between member states; and short-sea crossings are seen as essential links in growing combined transport routes. The EU has noted that three modes retain ample spare capacity for expansion of traffic, two of which (inland waterways and shipping) are in the maritime sector (CEC 1993a: 24). To this end, the Commission adopted, in July 1995, a communication (COM (95) 317) identifying three areas of action, namely: (1) improving the quality and efficiency of short-sea transport; (2) improving ports and infrastructures; and (3) including short-sea shipping within the general framework of the CTP's external relations. The EU's growing attention to multimodal development may already be translating into port operations; for example, in May 1995 the French port of Le Havre initiated overnight shuttle services of block container trains, to link the port with Lille's waterport, with direct connections to Channel Tunnel rail services—in effect creating a three-way port-river-train transport connecting system. Both the Fourth Framework (research) program of 1994–1998, and the TENs initiative, have targeted waterborne links, both information- and infrastructure-oriented, as warranting further budgetary attention.

A prime example of the potential competitiveness of sea routes has been the regeneration of the Channel ferries, which fought a losing battle with Channel Tunnel developers in the early and mid-1980s and seemed destined for decline as the fixed link usurped its business. And though the operative Channel Tunnel has captured up to 40 percent of the cross-Channel market, the emergence of a transport alternative instead has created substantial new markets and has galvanized the ferry industry, long noted for its indifferent services, into consolidation and upgrading, often sparked from outside (for example, Sweden's Stena Lines, the world's largest ferry group, took over Sealink's channel services in the 1980s). These measures have included the introduction of a new generation of superferries and, making a virtue of necessity, the shrewd marketing of shipboard amenities rather than speed.[22] The announced consolidation of Stena Lines and P&O's channel services in September 1996 is another indication of an attempted industry revival.

Retaining previous business, however, is less difficult than winning new markets and generating significant modal switching, which may depend more on the shock of crisis. One telling example has been the transformation of Adriatic ferry services following Yugoslavia's breakup. Despite the severe European recession of the early 1990s, ferry traffic from Italy to Greece more than doubled between 1988 and 1994, both for passenger and vehicular traffic,[23] far exceeding the 20 percent rise in tourists to Greece (8.4 m to 10.3 m) in the same period. This volume growth has been accompanied by a distinct upgrading of services and by the opening up of lucrative new destinations in the other direction, such as Trieste and Venice, and greater use of higher-revenue ports (e.g., Ancona) to accompany the traditional Italian ports of entry (Bari, Brindisi). Two lines, Minoan and Strintzis, share services on the Patras-Ancona run; and both Minoan and Attica now operate high-speed, high capacity (1500) superferries, with two additional deliveries planned for 1998. With the slow implementation of the Dayton peace accords for Bosnia, some doubt the sustainability of such heady expansion rates. Even so, it seems likely that the social and environmental savings (less fuel use; driver comfort) will continue to argue in favor of combined services coupling sea crossings with road and/or rail.

Two further concerns for the industry, and a source of political irritation between the Commission and member states, have been the problems of (a) shipping and shipyard subsidies, and (b) industry cartelization into liner conferences with leeway to set their own cargo rates. As noted earlier, liner conferences retained a block exemption under UNCTAD from EU competition rules as well as under the self-regulatory aspects upheld in Regulation 4056/86, an exclusion which the Commission has been keen to rectify because it implies an uneven industry playing field. The EU's Competition Commissioner, Van Miert, recently initiated retaliatory measures against two powerful conferences. One, the Far Eastern Freight Conference (with fourteen member companies) was assessed symbolic fines due to its practice of fixing prices on the land transport leg of seaborne goods, although the assumed exemption of price fixing for the sea legs of the journey was a problem left unaddressed.

The Commission has also sought changes in the practices of the fifteen-member Trans-Atlantic Conference Agreement, which effectively sets rates for North Atlantic traffic. The Commission's attempt to prevent land-leg price fixing in the latter case resulted in a European Court case; in a preliminary ruling, the Court in fact suspended the Commission's decision while ruling in favor of the shipowners, on the basis that competitive prices were crucial to maintaining the stability and regularity of maritime transport services (FT, 14 March 1995: 12). This action is expected to be preliminary to a more general future Court ruling on the overall legality of conference agreements. Here, the Commission was clearly allied with European shippers (exporters, via the European Council of Transport Users) against shipowner interests, by arguing that shipowners kept their landward rates (part of door-to-door operations) artificially high, thereby harming European exports.

Europe's shipowners have criticized the Commission as "dominated by a misunderstanding of the competition forces in the market that self-regulate [shipping] . . . (it) has a narrow, legalistic approach, ignoring economic realities" (ECSA 1993: 5). Shipowners have also complained about inter-modal imbalances in policy priorities, particularly within the TENs initiative, which they argue is heavily biased against maritime interests. Such arguments, however, lose force in light of the EU's decision in the early 1990s (strongly backed by shipowners) to continue duty-free privileges until 1999, and by their success in delaying application of the EU's Social Protocol to shipboard working conditions.

The Commission has found more capacity for shaping policy in national shipyard subsidies, which falls within the gamut of the 1986 regulations as well as within general Treaty restrictions on state aid. An important 1990 directive (684/EEC) allowed European governments to subsidize shipyards by up to 9 percent of contract value. The Commission has since been unwavering in its application of competition principles to Greece's big shipyards, such as Elefsis (sold in 1995) and Hellenic Shipyards, the latter being the largest in the eastern Mediterranean and a longstanding headache for the Greek government's still nascent privatization program, due to the lack of potential buyers.[24] Yet here again, EU preferences have had to be coordinated with key shipbuilding nations outside Europe. After years of negotiations within the OECD framework, an international ban on direct shipyard subsidies was approved in July 1994 (signed that December), effective in January 1996. The agreement attempted to put the long favored shipbuilding industry on a competitive footing so that market distortions, stemming from chronic oversupply, could be better aligned with demand. From a regional (European) perspective, there was an additional, urgent need to ward off a ruinous new subsidy race internationally, and a new round of American retaliatory measures (FT, 18 July 1994: 1; 8 Dec. 1994: 7).

From the perspective of common EU policy, the OECD accord was especially noteworthy insofar as it has been one of the very few international transport agreements negotiated by the Commission on behalf of the EU member states. Only the French government opposed the agreement, and even it relented late in 1994. Even so, the EU's position was forced by pressures from competing builders, especially the U.S., China, South Korea, and the Ukraine. But in a perverse if powerful display of domestic lobbying power, the U.S. Congress attached multiple amendments to the multilateral accord, which the Clinton administration had not only negotiated but had championed and pushed others (Japan, South Korea) into signing. Fears grew in mid-1996 that the deal might ultimately collapse (FT, 24 June 1996: 19), and the Commission accordingly proposed (COM (96) 309) that the 9 percent aid directive be extended until the end of 1998 should the OECD agreement fail to be ratified.

The dispute reinforced both the multilateral and contentious nature of maritime issues, such that the WTO agreement, signed in Marrakesh in April 1994, ultimately excluded maritime transport services from its provisions. And despite continued negotiations, the U.S. unilaterally dropped out of the WTO maritime services talks in spring 1996, claiming its own practices were more liberal than what was being negotiated as a common standard. Just as telling has been the shift from direct to indirect subsidies ("limited derogations" in the euphemistic jargon), because of loopholes in the OECD agreement; the French eventually agreed after receiving assurances that they would be able to maintain previous levels of aid during 1996–1998, despite the direct-aid ban. Meanwhile, Danish shipbuilders have criticized the EU Commission for allowing German subsidies for east German shipyards (FT, 18 July 1994: 3), a defensible position in light of the fraudulent practices uncovered in Germany's Bremer Vulkan episode.

Safety Concerns

The long-held reputation of shipping as the safest of all the modes has been badly tarnished by three major, and numerous minor, recent European shipping disasters that suggest a prioritization of economic over safety considerations. These have also heightened awareness of the vulnerability of ever-larger vessels to the twin dangers of fire and flooding, and have led to urgent calls for tighter security requirements—attention to safety concerns being, perhaps inevitably, a reactive rather than proactive element of shipping regulation. Though sinkings have drawn headlines, shipboard fires have also been a danger for passenger carriers; the blaze that destroyed the *Scandinavian Star* in April 1990, with the loss of 158 lives, occurred on a passenger ferry between Norway and Denmark, two states with otherwise enviable safety records. More recently, the gutting of the ill-fated Italian liner *Achille Lauro* in the Indian Ocean demonstrated that the danger is no less acute in the cruise industry, though few lives were actually lost.

The development of roll-on, roll-off ("ro-ro") passenger ferries has created new types of potential problems for the industry. These large capacity vessels contain entire ship-length compartments, at or near water level, for the storage of vehicles, which enter and exit through visor-type bow sections, thus offering greater space and convenience for both passenger and freight traffic. One of the cross-channel ferry industry's biggest claims in its earlier battle to retain a monopoly across the busy

Dover/Folkestone to Calais route was its enviable safety record. These cal-culations were upset in early 1987 with the sinking of the *Herald of Free Enterprise,* a ro-ro ferry which capsized (later revealed to have partially opened doors) upon departing the Belgian port of Zeebrugge for Britain, causing nearly 200 deaths. This tragedy mollified much of the fixed-link opposition in Britain, which had long argued that an enclosed undersea tube was a more risky travel alternative.

An even greater tragedy occurred with the September 1994 sinking of the *Estonia,* a passenger ferry plying the Baltic between Tallinn and Stock-holm, with a loss of over 800 lives, in what was Europe's biggest maritime disaster this century. Postmortem examination revealed structural prob-lems with the moveable bow section, which gave way in rough seas, al-though these findings continue to be disputed by some suspecting sabotage (*Economist,* 1 March 1997: 33). The year 1994 was the century's second worst in terms of loss of life at sea, reflecting a broader, fifteen-year nega-tive trend.[25] And though shipping incidents (unlike many airline crashes) frequently result from accidents rather than navigational error, both modes have suffered the mistaken impression of being less safe than roads: the to-tal loss of life at sea since 1980 due to accidents has been only one-fifth of the *annual* loss of life on Europe's roads and motorways. As always, per-spective is vital.

These and many lesser incidents nonetheless produced a flurry of ac-tivity designed to ensure greater safety of passenger shipping in general, and in ro-ro ferries in particular. Safety regulation of shipping has been the charge of the IMO, via its so-called SOLAS convention; since its initial conference in 1914 (prompted by the *Titanic* disaster two years before) it had pushed ship design in the direction of two separate compartments. Passenger ship subdivision was confirmed in the SOLAS 1974 convention, though the restrictions were tightened to cover damage stability, in which maximum angle of heel after flooding is not to exceed 15 percent (IMO 1995).

In turn, SOLAS 92, the current safety standard, applies a complex sys-tem known as residual damage stability value (or A/Amax) to ships on a progressive basis (according to ship size) from October 1994 until 2007. (Even so, these measures would not have affected the *Estonia,* which was relatively new and had a high A/Amax rating already.) Thus a panel of ex-perts appointed by the IMO to investigate the disaster urged in their March 1995 report that further steps should be taken, at high cost, to en-sure door stability and drainage of water from shipholds. This is part of a broader, safety-oriented thrust of international legislation under the rubric of an international safety management code, to be added to SOLAS as a mandatory requirement under Chapter IV, with a four year phase-in from 1998. Under shipowners' pressure, however, governments were unlikely to accept these recommendations unequivocally as the basis for an expected new SOLAS agreement.

European efforts have focused on more rapid and complete compliance with these international regulations for Europe-based ships, as opposed to creating a separate European safety regime. General standards are worked out in the IMO's Maritime Safety Committee; collective European initiatives, such as the February 1993 Commission communication proposing safe sea measures,[26] have aimed gradually to eliminate substandard ships from European waters. A November 1994 directive (CE 1994b) introduced elements of a common policy regarding safety and prevention of marine pollution. The European Commission proposed in February 1995 that the EU15 should adhere to the IMO's ISM code on ro-ro requirements two full years before other countries. Another recent development is the emphasis on the sharing of Community information, known as Vessel Traffic Management and Information Systems, which along with port development forms the main maritime component of the trans-European networks initiative; one result may be the mandatory shipboard use of "black boxes" as in aircraft. A third, safety-related European initiative is the 1982 Paris memorandum of understanding, under which the signatories agreed to inspect, at their own cost, 25 percent of ships under flags of convenience, to ensure their compliance with prevailing IMO and ILO standards (McDonald 1994: 18–22).

These limited EU steps led the British government to argue for more stringent requirements, proposing that transverse bulkheads be required for all ro-ro ferries (FT, 6 April 1995: 14). The Commission tread cautiously, noting that Community "standard setting ... will be limited to exceptional cases where efforts within the IMO have failed to produce a solution meeting the Community's particular needs" (CEC 1993a: 44). Huge gaps remain in the seaworthiness of EU fleets, with the loss ratio of the worst performers some fifty times higher than the level of the safest.

While most attention has focused on passenger ferry operations because of the human dimension, overall ship losses and environmental damage have been much greater in the cargo sector,[27] where the twin problems of thin profit margins and chronic overcapacity create pressures to cut corners in safety management. Deficient attention to safety rules were widely held responsible for the *Braer* incident in early 1993, when a Liberian-registered oil tanker was damaged off the Scottish coast, resulting in a large spill. The much larger *Exxon Valdez* oil spill in Alaska led directly to the stringent U.S. Oil Pollution Act (1990), attaching almost unlimited liability for oil spills in American waters caused by negligence, and mandating use of double hulls on tankers. This unilateral measure clashes with more flexible IMO (and Europe-approved) standards, which accept alternative safety protections to guard against oil spills, along with new tanker inspections (enhanced hull surveys), introduced in 1993. But with the prevalence of aging tankers under flags of convenience (as of 1996, 159 oil tankers fly the Maltese flag alone), combined with the IMO's relative lack of enforcement powers, will limit its overall effectiveness for many years. Under such conditions, shipowners have retained considerable power to shape the nature of regulations and the speed of expected implementation.

CONCLUSIONS

In brief summary, the European shipping industry has been affected by the broader trend toward transport industry liberalization, and the 1986 regulations collectively initiated a major, if still incomplete, basis of a common European shipping policy. More impressive has been the EU's ability to project itself as a collective negotiator in certain areas, being in the forefront of not only IMO and ILO standard-setting (e.g., port-state control), but in two substantive rounds, the OECD agreement banning direct shipyard subsidies and WTO negotiations on trade in maritime services. Such developments indicate the growing importance of the EU's common external commercial policy, particularly as three of the four regulations of 1986 (4055, 4057 and 4058) have directly external applications (including even the right to sanction foreign firms), despite problems of enforceability. In addition, it is hard to deny, in theoretical terms, the evidence of spillover tendencies into a policy area previously off-limits to EU decisionmaking bodies, facilitated by QMV rules in the Council of Ministers.

Nonetheless, more rapid change has been thwarted by a number of important factors including: the institutional presence and (partial) regulatory power of extra-EU international bodies (the IMO, UNCTAD, and ILO), whose efforts the EU is sensitive not to undercut by taking a divergent approach; widespread flagging-out and the drop in Europe's share (now under 20 percent) of the world's fleet; the powerful presence of Greek shipowners, espousing anti-regulatory, free market principles in the overall market, thus complicating the north-south national divide; the EU's history of acquiescence in an imperfect shipping market by allowing operators, via conferences, to determine prices and regulate themselves; and most generally, the strongly international nature of the industry itself, which prevents the EU from being a natural shipping market.

The crisis in west European shipbuilding in the face of lower-cost east European and Asian competitors, and the lack of a collective shipbuilding effort to match Airbus Industrie, also hinders collaborative efforts between what should be natural partners (builders and operators) in an overall industry. Naturally, shipping interests believe that Europe would be better served by redressing the supposed bias toward land-based modes. Yet even while demanding a level playing field in the intermodal competition for attention and funds, shipowner interests simultaneously claim that overall EU rules, particularly in competition and social legislation, should not apply because of the unique pressures on the shipping industry.[28] The desire to have one's cake while eating it too seems to be a universal one.

Yet another political complication is the split within the EU Commission itself, in which Competition and Transport (DGs IV and VII) have catered to differing interests, the former aligned with shippers and consumers via the European Shippers' Council, while the latter has been more sympathetic to the carriers' views. Other directorates are bound to become more involved as well, as other issues, such as the employment of non-European nationals onboard European-based ships, come to the fore. Two other political cleavages emphasized by recent analyses—separate national interests (Bredima-Savopoulou and Tzoannos 1990) and competing pressure groups (Aspinwall 1994, 1995)—further complicate the policy calculations.

In the end, the shipping industry demonstrates complicated EU and European political processes that defy easy characterizations of a trade-off between the interests of member states vis-à-vis Brussels. The relative lack of control by states over private operators defensive of their independently cosmopolitan traditions, and the EU's limited ability to shape a specifically European dimension in shipping, both find their causes in the transnational nature of the industry and in a set of rule-making bodies that maximizes global participation but minimizes enforcement potential. These industry characteristics also make it difficult to coordinate structurally with other modes in a combined networks approach now being advocated, as discussed next.

NOTES

1. For example, since 1963 the Rhine Commission (ICPR), a classic limited regime, has studied the origins and effects of pollutants in the river's basin. A 1987 action program set four aims: reintroduction of salmon to the river; improving water quality for drinking; making sediment harmless to the adjacent lands; and reducing fertilizer use (Europe 2000+ 1994: 88).

2. Turner with Nordquist 1982: 226. Comparative figures by Eurostat (1993: 135–136) show that even in 1990 the Norwegian fleet exceeded all EC states in both total size and number of oil tankers.

3. EC shipyard employment fell by over 100,000 from 1976 to 1983 (Hart 1993; Aspinwall 1995), and overall seafarer jobs dropped from around 307,000 in 1980 to barely 169,000 in 1986 (Smith 1993: 92).

4. See *Eurostat* 1993: 11; also Aspinwall 1995: 65, 76–78; Bredima-Savopoulou and Tzoannos 1990; Hart 1993: 51. Colonial ties led to flagging out to entities such as Hong Kong and Malta. The British figures were also distorted by

the Chunnel-related shakeout in the cross-channel ferry industry, led by Sealink's purchase by an outside group (Sweden's Stena Lines).

5. In 1992 Bremer Vulkan, under chairman Friedrich Hennemann, received German and EU funds to buy three east German shipyards at a large discount from the privatization agency, Treuhand. However, Hennemann was subsequently jailed and charged with breach of trust and misuse of public funds (DM 850 m), which led to the company's declaration of bankruptcy (FT, 22–23 June 1996, p. 2).

6. Commission members have since regretted this exemption, and the shipping industry fears that liner conferences, which encourage industry growth much as code-sharing in the air industry, will be challenged under normal EU competition principles (ECSA 1993).

7. The evidence suggests a direct correlation between ship costs and flagging-out practices. Most German newbuildings in 1992–1993, for example, transferred out because of reunification-associated rises in corporate tax rates. By 1993, German-owned ships flying foreign flags outnumbered those under the German flag.

8. To this end, four MIF panels have been set up to examine short-sea shipping, marine resources, ship financing, and electronic data exchange.

9. Cash 1995. After rising nearly fourfold in overall tonnage in the 1970s, the overall Greek fleet size was halved by flagging-out in the 1980s. After reaching nearly 10 percent of the world's total in 1980, it dropped to below 5 percent in 1990 (Eurostat 1993) before staging a substantial recovery in the 1990s.

10. Eurostat figures through 1990 (1993: 11) show Greece's share of the total EC fleet (in GRT) to be 34.7 percent, more than double its 1970 figure of 15.1 percent. In contrast, Italy, in 1990 the EU's second largest, accounted for only 13.5 percent of the total.

11. After a traumatic 1980s, the Greek shipowning community now reportedly has compiled reserves of up to $40 bn, which if accurate would make it the largest cash position of any industry in the world (Cash 1995). Verification is obviously problematic in an industry long noted for the opacity of its accounting practices.

12. Over 400 London-based Greek shipping companies, coordinated via the Greek Shipping Cooperation Committee, control up to a third of business on the Baltic (shipping) exchange. Inland Revenue tax raids on one such company in summer 1996 temporarily renewed fears of a capital flight from Britain.

13. Current fleet renewals are slowly changing old patterns of secondhand reliance, pioneered by niche operators like Eletson Holdings.

14. According to Lloyd's Register, in 1993 total Greek tonnage broke down into 22 percent tankers, 25 percent bulk carriers, and 20 percent general cargo ships. In contrast, just 18 percent was in passenger ferries. Greek oil tanker and dry bulk fleets that year represented, respectively, 7.1 percent and 8.5 percent of world tonnage (ECSA 1994: 25).

15. Public service-related need for total island coverage long has worked as a messy industry trade-off in which companies were granted access to routes made lucrative either by population (Crete, Rhodes) or by popularity for tourists (Myconos, Santorini) only in return for agreeing to service remoter islands (Sturmey 1994).

16. Unspecified Turkish threats if Greece extends its territorial claims to the

(UN-approved) twelve-mile limit have further underscored commercial and security shipping linkages in a volatile region.

17. In summer 1996 Greek ship unions repeatedly clashed with authorities over alleged violations of national cabotage restrictions by the British cruiser *Marco Polo*. It was repeatedly prevented from disembarking passengers, on one occasion embarrassing Patras's mayor, who had planned a quayside welcoming ceremony for the ship's arrival. Semi-comedic episodes aside, the image of hostile shipworkers concerns the tourist industry, since these two sectors are Greece's main sources of foreign exchange.

18. Though fleet renewal is a painstaking and costly process, demand shifts are reflected in wide swings in liner rate charges (much more dramatic, for example, than airline ticket prices). The industry was badly hit in 1991–1993 by rock-bottom rates for existing capacity and by unrelated developments (exchange rate turbulence). Overcapacity, an endemic problem, is a critical factor in recessions because of the great upkeep costs for idle ships.

19. Cunard and its then-parent company Trafalgar House were caught up in a transatlantic controversy over safety standards. A major refitting of the *QE2*, left unfinished during a 1994 Christmas cruise from Southampton to New York, resulted in a major class action suit by a group of aggrieved passengers, while the ship itself was impounded by the U.S. Coast Guard until the refit was completed. The comparison with relatively stricter American safety regulations proved an embarrassment to European regulators, who had allowed the ship to sail in the first place (FT, 10 Jan. 1995: 16).

20. As of early 1995 some 30 new cruise liners, valued at $7.5 bn, were under construction worldwide. Cruise industry growth is well into double digits, with the dominant U.S. market expected to rise to 8 m passengers annually by 2000. The Mediterranean, however, has seen wide swings; cruise arrivals in Greece fell from 459,000 in 1989 to just 235,000 in 1991, rising slowly thereafter (McDonald 1994: 6; FT, 11–12 Feb. 1995, supplement).

21. Fully two-thirds (67 percent) of the world's total cruise ship orders are accounted for by just two European shipyards, Fincantieri of Italy and Finland's Kvaerner-Masa (Cruising 1994), pointing to considerable industry overconcentration.

22. In the 1980s the main ferry operators, including P&O and Stena Sealink, introduced previously unthinkable shipboard amenities such as silver service dining. Comparative advertising techniques (one deriding *le Shuttle* as "a parking space and a lightbulb") were also effective, although the EU's continuation of duty-free services (which Chunnel trains do not offer) at least through 1999 remains the ferries' main selling point in competing for passengers.

23. Passenger crossings from Italy to Greece rose from 950,000 in 1988 to nearly two million (1,970,000) in 1994. Between 1991 and 1994 alone, carriage of commercial trucks more than doubled to over 200,000 annually. The current Adriatic fleet now stands at around 50 ships, with a cumulative capacity of 60,000 passengers and 15,000 vehicles (Yannopoulos 1995).

24. Intra-cabinet differences over the handling of Greek shipyard privatization caused the resignation in September 1995 of the Industry Minister, Costas Simitis, inadvertently paving his way to the premiership in January 1996.

25. Sixteen major ferry disasters during 1980–1995 caused 9500 deaths, though most were in non-European waters (the Philippines, Bangladesh). Numerous other near-collisions in the Baltic, and incidents such as the grounding and forced evacuation in rough seas of a Silja Line ship in December 1993, have revealed numerous technical infringements of shipping regulations, and increased pressure for new IMO action.

26. The February 1993 communication "A Common Policy on Safe Seas" (COM (93) 66 Final) proposed EU directives in these areas: (1) development of common standards for (ship) classification societies; (2) more port state inspections of third-country ships; (3) mandatory application of IMO resolutions on carrying hazardous cargos; (4) establishment of vessel traffic services akin to air traffic control; and (5) training programs for shipboard personnel.

27. Since 1986, an average of 230 ships (and 1 m gross tons) has been lost each year. These include general cargo ships (46 percent), followed by fishing vessels (26 percent), bulk carriers (6 percent), and tankers (5 percent) (CEC 1993a: 42).

28. Shipowners have argued that even the Single Market-generated reduction of paperwork in travel documents (hence time and cost savings) are largely negated by disallowing use of the simplified documents on cargo shipping runs that call at non-EU ports. But given the EU's geographical realities and the frequency of non-EU runs along the European periphery, the point is a valid one—even if it suggests a chip on the industry's collective shoulder.

Part III

EUROPEAN TRANSPORT
TOWARD THE 21ST CENTURY

Chapter Seven

Structural, Transnational and Multi-Modal Initiatives

A good road is the widest avenue to knowledge.
—AMELIA EDWARDS
Untrodden Peaks and
Unfrequented Valleys

From the individual modal focus of the previous four chapters, with its inherent emphasis on operations and services within separate transport industries, this chapter—and to some extent the final chapter—shifts the emphasis in two important respects. First, it brings the debate back toward what many regard as the essence of the transport question, namely the structural issues of overall systems development, centering on the EU's Trans-European Networks (TENs) program. Second, it discusses these structural elements in the broader overall context set by pan-European intermodal initiatives that are modifying, and to an extent overriding, traditional distinctions between the individual modal interests.

The chapter first examines the backdrop of structural transport questions, and the formalized infrastructure-related elements of the Maastricht Treaty. Then it discusses the main elements of the TENs program, including the means and methods by which the EU is attempting to ensure its rapid progress and broad acceptability. Third, it discusses major actual and potential problems of the TENs initiative, focusing especially on the crucial financing question. Later in the chapter, other elements of the initiative will be explored, with specific reference to four key infrastructure developments across the continent.

The EU's emphasis on overall networks development, largely though not entirely post-Maastricht, is a new departure insofar as it entails a concrete application of newly dynamic thinking about comprehensive transport development as an agent for integration. Equally, however, it represents a "back-to-basics" approach, in the sense that a working infrastructure network is a *sine qua non* of fully interoperative cross-border transport services; some of the projects envisioned, such as the Brenner north-south axis across Austria and the Egnatia road project in Greece, are in fact ancient routes revived and modified for modern transit needs.[1] Indeed the new emphasis on structural-type policies redresses a lagging element of the internal market program, which remains the bread and butter of future EU economic development regardless of what happens with higher profile questions such as enlargement. That said, however, the ever more crowded agenda at biannual European summits (exemplified by the submission of no less than eighteen different policy proposals for consideration at the two-day December 1995 European Council at Madrid) does not bode well for essential but arguably mundane initiatives in the structural field.

And in terms of policy prioritization, it represents the circle coming fully around, via a partial reemergence of harmonization as an explicit EU transport aim, after years of emphasizing market liberalization. Even so, the new initiatives are not simply 1960s redux; they accompany a much reduced and specified time frame (as opposed to the earlier, open-ended approach) and more importantly, they rely not on heavy handed EU dictates, but rather on a novel approach envisioned as "bottom-up harmonization."

THE TENS INITIATIVE: BACKGROUND AND FEATURES

The trans-European networks initiative represents an effort to synthesize diverse EU goals: reinforcement of economic and social cohesion between center and periphery; environmental protection without sacrificing growth (sustainable mobility); improving safety via more even traffic flows and standardization of corridors; ensuring freer operability across EU borders; creating more modal choice; establishing better transport links with eastern Europe; and forging a stronger common external commercial policy. Indeed two key features of TENs—cohesion and infrastructure—are both longstanding Community aims, if insufficiently realized either through common policies (the CTP) or regional programs like the ERDF. Nor has the EU been the sole, or even the primary, instigator of networks development. The Community of European Railways, for example, was an early backer of a comprehensive European high-speed rail network (CER 1989), while the International Road Federation (IRF) and the UN's ECE have backed the Trans-European Motorway initiative (CEC 1993c). Similarly, maritime interests have long argued that better port facilities would help the overall transport industry and boost trade.

Infrastructure building long has been almost exclusively a state pre-

rogative. Intermittent Community attention has focused mainly on establishing common guidelines for investment appraisal, aiming to minimize
distortions arising from different evaluation procedures (Vickerman 1991:
40). In keeping with its activist profile, the European Parliament first
brought infrastructure into EC budgetary consideration in 1982. In 1978 a
Transport Infrastructure Committee was set up to focus attention on critical bottlenecks in the system that hindered especially core-periphery and
transalpine traffic and raised overall costs to industry. The elimination of
such bottlenecks was in fact the first aim listed in the EC Commission's
1988 proposal for an infrastructure action plan.

The focus on infrastructure became urgent because of growing congestion on key transit routes caused by discrepancies between supply and demand. In overall policy terms the emphasis shifted in three ways. The first
involved a "decoupling" of transport infrastructure and services, with the
latter slated for progressive liberalization. The second shift involved identification of needed projects that otherwise would go unfulfilled at the national level, for budgetary or other (e.g., political) reasons. After the motorway building boom of the 1960s, overall levels of infrastructure
investment have declined in relative terms, despite continually rising demand,[2] though it stabilized by the late 1980s. A third, more recent development has been more emphasis in "soft" infrastructure relying on information technologies, such as telematics, aiming at "intelligent moblility"
especially in road use. The Fourth Framework Programme (1994–1998)
set out ecu 900 m for this purpose, with some 64 R&D projects underway
as of late 1996 in areas such as traffic management, new materials, energy
efficiency, electric vehicles, and installation of cockpit-type "black boxes"
for shipboard use.

A high-level Community group examining future European motorway needs estimated a near-doubling of passenger and freight use by
2015, with international intra-EU traffic growing even more, between
110 percent and 140 percent over the same period. The number of severe
bottlenecks could grow four- or even five-fold as a direct result (CEC
1993c: 23), involving up to a third of all Community motorways, especially in heavily trafficked areas such as Hannover-Dortmund, Brussels-
Antwerp, London-Manchester, and the Ruhr. Congestion is said to be
costing European states up to 2 percent of GDP; in Britain alone, the
Confederation of British Industry (CBI) estimates a cost of up to 15 billion pounds ($23 bn) annually due to time lost in transit delays. Aside
from direct costs, rising congestion has three other immediately negative
results. First, the space available in congested areas is declining, meaning
that expansion of supply ("hard" infrastructure) is an increasingly limited option. Second, environmental damage and energy wastage increases
in the stop-start traffic characterizing crowded roads. Third, relentless rises in traffic and overall vehicle numbers (now around 120 m in the EU)

more than negates the efficiencies generated by ongoing road cabotage liberalization (fewer empty runs by trucks).

The Commission's important 1986 proposal for a medium-term action program (CEC 1986a) included a proposal for a financial instrument to help fund infrastructure projects of demonstrated Community interest; and this was formalized in the 1990 Council regulation (CR 1990) allowed partial EC funding of projects (up to a quarter of total cost or up to half for feasibility studies). Though much of this funding could come from existing Community instruments such as the EIB, some could be taken, for the first time, directly out of the EC budget (Vickerman 1991: 42).

Behind these new EC commitments was a perception of growing inadequacy of national infrastructures, already straining to meet existing (mainly domestic) demands much less the additional cross-border needs anticipated by the internal market program; thus the need for an integrated transport network went hand in hand with the Single Market. Two key aims emerged: interconnectedness between different, often incompatible, national networks, especially by filling in "missing links" and eliminating bottlenecks; and the need to promote interoperability of transport services, via the removal of technical and organizational impediments in each mode, as well as the provision of more "meeting points" that would encourage intermodal freight usage. Together, these two aims were seen as promoting overall network efficiency and increasing access to that network by European firms and individuals—the "citizen's network" increasingly touted by the EU (CEC 1996a).

The second major element of the networks concept, cohesion, was introduced as an EC goal by Title V of the Single Act, which links the aim of harmonious development with specific policy instruments. The Maastricht Treaty, however, makes a more explicit connection between transport networks and overall cohesion aims, as well as tying both with EMU convergence criteria. Developments at the political level reinforced these linkages, since the entry of Spain and Portugal in 1986 shifted the EC political balance of power further to the poorer Mediterranean area. In the 1980s the Spanish (Gonzalez) government emerged as a formidable national proponent of greater EC attention to intra-EC development issues, and effectively used its veto threat to induce greater EC structural spending via creation of the Integrated Mediterranean Programs. Moreover the EEA agreement, which entered into effect in 1993, required the EFTA states, though still nonmembers, to increase their financial aid to Mediterranean states through a new financial mechanism. Spain's emergence as an effective national lobby for regional reform thereby introduced one of the key ingredients for change, conspicuously absent in earlier efforts to develop the CTP (Lindberg and Scheingold 1970).

Infrastructure-related EC documents in the late 1980s refer explicitly to Community-wide links forming "an essential condition for reinforcing its economic and social cohesion" (CE 1990b; CEC 1988). Economic in-equality, both a key obstacle to cohesion and a sign of its absence, has been at the heart of EC regional policies since the 1973 enlargement. Since that time, however, rich-poor divergences have increased, as has heterogeneity within the least developed regions (Category I), as pointed out in a detailed EU report on development of lagging regions (Europe 2000+ 1994). The relation between transport infrastructure and regional spending is also re-flected in ERDF spending priorities; between its 1975 inception and 1988 it directed nearly ecu 9 bn (8786.6 m), well over a third of its total outlays, to transport infrastructure in lagging regions (CEC 1993c: 23). In the four years following the 1988 structural program reforms, transport-related spending amounted to another ecu 5.6 bn.

Even so, this regional-transport linkage remained conceptually amor-phous, a problem which the creation of the new Cohesion Fund was in-tended to rectify. The Maastricht Treaty establishes economic and social cohesion as one of the main pillars of Union activity, and also as a key ele-ment of other EU policies (Treaty 1992). The twin goals of interconnection and interoperability were to "tak(e) particular account of the needs of its more geographically isolated regions" (CEC 1993a: 32). A crucial concern here was to counteract Single-Market related overconcentration of eco-nomic activity and infrastructure development in core areas (extending from southeast Britain to Paris, across the Low Countries and eastward into south central Germany), further skewing levels of development along the lines of Gunnar Myrdal's "cumulative causation" theory advanced in the 1950s. Poor infrastructure in developing regions would produce a drag on overall Community development, and the Commission has been quite sensitive to the need for action to counteract two-tiered development (Eu-rope 2000+ 1994). Even so, transport facilities in poorer regions have lagged to the extent that an EC study group questioned whether, without far-reaching reform, they could ever catch up (CEC 1993c). Accordingly, the new European motorway network plan (the "Horizon 2002" project) envisages new links that would triple the existing motorway network in both Greece and Portugal (now limited in both countries to single corri-dors of uneven quality mainly between the two largest cities), while in Ire-land a system would have to be built from scratch (CEC 1993c).

For these reasons, the EU's regional initiatives of the 1990s, under the rubric of the "Europe 2000" program, aim to combine cohesion and Single Market objectives, and explicitly recognize the spatial elements of regional development. Even so, many opposed separate creation of a Cohesion Fund, partly because its priorities seemed to overlap with other EU struc-tural funds. There are a number of important differences, however. First, Cohesion projects must strictly comply with the convergence programs of the EU, whereas the structural funds have no prior conditions. Second, their scope is limited to environment and transport infrastructures, where-

as the structural funds exclude no sector. Third, Cohesion projects are decided on a case-by-case, rather than programmatic, basis. And fourth, Cohesion Fund aid is limited strictly to the so-called "poor four" (Ireland,
Spain, Portugal, and Greece), whereas structural funds can be and are targeted, in line with a scale of objective regions (Categories I-VI), to any of
the member states. Yet another difference lies in the overall scale of the efforts. The Edinburgh summit of December 1992 designated ecu 15 bn to
be spent on Cohesion projects between 1993 and 1999, rising in yearly
terms from ecu 1.5 to 2.6 bn; structural funds spending, in contrast, totals
more than ten times these amounts.[3]

The Maastricht Treaty and TENs

The Maastricht provisions are quite clear on the EU's new priorities for
network development, and its relationship to regional and environmental
issues. One element is the strict separation between the CTP and TENs
programs; Article 3, which prioritizes twenty common policies and activities, mentions both "a common policy in the sphere of transport" (line f)
and "the establishment and development of trans-European networks"
(line n). EU publications, including the *Bulletin of the European Union,*
maintain this organizational distinction between the two, as does the annual Union budget.

The distinction is not surprising given that TENs are primarily, but
not exclusively, transport-oriented. Mirroring Maastricht's three-pillared
architecture itself, the TENs program is three-fold: transport, telecommunications, and energy sectors are all treated as network priorities. The first
two are increasingly interlinked in European R&D projects directly,
through incorporation of information technologies into transport systems
(e.g., telematics); and also indirectly, through promotion of mobile tele-
phony and telecommuting in order to reduce the need for business-related
travel as such (CEC 1993a). Transport nonetheless accounts for the bulk of
budgetary outlays for TENs (around three-quarters), and the EU transport
commissioner is responsible for coordinating and implementing them. Additionally, the initiative's transport component is the only one with a firm
foundation in the Treaty of Rome; one of the EU's priorities has been to set
the other two (energy and telecommunications) on a similar legal footing, a
point underscored by Commission President Santer in his inaugural address to the European Parliament in early 1995 (CEC 1995a).

Under Maastricht Title XII, TENs aim at "promoting the interconnection and inter-operability of national networks as well as access to such
networks ... in particular of the need to link island, landlocked and peripheral regions with the central regions of the Community" (Art. 129b).
To this end the EU would establish guidelines for objectives and priorities,
identify specific projects of common interest, and implement measures to

ensure network interoperability. Any such measures were to be decided upon by the member states "in close cooperation" with the Commission; in turn, the Community could decide to cooperate with third countries "to promote projects of mutual interest" and to ensure interoperability (Article 129c). The marriage of infrastructure, environmental, and regional policy was underscored in the Cohesion Fund discussed above, aiming "to provide a financial contribution to projects in the fields of environment and trans-European networks in the area of transport infrastructure" (Article 130d).

The TENs program emerged as an increasing focus of the EU's eastern thrust and its comprehensive pre-accession strategy for east European states, developed between the Copenhagen (June 1993) and Essen (December 1994) European summits, and set out in its association ("Europe") agreements with eastern states. TENs are bound up in numerous interregional cooperative agreements: via Phare and Tacis (involving eastern Europe and Russia respectively, the former being slightly more transport-oriented); in the Balkans via the nascent Royaumont initiative; in the Baltic region; and, stemming from the 1995 Barcelona conference, as part of the Euro-Med partnership (focusing on port development). Taken as a whole, TENs are emerging as a key plank in the EU's "semi-foreign policy" and with tangibly greater success than higher profile CFSP initiatives have met (e.g. Bosnia, Albania).

Overall, the TENs program reinforces three main EU transport priorities: (1) use of (transport) infrastructure as a development tool; (2) institutionalization of both policy linkages (communications, energy, environment) and programs (Cohesion Fund, ERDF, EIB lending); and (3) externalization of transport interests in non-EU regions in order to promote Europe-wide development.

Prioritization of Projects

Notwithstanding the general, network-oriented conception of TENs, the overall initiative is characterized by great specificity, in the sense of being strongly project oriented. From the outset the Commission's task was to identify and prioritize separate projects on the basis of their individual importance for the overall goals outlined. This complicated task was entrusted to an expert advisory panel, the so-called Christophersen group chaired by the Commission's vice-president, created in December 1993 upon a decision at the Brussels European Council to speed up TENs progress. (Information systems were handled separately by a group chaired by Industry Commissioner Bangemann.) It produced an interim report in June 1994 (Trans-European 1994a), setting out a proposed list of eleven specific projects considered first-level priority. To this list, which was approved by the heads of state and government at Corfu in June 1994, were added three ad-

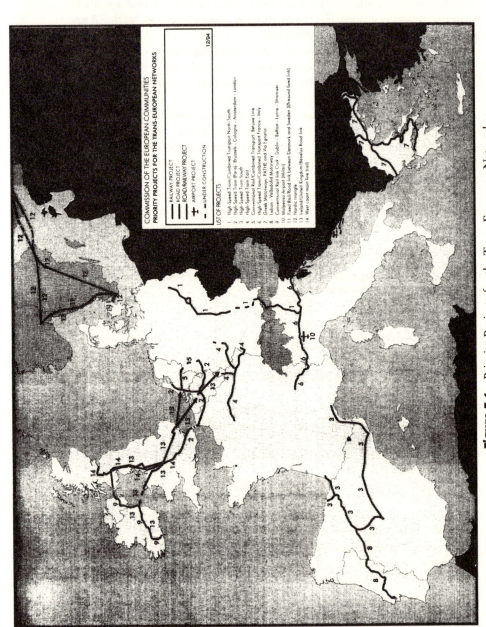

Figure 7.1 Priority Projects for the Trans-European Networks.

COMMISSION OF THE EUROPEAN COMMUNITIES
PRIORITY PROJECTS FOR THE TRANS-EUROPEAN NETWORKS

12/94

RAILWAY PROJECT
ROAD PROJECT
ROAD/RAILWAY PROJECT
AIRPORT PROJECT
UNDER CONSTRUCTION

LIST OF PROJECTS

1. High-Speed Train/Combined Transport North-South
2. High-Speed Train (Paris) Brussels - Cologne - Amsterdam - London
3. High-Speed Train South
4. High-Speed Train East
5. Conventional Rail/Combined Transport Betuwe Line
6. High-Speed Train/Combined Transport France - Italy
7. Greek Motorways: PATHE and Via Egnatia
8. Lisbon - Valladolid Motorway
9. Conventional Rail link Cork - Dublin - Belfast - Larne - Stranraer
10. Malpensa Airport (Milan)
11. Fixed Rail/Road link between Denmark and Sweden (Øresund fixed link)
12. Nordic Triangle
13. Ireland/United Kingdom/Benelux Road link
14. West coast main line (rail)

ditional projects (two in Britain, one in Scandinavia). The list of fourteen (listed in Table 7.1) was analyzed in detail in the group's final report to the Essen European Council (Trans-European 1995), which gave its approval. However, it was not until July 1996 that a Council Decision, with EP approval, was forthcoming (1692/96/EC).

Despite being Commission-led, the Christophersen group consisted largely of national representatives, charged with three main tasks: identification of problem areas; targeting of projects; and arranging for their financing and completion. The gathering of information was a matter for Commission-initiated project seminars, in which diverse interested parties (national and regional authorities; industry promoters; financial institutions like the EIB; user groups) convened to discuss common problems and work toward their resolution. A key aim was the promotion of public-private partnerships (PPPs) in infrastructure development, the special problems of which are discussed below. Member state involvement is critical given the need for states' approval of Commission guidelines; and the fact

TABLE 7.1
High Priority EU Trans-European Networks Transport Projects (work due to begin by the end of 1996)

Project	Est. Cost (billions ecu):
1. High-speed train/combined transport north-south (Berlin-Nuremberg; Brenner axis Munich-Verona)	20.8
2. High-speed train Paris-Brussels-Cologne-Amsterdam-London (PBKAL system)	15.7
3. High-speed train south (Madrid-Montpélier/Dax)	12.9
4. High-speed train east (Paris-Appenweier/Karlsruhe), with junctions to Metz-Mannheim and Metz-Luxembourg	4.5
5. Conventional rail/combined transport: Betuwe line (Rotterdam-Rhine)	3.3
6. High-speed train/combined transport France-Italy (Lyon-Turin and Turin-Trieste)	6.8
7. Greek motorways (Rion-Athens-Bulgarian border and Via Egnatia; Igoumenitsa-Turkish border)	6.4
8. Motorway Lisbon-Valladolid (Portugal-Spain)	1.1
9. Conventional rail link Cork-Stranraer (Ireland)	.24
10. Malpensa Airport (Milan)	1.1
11. Öresund fixed rail/road link (Denmark-Sweden)	3.1
12. Nordic triangle road and rail connections	4.4
13. Ireland-United Kingdom-Benelux road link	2.9
14. British west coast main line (rail)	.8

that project implementation is left to the relevant national, regional, and local authorities ensures maximum flexibility while reinforcing subsidiarity aims.

The group adopted six selection criteria: (1) a common European interest for each project; (2) large size; (3) economic viability and scope for private involvement; (4) contribution to Union objectives, particularly economic and social cohesion; (5) respect for other Union policies, especially on the environment; and (6) degree of maturity (CEC 1995b; Stassinopoulos 1995). The last-mentioned (maturity) received special emphasis, since only projects scheduled to be underway within two years (end of 1996) were prioritized. The final list was selected to meet two essential goals: first, the projects must have a "strategic character," in keeping with the integrated networks approach of the entire initiative; second, they must contribute to growth and employment.

The majority of the priority projects (and the great bulk of expected appropriations) are for dedicated rail development, and another tenth for combined road-rail, while the other modes also figure to a lesser extent. The rail emphasis helped blunt the worst criticisms of the program, that it merely duplicates the deficiencies of traditional supply-side national solutions. Even so, it has attracted criticism in both air and maritime sectors, respectively the *Comité des Sages* and the EC Shipowner's Association (Expanding Horizons 1994; ECSA 1994). The most ambitious (in cost terms) are the HST systems (e.g., trans-alpine and the intercity PBKAL), along with the Betuwe combined transport link involving a new freight rail link between the Rhine/Ruhr region and the port of Rotterdam (Table 7.1). It is no accident that the fourteen projects also happen to involve the entire EU15, an important selling point to the Transport Council.

In addition to the priority projects, the Christophersen report also listed nine "further projects of importance," twelve projects requiring further examination, and a number of additional Europe-wide projects in traffic management, as well as a separate list of projects connecting to third countries (mainly in eastern Europe). Priority energy projects were detailed separately. The Corfu summit also produced a highly unusual, midstream initiative by the EU member governments to expand the group's mandate, by its explicit request for the group to spell out potential "environmental networks" alongside the transport, information, and energy fields. Strong Council support for TENs, in fact, has distinguished the program almost from the outset; and at the Madrid summit in December 1995 EU leaders reconfirmed their belief that TENs would contribute fundamentally to EU competitiveness, job creation and overall cohesion.

The scale of the effort is measurable both in the time period and expenses involved. The EU aims for completion by the year 2010, although this is likely to extend much further when considering the second-tier projects or those still in the initial planning stages. The total needs have been

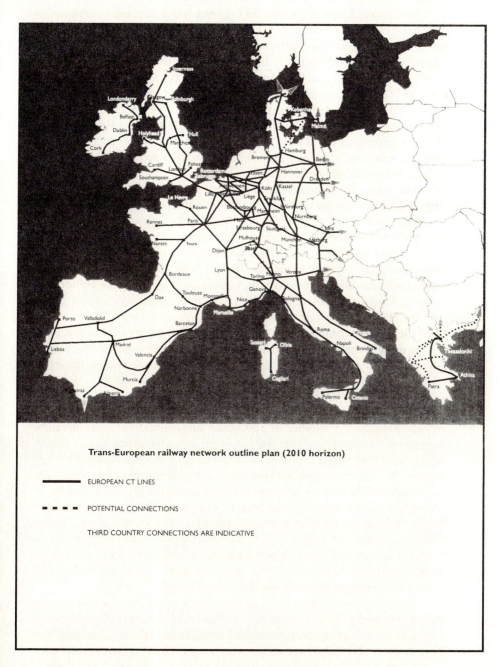

Figure 7.2   Trans-European Railway Network Outline Plan (2010 horizon).

estimated at up to ecu 400 bn, the majority of which (ecu 230 bn) was to be spent by 1999. Of this total, the fourteen main projects will account for approximately ecu 91 bn (of which only 34 bn will be spent by 1999).

The overall network envisioned in the master plan includes some 56,000 km of motorways and expressways (15,000 km due for completion or upgrading over the next decade), via the so-called Trans-European Road Network (TERN), the ten-year (1994–2004) plan for which was set out by a Motorway Working Group within the Transport Infrastructure Committee (CEC 1993c) and adopted by the Commission in June 1992 (see Figure 7.3).

The rail network, as set out by a HST working group and finalized in February 1995, would cover 70,000 km, including some 23,000 km of high-speed rail lines (divided roughly half and half between dedicated lines for speeds above 250 kph, and upgraded track for speeds up to 200 kph) (see Figure 7.2). Network development is also envisioned for airports, inland waterways, ports, and traffic management, as well as the environment; the term network itself seems to have become, in rapid fashion, a permanent component of the EU policy lexicon.

The TENs initiative is particularly noteworthy in that it combines long-range ambitions for a systematic, comprehensive network with carefully crafted, pragmatic working methods employed within the so-called bottom-up approach. The Keynesian overtones often attributed to TENs probably derive from Jacques Delors's last major initiative as Commission President, the competitiveness initiative embodied in his White Paper on Growth, Competitiveness, and Employment, submitted to the European Council at Brussels in December 1993. In the Delors (1993) conception, network development would promote long-term European competitiveness in the world economy via increased intra-EU efficiency, while major new public infrastructure works would also boost economic growth and reduce unemployment in the short- and medium term. The linkage with other Maastricht priorities was underscored by the focus on promoting EU-wide development, enhancing cohesion aims and making monetary union itself a more viable prospect. It could almost be said that this interpretation was tantamount to shifting transport's traditional public service obligations from the national to the international (EU) level, built around overarching conceptions of European need, though lacking such an explicit legal foundation.

PROGRESS AND PROBLEMS IN TENs DEVELOPMENT

One of the outstanding elements of the EU's effort has been its careful analysis of potential problems involved in the relative *terra incognita* of cross-border European infrastructure planning. The initiative is ambitious

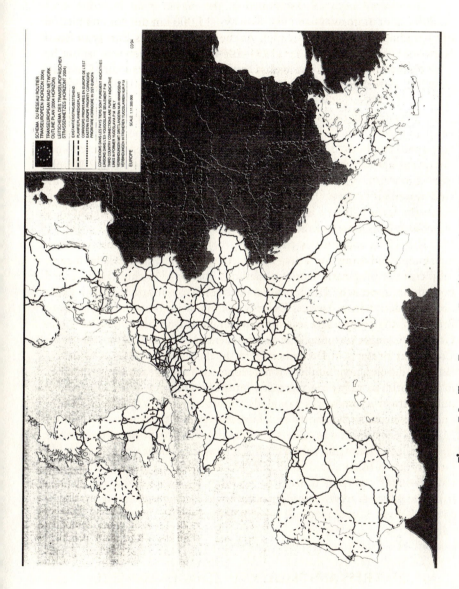

Figure 7.3 Trans-European Road Network Outline Plan (2004 Horizon).

because of its sheer size and overall expense; further, it is groundbreaking because the Union is attempting a number of unprecedented steps at one stroke: by directly funding infrastructure development; by actively planning and promoting such development across borders and within a long time frame; by its extension of EU transport linkages to third countries;[4] by its special emphasis on the historically difficult and neglected rail sector; and, perhaps above all, by its emphasis on enticing private-sector involvement in infrastructure building. These same groundbreaking elements are also, however, the source of concern from financial and risk perspectives.

The Financing Issue

Administrative, regulatory, and technical hindrances to harmonization, including the lack of a common legal framework, were highlighted by the Christophersen group as formidable barriers to timely completion of infrastructure projects (Trans-European 1995: 85–92). Even so, the question of project funding looms as critical in the years to come. The initiative's success will likely hinge on whether or not a viable mixture of private-public funding (PPPs) can be found: the priority projects are either too vast and expensive, or administratively problematic as cross-border ventures, to rely solely on traditional sources of funding (national budgets). The Christophersen group identified five special finance-related problems: (1) political intrusion in large projects; (2) splintering of projects into two or more national sections; (3) lack of a single promoter; (4) changing status of EU transport operators due to industry liberalization; and (5) technical difficulties. For the Commission, these problem areas require "more imaginative combinations of public, private and Community funding" (ER 1994a), but the task of finding these combinations lies primarily with the states themselves.

Though an EU initiative, TENs development can rely little on direct Community financing. EU aid is limited to three functions: pre-investment feasibility studies; interest subsidies on loans; and aid guarantees. A draft Community regulation in March 1994 set out around ecu 2.4 bn for 1993–1999 out of the Commission budget, two-thirds of which (ecu 1.87 bn) was transport-oriented (ER 1994b). Under Regulation (EC) 2236/95, the Commission allocated ecu 240 m from the 1995 budget for TENs feasibility studies, out of ecu 274 m for the three TENs policy areas. Such sums are but a drop in the bucket when considered in the overall context of needed expenditures (ecu 400 bn, including ecu 230 bn by 1999), and the Commission frankly asserts that its own financing is marginal and meant to serve as incentive or "seed money" to unlock larger sums from elsewhere and to help projects already underway.

That said, however, direct EU outlays for TENs have grown impressively. The Union budget for 1996, which Budget Commissioner Erkki Liikanen of Finland described as "marked by austerity," nonetheless shows double-digit increases in TENs spending (against an overall 8.5 percent rise). Commitments to TENs (priority and secondary projects) rose by ecu 64 m over 1995, and of a total figure of ecu 445 m, ecu 282 m is targeted for priority transport networks, which represents a (transport) year-on-year increase of a full 17 percent. These figures are against an overall total of appropriations under Heading 3 (Internal Policies) of just 4.2 percent, and makes TENs the second largest sector recipient in the Internal Policies segment of the budget, after Research.[5]

Despite increasing EU capital commitments, already by mid-1994 the Commission was estimating a potential financing shortfall of its priority TENs projects of up to ecu 4–5 bn between then and 1999 (EIS 1994). To make it up, other EU-associated facilities and bodies are expected to take a much stronger financing role, including the Cohesion Fund in its four target states. An increasingly pivotal role is to be played by the EIB, which already provided infrastructure loans totaling over ecu 25 bn in 1988–1993 alone (10 percent for non-Community countries), and infrastructure accounted for nearly a third of all its lending (EIB 1994a); much of this went to high-speed rail development.[6] Already in December 1992 the EIB was invited by the European Council to contribute toward the EU's growth initiative; at that time the so-called Edinburgh facility was established to provide a window for channeling an additional ecu 5 bn in loans for TENs-related projects (later increased by a further 3 bn), which allows the EIB, if necessary, to extend its lending beyond the normal cutoff of 50 percent of the project's total. The EIB has also been a key partner in Commission-sponsored project seminars, by virtue of its collective financial expertise and experience with structural issues. Still other EU-related bodies tapped include the European Coal and Steel Community, for projects promoting steel use;[7] and the new European Investment Fund (EIF), constituted in June 1994 with an initial capital of ecu 2 bn, through long-term guarantee facilities and, later, also equity finance.[8]

The Problem of Risk

The Commission expects not only the TENs funding shortfall, but the bulk of overall financing, to come from the private sector and from the member states. Not surprisingly, the financing question has become a crucial bone of contention, especially after the June 1996 Florence summit when the European leaders, led by Britain and Germany, rejected an attempt by Commission President Santer to make an intrabudget transfer of EU funds (amounting to ecu 1.2 bn) to boost the TENs program,[9] reinforcing prevailing images of public infrastructure as something of a political hot potato.

In some respects it is only natural to expect private sector involvement in infrastructure development, not least because firms directly benefit from better transport facilities that link producers with consumer markets and have a multiplier growth effect. As discussed in the modal chapters, 19th century precedents in canal, road, and rail development demonstrated that private capital can be marshaled effectively for major undertakings. There is no lack of individual examples of market involvement, even in today's Europe; motorways in Italy, France, and Britain have been partly debt-financed, and France's SNCF has tapped the capital markets for initial TGV funds. The Commission sees its task as enticing, through various incentives, further such involvement.

But just as baiting the hook is no guarantee that the fish will bite, the EU faces potentially great difficulties in ensuring that private sector help is not only forthcoming, but becomes a reliable and consistent partner in future development. Banister, Andersen, and Barrett (1995) have argued that of all the potential types of infrastructure partnership, those involving a combination of public and private players have the greatest potential but also require the most effort to realize. The biggest difficulty lies in establishing an equitable sharing of risk between the two. From the perspective of the private sector, the problem can be sub-divided between *financial risk* and *public policy risk*.

Financial risks stem from the complicated nature of infrastructure itself, requiring longterm planning, based on (inevitably unreliable) traffic forecasts years into the future. The sheer scale of major works limits any such involvement to the very largest firms or, more commonly, conglomerates or consortia. Another is the long time horizons involved, often measured in decades, which require major adjustments in thinking by firms used to concentrating on short-term priorities and bottom-line considerations—a tendency being reinforced by growing attention to shareholder value even in Europe. Thus firms require not only an adequate return on capital but some likelihood of future profits.

The question of capital return here merges with the second issue (public policy risk) because private capital will demand higher-than-normal returns for infrastructure involvement to offset these inherent problems. In the case of TENs projects, most of which (10 of the 14 on the priority list) straddle borders and often cross geologically difficult or ecologically sensitive areas, there are untold possibilities of planning disruptions due to political confrontation on a local, regional, or even national scale, the intensity, duration, or outcome of which is impossible to foresee. But the sensitivity of governments to environmental pressures and/or budget restrictions means that the possibility of delays, government-mandated changes in project specifications, or outright cancellation—all forms of public policy risk—are never absent; and these possibilities multiply when the project involves several countries, in which one country's refusal to carry on with a project can effectively sabotage the entire endeavor.

For this reason, private capital often demands governmental guarantees against such unforeseen changes arising at the political level. Traditional means of building infrastructure at the national level, such as governments franchising out projects to the private sector, have worked because capital markets regarded the possibility of cancellation as low, due to explicit or even merely implicit public guarantees. For example, in the case of French rail (SNCF) the national company operates under favorable economic conditions and relative investor comfort because of the lower costs of capital deriving from a beneficent state attitude and the ultimate probability of bailout in case of need.

However, for major international projects this comfort zone is largely absent, because no single entity (whether national governments, the European Commission, or even the EIB) is positioned to act as guarantor. Such conditions inevitably raise the cost of money, and act as a barrier to the entry of private capital in the absence of the prospect of superior rates of return to offset the interest rate premium. At the international level, still other public policy-related risks could include changes in EU taxation policy, or (a more immediate concern) EMU-related interest rate rises. As the Channel Tunnel case has amply demonstrated, even minor rate fluctuations can have enormous adverse impact on major projects saddled with heavy long-term debt.

One option, though limited, would be greater use of alternative financing via toll roads, already used extensively in the "olive belt" (Spain, Portugal, Italy, France, and Greece), though there are wide discrepancies between national toll rates and no ready plans to harmonize them at EU level. Efforts are also under way in Britain, via its Private Finance Initiative (PFI) to entice private capital to infrastructure development (discussed briefly at the end of Chapter 3), though so far the key questions revolve around similar problems of transfer of risk from the public to the private sector. Even Italy, with its bloated state sector, has taken steps in this direction, via its TAV project to link Turin and Naples via a $10 bn rapid rail line; it involves 29 different shareholders, several of them non-Italian, and relies on private capital for 60 percent of the total cost (FT survey, 13 Dec. 1995: vi).

For all these reasons, EU coordination is a critical element in the entire TENs program, as it creates a supportive political climate but short of outright public guarantees. The consultative procedures, with the Commission itself acting as a convener and catalyst, resemble national neo-corporatist economic arrangements prevailing in the 1960s and 1970s, with major economic groupings meeting periodically for the purpose of hammering out compromises on economic policy minimally acceptable to all. Streeck and Schmitter have argued (1991) that neo-corporatist practices have not been transplantable at Community level because of the fragmentation of interest groups themselves, especially labor. Successful collective bargaining presupposes a high degree of centralization among the participants, which is inevitably much harder to achieve across national boundaries where bonds, though developing via Brussels-based trade and interest associations, remain rather loosely established (Richardson 1996). Yet TENs procedures bear many corporatist hallmarks, both in their inclusive consultation process and in their largely pragmatic, project-oriented emphasis. Another possible model might be that of *Gleischaltung,* the coordination of diverse interests by a central body, akin to a magnet attracting metal filaments toward one goal.

Given the complexities of co-decision legislative procedures and the post-Maastricht, anti-centralization political backlash against Brussels, there appears to be little alternative to an arrangement whereby the Commission is first among equals. Even so, the TENs program can fairly lay claim to being an unprecedented experiment in international policy coordination that will be closely watched in coming years as plans translate into action. There are also favorable parallels with development of the Single Market project itself, insofar as both have benefited from an early establishment of political support, a clear set of priorities, highly pragmatic working methods, and a specified timetable.

Shifting Emphasis of TENs Planning

The process of winnowing out EU priorities has brought about little-noticed but discernible shift in TENs emphasis. The earlier Delors conception revolved around major public works projects under an overarching EU regulatory umbrella and having primarily economic growth and employment objectives. Since 1993–1994, however, the emphasis has shifted to more directly financial considerations and tests of individual project viability. For example, in early 1994 the Christophersen group agreed that, while each new TENs project "must satisfy a test of economic viability," there was no insistence that each project pay for itself; indeed it held that "few of the transport projects are likely to satisfy this test" (Trans-European 1994: 58). In contrast, European finance ministers, through Ecofin (the Economic and Financial Council of EU Ministers) at their November 1994 meeting, gave much greater weight to financial issues, even stressing that economic and commercial profitability was an essential condition.

With Delors' departure in December 1994, overall TENs planning has tended to deemphasize top-down, Commission-led central planning, in favor of a more bottom-up emphasis given to the nation-states and to the private sector. A second change has been a shift from the overarching, conceptual network elements to a more "micro" emphasis, in which each project's viability is scrutinized individually. A third change relates to the telescoping of viability measurements themselves, with a growing focus on

bottom-line considerations and a corresponding deemphasis on social issues relating to employment and quality of life.

Three factors seem to have caused these changes. One was the changing macro-economic environment; the Delors notion of an EU-generated
economic stimulus, first spelled out late in 1992 in the depths of a severe
European recession, seemed less urgent by the spring of 1994, when most
economies were recovering (though with disconcertingly little positive effect on unemployment figures, persistently above 10 percent of Europe's
workforce). (At any rate, an internal Commission report, leaked to *The
European* newspaper (9 January 1997: 1), suggested that the macro-economic growth effect of TENs works was far overestimated.) The second
factor was the post-Delors changing of the guard within the Commission
itself, in which the Gallic-style *grand projet,* often seen as a shift back to
the political left by Delors,[10] was submerged in favor of greater pragma-
tism under his successor, Santer.

The third reason for the shift in emphasis was the working method of
the Commission's Christophersen group, which inevitably focused on the
individual elements of projects themselves, and on the relative economic
feasibility of each. The group's approach was deliberately, and perhaps inevitably, ad hoc; and reflecting prior Commission efforts, it focused on a
small number of priority projects (pared down from an original list of 34).
Though the Commission had in mind the overall European interest in networks development, the emphasis in both prioritization and funding has
remained with the states and their own identifiable needs.

The overall policy context of TENs also shifted during 1994 when a
major Delors financing initiative failed to see the light of day. His idea,
based on a successful initiative launched in the late 1970s,[11] was to tap the
international capital markets via so-called Union Bonds, in which the EU
would act as a borrower for infrastructure development purposes, anticipated at around ecu 7 bn a year. However, key governments (Britain and
Germany) opposed the idea, though for different reasons—the British as an
unwarranted EU intrusion into issues better left to the market, and the
Germans because of a fear that excessive EU borrowing would unsettle financial markets and jeopardize progress toward monetary union.[12]

Another source of opposition is the EU's Council of Finance Ministers
(Ecofin), whose collective power is already under threat because of common monetary provisions and the European Monetary Institute (EMI) set
up in 1994 to oversee the transition to a single currency. In the absence of
either an overall funding instrument or broader political agreement on the
means to provide it, the Commission has had to proceed painstakingly on
a case-by-case basis, often having to rely on incomplete information or ed-
ucated guesswork regarding the extent of private sector interest in the individual projects. Even by 1995, only three of the fourteen priority projects

had financing firmly in place, one of which (the Öresund bridge-tunnel between Denmark and Sweden) was to be paid for by wholly traditional means (government guarantees).

Future Questions

Despite its promising launch, the TENs initiative faces numerous problems in translating from conception to reality. One danger is excessive attention to market-driven, micro-oriented solutions which, by hiving off projects with the greatest likelihood of self-generated financing, would diminish the overall network emphasis. Another problem area derives from the non-economic barriers to cooperation stressed in the Christophersen group's December 1994 report, including technical and administrative constraints on cooperation, particularly the lack of a common legal framework for cross-border projects, which tend to create multispeed (hence uneven) development even within single projects. Progress on the intercity PBKA fast rail network, for example, has suffered due to delays on the Belgian section, resulting from financial difficulties at Belgian rail (SNCB).

Another potential issue could be political divisions over objectives. Despite its workmanlike emphasis on bottom-up planning and extensive consultation procedures, the Christophersen group nonetheless insisted that its own work "constitutes an exceptional and primarily political effort" (Trans-European 1995: 32), focusing on attempts to coordinate various parties having divergent interests. Conflicting political objectives were most pronounced in regard to the controversial TERN roads network. While it developed in response to state-level political demands, it has aroused opposition on environmental grounds that it will merely promote road use at the expense of parallel modes (rail), thus undercutting sustainability objectives. Indeed, environmental impact assessments must still be made for each TENs project. The continued split between the states and Brussels over funding infrastructure seems bound to remain a factor, particularly given the hostile response to the Union bonds issue by the German government, otherwise a staunch supporter of pan-Europeanism. Differing state attitudes also reflect wider philosophical differences regarding the usefulness of market-oriented solutions to public issues.

Infrastructure development could also emerge as a divisive issue even within the EU's organizational structure, as a result of the evolving trilateral political nexus linking the Commission, Council, and Parliament. As it stands, the Commission must report on TENs progress every five years to the EP, Council, ESC, and Regions Committee. Three potentially disruptive elements have already arisen. One is the apparent divergence between Commission and Parliament, highlighted by the latter's post-Maastricht political assertiveness. Their respective priorities, set out at the outset of the Santer era in January 1995, were clear enough. Whereas the new Commission president asserted that his first priority was "a strong economy to create new jobs" (CEC 1995a: 8), the EP's official response held that "the European Union's first priority [is] to be the fight against unemployment," and called for a jobs program aiming at creating 15 million new jobs over five years, along with the creation of a "genuine industrial policy" and a "revival of the social dialogue at European level" (EP 1995: 64).

As both organs are now, via co-decision procedures, jointly responsible for legislation pertaining to networks development, such differences have important implications for infrastructure works. The Parliament has recently (though arguably, unjustly) criticized the Commission for insufficiently emphasizing the environmentally sounder railway and inland waterway elements of TEN-related Cohesion Fund priorities, an indication of the increasingly "green" element of Parliamentary opinion.[13] More generally, the overall political tone of the EP, which since the 1994 elections has been led by the Socialist bloc, is diverging from the Santer Commission, led by a nonideological pragmatist in contrast to his predecessor (Delors), a French Socialist.

A second institutional problem could arise from the uneven Commission-Council relationship. As noted, the TENs program has been a fortunate recipient of high level Council support for Commission priorities; and as Corfu demonstrated, the European Council is capable of even extending the Commission's mandate, given sufficient collective political will. Just as easily, however, such political backing can evaporate or be compromised; by mid-1995, the Council was requesting the Commission to reexamine its priority transport list (which the Council had already approved) to see if further financial savings were not possible (BEU 6/1995: 63). The Council's rebuff in June 1996 was more direct, and indicated states' determination to keep the Commission on a short leash by restricting Santer's scope for creative license in TENs budgeting. While it may be premature to dismiss the Council's earlier support for TENs as mere rhetoric, such mixed signals could undermine confidence. There are already signs of a slowdown in major works, as pointed out in the Ciampi group's competitiveness report to the Madrid European Council (December 1995), which lamented lack of national progress in establishing PPPs.

Thirdly, even within the Commission, the growing involvement of different directorates apart from Transport raises the potential for inter-directorate wrangling. Revealingly, the Motorway Working Group, set up to establish EU road network priorities, included no less than six different Commission Directorates (DGs II, III, VII, XI, XIII, and XVI), along with other interested bodies (states, industry and unions, the ECMT, the IRF, the ECE). The rapid turnover of the Transport portfolio itself, which has seen four different Commissioners in just the first half of the 1990s (Karel Van Miert; Abel Matutes; Marcelino Oreja; and, from 1995, Neil Kinnock), each with his own interests and priorities, has been an additional, and unnecessarily unsettling, influence.

The problem here may be akin to the growing issue, in the American political context, of "unfunded mandates," that is, new political initiatives taken at the center (Congress) for the individual state governments to carry out, though without firm guarantees that the political commitments will be backed up by the requisite appropriations. But with TENs, public appropriations from whatever source are neither the sole nor even the main source of funding. It may be more accurate to regard TENs as guidelines, not mandates, since the EU commitment to the entire range of the TENs program remains firm but not ironclad, which may insulate it (the Commission) from being forced, in future, to become a lender of last resort to troubled, over-budget, cross-border infrastructure projects. Equally, states are under no obligation to develop the designated projects according to EU-wide technical standards or, for that matter, to complete them at all. Ample opportunities remain for passing the buck in terms of ultimate financial and political responsibility. The need to craft individual financing schemes on an incrementalist basis also gives scope for projects to falter in the absence of firm guarantees from any single source. Such mid-project failures would be doubly damaging, in terms of both wasted resources and, ultimately, diminished public confidence in what has been, thus far, a high-profile EU initiative.

Most broadly, the TENs program relies on an extraordinary balancing act: between goals (efficiency vs. social concerns), scope of development (overall networks vs. individual projects), economic partners (private and public), and public institutions (cooperating governments; EU organs). This factor, coupled with its still incipient nature, makes the program especially vulnerable to shifts in the political climate, while a general European recession would threaten many of the projects themselves. And the sober budgetary climate of the mid-1990s, with Britain and Germany pressing for 0 percent nominal growth in the EU budget for 1997, has cast an unspecified chill over major EU programs, especially the CAP and structural spending, both of which would hit peripheral and Cohesion states and other developing regions the hardest.

The main danger would thus seem to lie, not with overall program collapse, but rather with an excessive concentration of resources into those relatively few projects with the greatest likelihood of meeting narrow (financial feasibility) rather than broad (cohesion) objectives. And though the Cohesion Fund's aim is to ensure that core development is not at the expense of the poorer member states, the danger of a two-tiered development remains evident, and may be averted only insofar as the EU itself can avoid a severe budgetary crunch in coming years.

EUROPEAN INFRASTRUCTURE DEVELOPMENT IN PRACTICE

For all the EU's progress toward establishing the ground rules for a transport infrastructure policy, EU-level conceptualizing about future pan-European needs has tended to follow practice, rather than the reverse. Cross-border infrastructure already has featured in Europe's postwar political geography (e.g., the Mont Blanc road tunnel linking France and Italy, opened in the 1960s), though needs have increased as national infrastructures are pressured by rapid rises in international traffic. Recent and ongoing projects allow some tentative conclusions to be drawn about the problems and possibilities of building transport infrastructure with directly international ramifications. Discussion here will focus on four such cases illustrating, respectively, questions of private finance (the Channel Tunnel), development in lagging regions (structural projects in Greece), the environmental dimension (transalpine transport), and the spatial dimension (Nordic infrastructure).

The Channel Tunnel

By virtue of its great size, expense, and symbolic significance linking Britain with Europe proper, the Channel Tunnel project, which opened in stages during 1994, emerged as the quintessential test case for cross-border infrastructure development. The Chunnel has been pathbreaking in a number of important respects: it is the largest and costliest infrastructure project ever undertaken, and completed, in Europe; it was facilitated by bilateral political agreement, followed by an extensive network of cooperative intergovernmental supervision; and it was financed entirely from the private sector, without governmental financial guarantees or direct EU aid. In addition, it has initiated new forms of corporate governance, in this case via a binational enterprise (Eurotunnel) responsible for arranging its financing and construction, and now for operating the system itself, via a longterm monopoly concession extending for another half-century. Yet despite such features, the precedent it sets is partly a negative one, in which a loose corporate structure, stringent yet uneven governmental regulation, project delays, endless infighting and cost overruns have all led to a series of dramatic financial crises—including an unprecedented shareholder revolt—from which it has still not emerged despite a much-touted debt-for-equity swap in 1996.

The Chunnel frequently has been cited as an influential factor in the consolidation of the EU's own plans for network development, particularly in rapid rail. The initial Paris-Lyon TGV line opened in 1981, the same year as the first verbal agreement to pursue a new Channel Tunnel attempt between the British and French governments; the agreement firmed in 1984, and the formal Chunnel treaty was finally signed in February 1986.

Chunnel progress also went hand in hand with France's TGV-Nord initiative to link Paris to London and Brussels via Calais and Lille. The details of the project's development have been well covered elsewhere (e.g. Holliday et al. 1991; Vickerman and Flowerdew 1990), so here only a brief mention will be made of its potential lessons.

On the positive side, Chunnel completion is a boon to hopes for greater system intermodality in Europe. Its physical structure is itself multi-modal, insofar as the tunnel itself, a dedicated twin-bore rail system, connects both with road systems (via drive on and off shuttle trains) and rail networks (via intercity Eurostar trains) on the British and French/Belgian sides. Moreover, operations since the May 1994 opening have introduced new forms of intermodal competition for customers on cross-channel routes, in two respects; the shuttle services compete with the channel ferries, forcing a price war and later a consolidation of ferry operators P&O and Stena Lines; while Eurostar (despite disappointing results) has drawn away some of the airline business, especially on the lucrative London-Paris route. Yet while the Chunnel has captured much of the existing air and sea market (now accounting for about 40 percent of cross-channel traffic), equally striking has been the overall rise in traffic, a full 20 percent in both 1994 and 1995, reinforcing the notion that new infrastructure creates new markets—economically if not environmentally appealing.

The negative lessons of the Chunnel have, alas, been no less dramatic, even before the disastrous fire aboard a freight train in November 1996, which halted operations for many months. The most obvious problem has been the huge overall debt load, amounting to some 8 bn pounds ($13 bn), requiring roughly 2 m pounds in payments daily just to service the debt. One year after the startup of operations, in fall 1995, Eurotunnel abruptly halted interest payments on its debts amid rumors of an impending restructuring of the finance package involving a large debt-for-equity swap or even a forgiveness of part of the debt itself by the lending banks. Meanwhile, the listed share price sagged below 1 pound (from over 5 pounds in early 1994, and over 10 pounds at its peak). The company has alleged that its financial burdens have been greatly compounded by punitive governmental treatment, both indirectly (via hidden subsidies to the ferry industry and favorable treatment of BA and Air France) and directly (via the supervisory, bilateral intergovernmental commission, or IGC) which imposed safety and security requirements which Eurotunnel claims are far in excess of those required in competing cross-channel air and sea services.[14]

Eurotunnel has also been involved in legal action against the railways, because of Britain's failure to build a high-speed link from the tunnel terminus to London, slowing city-to-city travel times and thereby limiting the project's attractiveness to business customers.[15] Inherent in much of this ongoing saga is the crucial issue of risk allocation between the public and private sectors, in which governments remain chary of granting contracting firms adequate terms to compensate for the political and public policy risk of infrastructure development. By the same token, as Holliday (1995) rightly points out, large projects can have an inbuilt safety feature in the form of implicit government guarantees; in this case, the huge sums involved mean that the Chunnel project has long since passed the stage at which it could simply be allowed by the French and British governments to collapse as a failed private-sector venture. Joint public takover, while unlikely (and denied by both governments), remains an ever-present possibility. At any rate, Chunnel development seems less a case of public-private collaboration than of continuous high-level brinksmanship (in what has been called "management by confrontation") by its pugnacious co-chairman Sir Alastair Morton, vis-à-vis the two governments, their rail systems, and the lending institutions.

Greek Infrastructure Development

The case of infrastructure development in Greece illustrates both the transformative potential of EU infrastructure commitments and the multiple problems that can arise in translating commitments into working transport systems. Greece, which entered the EC in 1981 as its tenth member, bears many of the hallmarks of a developing economy, with up to a quarter of the workforce engaged in agriculture, uneven urbanization patterns, serious environmental problems, and public sector inefficiencies. Further, the problems of peripherality and distance have been greatly worsened by the disruptions of the Yugoslav war: doubling the time needed for overland road traffic to central Europe; increasing the importance of the Italian seabridge; and newly prioritizing east-west, rather than traditional north-south, linkages across Greek territory.

The country has already received substantial Community development monies via the structural funds and the first Community Support Program (1989–1993), and is also, along with Portugal, Spain and Ireland, one of the four designated recipients of Cohesion Fund aid. The Greek network also figures prominently in the TENs initiative; two main motorways (PATHE, or Patras-Athens-Thessaloniki-Evzoni) and Egnatia (Igoumenitsa-Alexandropoulos) are targeted EU road projects; another (a new airport at Spata, outside Athens) is one of nine second-tier projects; and Greece figures directly in two of the eight priority energy network projects.[16]

Still other related projects include a new suspension bridge across the Gulf of Corinth from Rion to Antirion, an underground railway system for the northern city of Thessaloniki, metro extensions in Athens, and two ring-roads around the capital to service the shipyards at Elefsina and the new airport. During 1995–2000, Greece is due to receive EU infrastructure aid totaling around ecu 32 bn ($40 bn) from the Community Support Framework, the Cohesion Fund, and the TENs package; in addition, "soft loans" from the EIB, and private investment, is to cover ecu 5.6 bn, with the Greek government supplying another ecu 4 bn in matching funds. EU support during this period is expected to amount to nearly 5 percent of national GDP, raising national growth by nearly 1 percent annually, and creating an expected 100,000 additional jobs (McDonald 1996).

The vast scale of these new investments, in a country of 10 million inhabitants, gives the distinct impression of a country in which seemingly every transport facility is an EU construction site, especially the Athens metro works with their disruptions of the capital's already sclerotic traffic flows. Indeed EU-sanctioned *megali erga* (big projects) are a key facilitator of overall economic growth and a centerpiece of a much-heralded domestic modernization program, to an extent unmatched elsewhere in the Union, and have, in turn, transformed the once-hostile views of the ruling PASOK party toward the Community.

However, Greece's inadequate absorption of EU structural funds caused the Commission, in October 1994, to place a temporary block on some ecu 4 bn of aid to Greece, in an attempt to gain leverage by facilitating the overhaul of traditional Greek infrastructure practices. This block was (partly) lifted in April 1995, only after a direct intervention by Greece's then-prime minister, Mr. Papandreou, to Commission President Santer (FT, 11 Oct. 1994: 2; 15 March 1995: 2). Even with funds already allocated for 1994–1995, it is estimated that some 260 bn drachmas ($120 m) failed to be absorbed due to bureaucratic inertia and a severely weakened government. In addition, high public deficits (of the four Cohesion countries, Greece's, at over 7 percent of GDP for 1996, was the highest) have led to Commission threats to cut off Cohesion aid unless the figure is reduced. Though the government claims much higher absorption rates by 1996–1997, these delays and problems shed valuable light on the potential problems of future European infrastructure development, both for current members and, in the longer term, for eastern Europe and subregions such as the Balkans. These problems include:

1) *Antiquated tendering procedures.* Greece's method of awarding public contracts has been characterized by a lack of transparency, coupled with the inefficient practice of allowing such contracts to be split up among numerous small, local construction companies, effectively giving a large number of firms control over individual sections of projects. Such methods are generally seen as handouts to political allies in industry, often privy to inside information regarding the timing or other details of the tender competition, but they have persisted because of inadequate managerial control over overall project planning. Companies have been able to win contracts partly by severe underpricing, offering price discounts of up to 80 percent below the expected overall costs, inevitably leading to huge cost overruns and eventually, as corners are cut, to inferior overall quality. Complaints and legal action by losing bidders also delay progress. Govern-

ment policy has also been partly to blame; since the 1960s there has been a limit of Dr 5 bn to the value of any contract to a single company, although the ceiling is set to move up to Dr 12 bn in response to EU pressure for greater efficiency. Such reforms will likely lead to mergers in the construction industry, hitherto characterized (in an economic sense) as immature, with numerous smaller firms competing both for government contracts and private capital on the Athens bourse.

European Commission objections have centered on two projects in particular, the Rio-Antirio bridge near Patras and the Spata airport outside Athens, due to inadequate procedures being followed. The bridge project was delayed by lengthy wrangles with the Commission regarding inadequate technical specifications and overoptimistic traffic projections. The formal (revised) contract was finally signed in January 1996, and went to the Greek-French *Gefyra* consortium, which expects completion in 2003. The Spata airport project suffered from political maneuverings (see below) which led to an ill-tempered struggle between French and German contractors over the propriety of the contract-awarding process and has had major reverberations in Greek domestic politics. Thus a key Commission aim is for greater transparency of overall tendering procedures to enable adequate scrutiny of projects awarded or under consideration.

2) *Political intrusion.* Another major problem in the Greek case has been a splintering of transport priorities between three different ministries (Transport; Shipping; Environment and Public Works) and a reluctance on the part of the last-mentioned to share planning control despite a lack of management expertise in handling technical and financial issues of large infrastructure projects. But with the Commission's insistence on mixed private and public funding for infrastructure, the need for streamlining political proceedures, and for independent and nonpolitical project management, is growing.[17] High-level political intrusion has been most obvious in the Spata example, which involves construction of a new airport at a cost of some ecu 2 bn. After lengthy negotiations, the Conservative government of Constantine Mitsotakis awarded the airport contract to Hochtief, a German company, over its French competitor, a French-Greek consortium (Dumez GTM), led by Aéroports de Paris. The terms at the time included the right for the company, holding a majority stake of 60 percent, to build and operate the airport for a fifty-year concession period.

However, the government fell before Parliamentary approval could be gained, and the ensuing election campaign was fought partly over the airport issue amid Socialist charges of a sellout of Greek interests. Once back in office, Papandreou proceeded to reopen the negotiations, and though Hochtief retained the rights to build it, its stake was reduced from 60 to 45 percent and its operating concession from 50 to 30 years. These unilateral changes in the terms led to a Commission inquiry into the way the contract had been handled, prompted by strenuous objections by the losing contractor (Dumez GTM), which enlisted the support of Roland Dumas, a former French foreign minister, to intervene with the Commission and with Santer personally in order to block an EIB loan. At the other end, Klaus Kinkel, the German foreign minister, defended the contract's terms in a direct representation to the Commission president. What emerged for a time was thus a three-level political involvement (Greek interparty; two other European governments; the Commission itself) in an ostensibly nonpolitical decision.

In the end, however, the Commission decided not to take Greece before the European Court, and by the summer of 1995 the government had achieved the necessary parliamentary approval and finalized the contract, fourteen months late. The clear lesson of such political maneuverings is that private firms, especially in developing areas, face very real, continuing public policy risks in undertaking infrastructure works, whether alone or in partnership, and can be subject to unexpected delays and to unilateral reopenings of supposedly agreed-upon conditions.

Against such possibilities, firms will demand very favorable terms in order to entice their participation in projects of such long duration;[18] and the problem is especially acute in precisely those (relatively poorer) countries targeted by the Cohesion Fund. Greece, for example, was exempted from EU public procurement regulations through 1998. One major irony which could emerge from the EU's Single Market-related efforts to open up the traditionally murky public procurement process in Europe is that, while possibly reducing the potential for domestic political wrangling, it may actually increase the potential of Spata-style, bottom-up politicization of the process at the European level, via individual governments championing their own companies at the expense of those based in other states, and challenging future contracts awarded on the basis of improprieties, actual or alleged.

3) *Uneven development patterns.* Greece is also somewhat typical of other poorer European countries in that its development is highly skewed, with 30 percent of the population concentrated in Athens, and other cities (e.g., Patras, Thessaloniki) separated from the capital by large stretches of relatively undeveloped territory. The via Egnatia highway currently being constructed across northern Greece, part of it straddling the remote Pindus mountains, is a particularly difficult case, made worse still by an international outcry over a possible environmental threat to the ancient theater of Dodoni.

The financial risk for private sector companies under such conditions is great, because of the wide variations in relative viability even within a single project. For example, a company contracted to build stretches of motorway in return for rights to operate tolling facilities can expect very different volumes of traffic, and hence revenue potential, near cities as opposed to rural stretches. For this reason, suggestions have been put forth to divide projects between urban-based, using private sector funding, and rural-based, relying on public funds either directly or via public bond issues. While in keeping with the Commission's pragmatic aims of financing TENs projects, breaking up such projects in this manner would be difficult to realize in practice, and may well tend to undercut the Commission's own efforts to streamline overall tendering procedures.

Transalpine Transport Issues

Differing north-south transalpine transport priorities have been yet another obstacle in the way of seamless network development in Europe. But whereas the Chunnel is representative of the challenges of private financing and Greece of special problems in remote or developing areas, the Swiss case is *sui generis* insofar as its anomalous position, an EU nonmember straddling Alpine passes and adjacent to huge German, French, and Italian markets, has been reinforced by the EU accession in 1995 of its Alpine neighbor Austria. It is no exaggeration to say that the single biggest obstacle to closer Swiss-EU relations in the 1990s has been a fundamental divergence over transport priorities. Swiss obstructionism has become a major headache for both EU planners and road hauliers, which depend on open Swiss transit routes through the Alps or else must be diverted several hundred kilometers into France or Austria. Environmental issues have come to a head because the huge increases in EU hauliers using Swiss roads has been compounded by ever-larger trucks, adding to congestion, air and noise pollution, and damaging roadbeds in a fragile ecosystem.[19]

In 1992 the Swiss government negotiated an agreement with the EU which limited the size of trucks using Swiss roads to 28 tons, for use only on weekdays, which had a profound impact on traffic flows.[20] Furthermore, in a February 1994 referendum, Swiss voters defied the government's desire for closer relations with the EU by narrowly approving an outright ban on foreign (effectively, EU) trucks from Swiss motorways after the year 2004, when the 1992 agreement expires (*The Economist*, 26 Feb. 1994: 34). At the same time, in a rare display of economic largesse, Swiss voters approved a major extension of their transalpine rail tunnel system, involving the construction of two new north-south rail tunnels within the next decade, in order to divert road traffic to piggy-back rail services. In an apparent tit-for-tat response (and defying its own stated interest in promoting intermodal development), the EU deliberately delayed progress in establishing schemes for research collaboration involving the Swiss, and it was conspicuously slow before finally allowing the Swissair-Sabena air alliance to proceed.

The Swiss case demonstrates several different transport problems with wider applicability: tensions between European road and rail interests, which has grown along with the rise in overall traffic; the knock-on effect of transport problems onto broader economic and political relationships;

and perhaps foremost, the growing potential for political obstructionism, often based on localized needs and concerns, which can hinder attempts at centralized coordination of transport priorities (Maggi 1992). All this indicates the potential for transport questions to become the focus of broader struggles over decision-making authority itself when it comes to quality-of-life issues. In neighboring Italy, for example, the planned Rome-Naples section of the TAV high-speed rail project has been slowed by the necessity of holding roundtables with over sixty different local communes over environmental concerns.

The Nordic Dimension

Finally, the case of infrastructure development in the remoter Nordic region has highlighted the new problems to be faced in transport because of the major expansion of EU territory to areas north of the Baltic Sea. It has also illustrated the potential for high-level politicization of transport decision-making processes, and for suboptimal outcomes resulting from such politicization. The decision by EU leaders, at the Corfu summit in June 1994, to add the so-called "Nordic triangle" to the EU's priority list of TENs projects was itself transparently political, being tacked on late in the day in hopes of favorably influencing imminent national referenda over EU membership in Norway, Sweden, and Finland. (The same could be said for the EU's decision, under its regional programs, to create a new category (Category VI) of regions, those with sparse populations, qualifying for EU aid.) The Nordic triangle project otherwise did not meet the Commission's rather strict criteria for priority projects (expected to begin work by the end of 1996, and with some private sector commitment); the Christophersen group itself admitted that the project was at a nascent stage of development and lacked reliable financial estimates (Trans-European 1995: 151–153). Norway's rejection in November 1994 of EU membership obviously raises serious questions about the ultimate feasibility of the project itself, at least from the EU's perspective as a project of declared European interest meriting direct support.

Another EU high priority Nordic project, involving a bridge-tunnel link across the Öresund between Copenhagen and Malmö, has also been heavily politicized, though in very different ways. In Sweden, what originated as a low-level, localized issue for the Malmö region erupted into a major national political controversy and a persistent headache for the Bildt government (1991–1994) because of the vocal opposition to the project of a major coalition partner, the Center Party, and its leader, Olof Johansson, on environmental grounds; in turn, these problems spilled over and negatively affected Danish-Swedish relations and even Sweden's ongoing negotiations with the EU over the terms of its membership (Ross 1995). In Denmark, meanwhile, decision making on the domestic Great Belt project, designed to link that country's islands and peninsulas via road and rail tunnels and bridges, has been allegedly beholden to special interests and thereby skewed.

Indeed Kai Lemberg (1995) holds that the Great Belt and Sound bridge projects together are classic examples of national prestige projects, pursued by politicians and powerful industrial interests in spite of a lack of evidence that such development is economically justifiable, and that an initial emphasis on rail tunnels was gradually converted, through political pressure, into less environmentally sound (but more "visible") combined motorway/rail bridges. The implication is that considerations of national prestige often take precedence in major projects, often to the detriment of environmental and even straightforward economic considerations, and even in two states otherwise noted for the soundness and openness of their planning procedures and for their relative sensitivity to environmental concerns.

CONCLUSIONS

The evolution of these and other projects will provide valuable lessons for industry and public officials alike in the effort to identify and minimize infrastructure risks. The potential problems are diverse, with single large intrastate projects (such as Italy's long-discussed suspension bridge across the Messina Straits between Sicily and the Italian mainland) involving one set of issues, and international collaborative ventures (such as the mooted tunnel under the Straits of Gibraltar between Spain and Morocco) quite another. Two points do seem clear: first, that international projects of ever-growing size, cost, complexity, and sheer ambition will continue to have their backers,[21] making collective political will a crucial prerequisite for success; and second, that major projects will require careful balancing of economic and social factors, between efficiency and equity. In both, the role of the EU as planning coordinator, provider of seed finance, and (not least) cheerleader will remain crucial.

While the problems outlined above are not insurmountable, they do suggest limitations on the EU's ability to formulate a Europe-wide networks strategy with operational potential that matches its conceptual elegance. Political intrusiveness into infrastructure development is likely to continue, though more splintered among governmental levels (local, regional, national, international) and less purely national-based. EU efforts to open up tendering procedures for public works projects are still nascent and will prove difficult to apply throughout the EU. The growing complexity of projects, with expensive technology requirements, will continue to demand long-term capital commitments from mixed sources.

In turn, the need for market involvement means that major projects will be exposed to macroeconomic developments such as currency movements, energy price rises or Euromarket interest rate fluctuations. An ongoing need is to ensure that these economic imperatives do not blind policymakers to the equally vital, and traditional, social and distributional elements of infrastructure. The transport sector is, and doubtless will remain, a highly imperfect market, in which the economics of infrastructure building can never be divorced from its wider social and political context.

Despite the multiplicity of actual and potential problem-areas, there is reason for hoping that the networks strategy will evolve in positive ways, even short of total eradication of what R. W. Vickerman (1991) calls the "shadow effect" of national borders on the Single Market. One crucial reason is the establishment of intermodal linkages even outside of the EU's aegis. The Channel Tunnel was completed binationally, using private capital. Road and rail interests are discovering the lost virtues of cooperation via combined transport projects. Airlines, such as Lufthansa and (more recently) Virgin, have become providers of rail services. New airport projects are being designed as separate stops on the emerging high-speed rail system. Port development is increasingly linked to rail connections for cargo as well as passenger traffic. Such ventures indicate a growing realization that better networks benefit all, and that intermodal cooperation results in a growing pie rather than the zero-sum game traditionally assumed.

An optimistic perspective is also warranted if it accompanies realistic expectations in terms of behavioral changes and modal elasticity, in two respects. HST development, for example, is expected to reduce road use on parallel routes from anywhere between 2.5 and 10 percent (4 percent in France). Second, raising the cost of car transport would reduce mobility by about 4 percent, and fuel use by about 3 percent (CEC 1995c: 74–75). The overall savings are thus potentially substantial while hardly revolutionary.

In addition, network development has benefited from the gradual convergence of a substantial EU policy community, particularly in favor of HST development, in which the Commission and European governments, after years of being at loggerheads on transport questions, appear to have achieved something of a *modus vivendi* on infrastructure development. Growing EU outlays, both directly through the TENs budget and indirectly via the Cohesion and structural funds, speak to a commitment to coordinating different projects within an overarching strategy, and suggest that continuity could well replace inconsistency as a characteristic description of EU efforts in this area. The main potential difficulty seems likely to be related to the need to maintain an overall networks concentration despite different project needs, particularly after 2000 when additional demands from new member states will make themselves felt.

NOTES

1. The via Egnatia, one of the key east-west routes linking Rome with the Balkan peninsula and the Black Sea, facilitated the eastward expansion that culminated in the shifting of the empire's capital from Rome to Constantinople in 323–329 A.D. It extended from Dyrrachium (Durazzo), the present-day Albanian port of Durres, southeast toward Thessaloniki and Constantinople (Istanbul) (De Burgh 1953: 246 n. 1). Thus in strictly historical terms, the mooted East-West Axis, a competing (non-TENs) Balkans road project (see Chapter 2), more closely reflects the historical pattern.

2. Overall Community transport infrastructure spending dropped from around 1.5 percent of GDP in 1975 to just .8 percent in the late 1980s. At the same time, demand for goods transport rose around 2.3 percent yearly, and that for passenger transport even more, by 3.1 percent (*Trans-European* 1994: 3). The increase in motorway use between 1985 and 1989 alone averaged over 10 percent, ranging up to 16.4 percent in Portugal (CEC 1993c).

3. Total structural funds for the same period (1993–99) amount to ecu 172.5 bn. In the 1996 budget, Cohesion spending accounts for 8.4 percent of all structural expenditures, while the structural funds overall account for over 90 percent of the total (CEC 1995d).

4. The developmental effects of TENs on non-EU states has been increasingly emphasized since a joint Commission-Council of Europe conference in Dresden in November 1993 (*Trans-European* 1995). The second pan-European transport conference, in Crete in 1994, set nine priority multimodal corridors in eastern Europe; and the following year, transport ministers launched a transport infrastructure needs assessment mechanism to identify needs and project viability. A third conference, in Helsinki in June 1997, was to follow up these initiatives.

5. In addition, normal transport spending, dealt with under a different heading, also received major new commitments, totaling ecu 11.5 m (a rise of 47 percent); and the Cohesion Fund, which involves additional transport expenditures, also rose by nearly ecu 300 m (13.6 percent) compared with 1995 (CEC 1995d).

6. During 1988–1993, the EIB provided around ecu 5 bn for rail development in Europe, of which 1 bn went to the France's TGV Nord initiative to link with Lille, Brussels, and the Channel Tunnel. Other sums have included ecu 350 m to France's TGV Atlantique link; 777.5 m to Spain's AVE high-speed line between Seville and Madrid; and 250 m to Belgium for upgrading links to TGV-Nord (EIB 1994a).

7. The ECSC is, however, limited as a long-term funding instrument due to expiration of its fifty-year mandate in 2002.

8. The EIF is a joint venture between the EIB, the Commission, and public and private banks in the EU. The limited initial capital (ecu 2 bn) is nonetheless expected to guarantee financing worth up to ecu 16 bn. Support is intended for both infrastructure and small and medium-sized enterprises (SMEs).

9. British opposition to Santer's proposal was based on antipathy to EU intrusion in national issues, while Germany was concerned to demonstrate that the budgetary discipline being asked of member states to meet EMU convergence criteria could not be simply be made up at will by Brussels.

10. Delors was granted a special two-year term (1993–1994), amid expecta-

tions (ultimately unrealized) that he was preparing a run for the French presidency in May 1995, the success of which would ride largely on his obtaining the formal backing of the French Socialist party.

11. The reference here was to the so-called Ortoli facility, created in 1978 as a "New Community Instrument" (NCI) to support investment by SMEs in the energy and infrastructure sectors. Prior loan launches in the 1980s, including NIC I, II, and III, raised a total of around ecu 5 bn for such purposes (*Trans-European* 1994).

12. Germany's argument for maintaining fiscal rectitude by denying the EU the right to borrow on capital markets was, however, undercut by the limited size of the Union Bonds proposal (initially ecu 7 bn), which according to Delors accounted for less than 1 percent of Eurobond and bank credit markets (*The Economist*, 11 Dec. 1993: 27–28).

13. See e.g. BEU 6/1995: 63. Such criticisms seem excessive given the Commission's strong emphasis on dedicated and combined rail projects. The Christophersen group estimated that, of the eleven projects first prioritized in spring 1994, costing some ecu 68.5 bn (excluding the government-funded Öresund fixed link), a full 88 percent of these costs were rail-related (*Trans-European* 1994: 71). The EP's point is more justified when considering the lower-priority projects, where a motorway emphasis is more evident.

14. I am indebted to Mitchell Strohl for earlier clarification on this point. There is also evidence that the freight industry has suffered because of security-related delays on through-Chunnel rail services, forcing business back to road hauliers.

15. However, a breakthrough came in January 1996, with the government's choice of London and Continental Railways, led by Virgin Airlines, to build the rail link by private funds. After years of delay, the Chunnel rail link is now a central plank in its Private Finance Initiative (*Sunday Times*, 28 Jan. 1996: 2, 1).

16. The two TENs energy projects involve a submarine electrical connection from Italy and natural gas networks in Greece. The latter has suffered long delays, leading the EIB, its main backer, to suspend support in June 1993. Equally significant has been a planned transBalkan oil venture to bring Russian oil to Greece via ship and pipeline between the Black and Aegean Seas. This project has also been held up, over the sharing of oil processing rights (*Trans-European* 1995).

17. Steps in both directions have been taken recently. One of Simitis's first acts as premier was to create a "superministry" of development under Vasso Papandreou, charged with speeding up privatization and overseeing EU projects. And in 1995, Economics Minister Yiannos Papantoniou initiated the formation of an interministerial committee to oversee state procurements, to promote more independence in project management.

18. Even so, after the contract revisions Hochtief still expects a substantial return (close to 20 percent).

19. For example, whereas in 1980 an average of 80 trucks passed through the St. Gotthard pass daily, the average is now some 2500 per day. The numbers are expected to surpass 6000 by the year 2000.

20. These Swiss road restrictions have effectively doubled such traffic in neighboring Austria, eliciting derisory commentary on the "tail-to-tail truck trail" through the Arlberg. Truck traffic through France has increased fourfold despite

the longer distances involved. In all, transalpine traffic in Switzerland is only 10 percent of that crossing these two other countries (Rossera 1995).

21. Plans for projects once dismissed as foolhardy are now taking active shape, including possible fixed links between Scotland and Ireland (32 km), Finland and Estonia (64 km), Italy and Albania (75 km), and even Italy and Tunisia (144 km). Against these the 3 km separating Sicily from Italy's mainland, or even the 14 km between Spain and Morocco, seem modestly challenging.

Thinking has become truly globalized, best indicated by ongoing plans for the immodestly denoted "inter-hemispheric," 73-km rail bridge link across the Bering Straits separating Russia and the U.S. off Alaska, truly a bargain at a projected cost of a mere $40 bn+ at current prices. An international symposium on the project, scheduled for September 1995 in London, was rescheduled, supposedly because of overwhelming interest.

Chapter Eight

Europe's Incomplete Transport Revolution

Travel teaches toleration.
—BENJAMIN DISRAELI

This volume opened by remarking briefly on the unevenness of transport's role in the EU milieu. The point is scarcely less valid in regard to the likely future evolution of transport systems, because the newfound policy attention has rested uneasily with the varying pace of progress. On the one hand, the European approach unquestionably has undergone a sea change since the mid-1980s, in substantive as well as rhetorical terms. The move away from national transport monopolies seems irreversible; national champion strategies are giving way to incipient internationalist ones; there is broad agreement on the technical obstacles to harmonization; Europe-wide networks are being championed by powerful interests; public-private links are expanding; transport seminars and conferences abound. The sheer range of activity and the amount of energy being expended is impressive, even if it attests as much to intellectual ferment as to focused policy priorities.

In the same vein, reformist pressures are no longer driven solely by the pervasive sense of crisis discussed early on, but are increasingly counterbalanced by the pull of positive developments: of the market-altering potential of new transport systems, such as rapid rail; of the willingness of companies (such as Hochtief in the Spata airport example) to undertake long-term infrastructure development despite the inherent risks involved; of a $16 bn Channel Tunnel completed without governmental funding; of dramatic, post-privatization turnarounds of chronic lossmakers like British Airways. Even if slow, incremental, and subject to negative pressures, progress is happening on many fronts. The chronic pessimism attending the debate over the consequences of transport overuse may be overdone, just as markets often overshoot their point of equilibrium, and appear far removed from the earlier hopes induced by Concorde, the 747, catalytic converters, and the "white heat" of Harold Wilson's technological revolution.

On the other hand—and in the European transport policy debate, there is always another hand—initiatives aiming at a borderless European transport environment remain disturbingly at odds with present and foreseeable future realities. The term "transport policy" could easily be substituted for "travel" in the chapter-opening quote, for in many ways the EU is engaged in a permanent game of catching up with developments. It is striking that the same symptoms that precipitated all the recent attention still abound. Infrastructure investment lags behind likely future needs; loss-making state airlines and railroads continue to drain public purses; road transport's continuing dominance negates environmental advances; proprietary governmental attitudes toward home industries continue to distort competitive conditions and perpetuate high costs; hortatory EU calls for denationalization too often fall on deaf ears, or elicit dilatory, "one last heave"-type bailout programs for troubled firms, with grudging Commission acquiescence.

Amidst all the competing evidence of progress and problems, and the definitional fog surrounding newly enunciated policy goals, it is possible, nonetheless, to identify two broad changes over the past decade. One is the internationalization of the transport policy and industry environment; the other, partly counteracting the first, is the gradual, if belated, emergence of an overarching Community transport policy.

The internationalization of industry profoundly has altered the macroeconomic environment in which European transport services and manufacturers operate. According to some prominent analysts (e.g., Hall 1993; Wright 1995) globalization has constituted no less than a paradigm shift in thinking, from Keynesian, statist industrial policies to neoliberal approaches reflected in Community policies and leaving no state unaffected. The impact of recent market reforms and outside pressures from the Far East and the U.S. have been particularly forceful agents for changes, including: loosening state ownership and regulatory control over national industries; "bringing the firm back in" and promoting industry strategies independent of governmental fiat, necessitating recourse to global capital markets by firms; refocusing conglomerates' attention on core activities; and requiring transnational as opposed to strictly nationalist strategies (with all the paradoxes that an internationalized national champion may imply), often involving cross-border alliances. Europe's industries can no longer hide behind national borders nor rely on proprietary governmental policies to disguise inefficient practices.

Internationalist strategies have emerged not only in transport operations but, increasingly, in manufacturing as well, in the airframe, rail engine, shipbuilding and especially auto sectors. The effects of globalization on the transport sector can work both ways: while encouraging (even forcing) transnationalist strategies on companies, it shows that the transport industry can, itself, "function as a lubricant for world-wide economic integration" (Grant 1995: 84). Closer to home, commitment of EU resources for trans-European infrastructure is similarly predicated on faith in transport's potential for integrating two halves of Europe so long separated by political ideologies and military divisions.

The trend toward industry consolidation poses special challenges to the EU's competition directorate in ensuring that the creation of transport mega-carriers capable of competing worldwide does not crowd out all competitors and merely recreate, in the private market, the monopolistic conditions that so long dominated the public sector.[1] The war of words between the Competition Commissioner (Van Miert) and BA's chairman (Robert Ayling) over the EU's right to investigate the BA-AA alliance vividly demonstrated the potentially explosive issues involved. Another likely effect with operational consequences is the ongoing shift from the hitherto separated modal operations, dictated by the existence of national borders, to a hiving-off of operations on the basis of journey distance and speed. Strict modal separation is becoming a thing of the past, indicated by: the nascent division between fixed rail infrastructure and operations and between long-distance HST routes and domestic services; trans-European motorway networks operating separately from domestic road systems; the gradual separation of long-haul, international air routes from smaller domestic markets; and the traditional separation of inland waterway and deep-sea operations, the latter dividing further into separate markets such as for passenger ferries, dry goods, and container shipping. In each case the likelihood is growing for profitable, privately-run long-haul operations in contrast to loss-making sub-national services.

Still, the transport sector has been slower than many other industries to respond to these cross-pressures and has been partly insulated from the worst effects of rapid globalization. The exogenous pressures to liberalize and rationalize have been attenuated by the highly imperfect nature of the transport market, in which economic considerations continue to coexist with lingering public service obligations for operators, direct or assumed, and by the ever-present social implications of transport operations, which are never environmentally neutral. Other complicating factors include the differing market structures and policy environments of the different modes, which fostered the multi-speed introduction of individual modal common policies; and the persistently solicitous governmental treatment of home-based operators, even if no longer state-owned. Overall, transport resists generalization; both the intergovernmentalist and institutionalist explanations for change offer static alternatives to a much more complicated reality. Similar arguments have been made for competition policy (McGowan and Wilks 1995) and for the Single Market itself (Cowles 1995), suggesting that transport is far from unique in this respect.

The fact remains that most European transport companies retain their national bases and have pursued internationalist strategies not in spite of these national roots but because of them. The formation of global air alliances, even those involving equity cross-holdings, has not meant the end of the European flag-carrier itself but rather shows shrewd survival instincts. Similarly, recourse to international capital markets, inaugurated by Daimler-Benz's New York listing in 1993, remains a trickle rather than a flood. Indeed the debate over whether or not national champion strategies are outmoded is somewhat sterile; it is far more important that states remain vitally interested in enhancing the competitive position of home transport companies and show increasing ingenuity in doing so. Evidence of genuinely pan-European, non-national transport companies remains scant; and those few emergent cases—ABB in rail and engineering systems, Easyjet and Virgin Express in the air industry—tend to be smaller, leaner, more flexible and less tied to national bases; and they often allege discrimination by governments in favor of larger, established operators.

The second major trend has been the gradual emergence of an overarching EU transport strategy. In some respects the elimination of internal European borders neatly parallels the opening of the world economy; in others, however, global transport operations make it difficult to isolate a specifically European component of an increasingly international industry, as indicated by the growing web of air alliances, flagging-out maritime practices, and disputes over "domestic content" in car manufacturing. From tentative beginnings, hindered by restrictive national practices, vague treaty guidelines and occasional pusillanimity in Brussels, transport has now largely shed its image as an embarrassing exception to the Single Market and has emerged as a central, even dynamic, element in European integration processes. The EU, especially the Commission, has carved out a significant niche for itself in policy prioritizing, industry regulation, structural planning, and even, in some fields (shipping and more recently air), having traded implied for actual competences in negotiating responsibility. Furthermore, the EU's overall gamut of policy concerns has widened significantly from the Rome Treaty's modest provisions; the old dismissive, "old wine in new bottles," hardly characterizes the new, expanded CTP.

In some respects this trend represents an extrapolation to the European level of the earlier (19th–early 20th century) trend by states to co-opt private transport systems into the public domain as crucial components of developing national economies, military strategies, and even imperialist ambitions. Similarly, the EU's shift from a reactive to a proactive strategy implies recognition of transport's broader strategic character for the pan-European economy and for Europe's global competitiveness. The difference, of course, lies in civilian/economic, not military/strategic, motivations; with no powers to requisition transport systems and no workable CFSP, the EU must tread carefully in asserting its authority. A second historical parallel is evident in the present post-Maastricht climate, namely the renewal of the 1950s emphasis on promoting "lesser" policy areas as integrative vehicles in the absence of rapid progress in more visible areas (e.g., monetary union).

The EU has prioritized the transport sector in two respects, first as an internal/European element (completing the internal market, maximizing the cost-savings of borderless travel, and linking east and west Europe) and a less obvious, but no less crucial external/international element (enhancing the competitive position of major European firms and raising Europe's collective profile in the international political economy). Both elements converge in their reliance on neoliberal economic means to achieve broader political ends; and both have been advanced through the enunciation of common modal policies together with multimodal and structural initiatives, all aimed at an overarching CTP strategy which is more, rather than less, than the sum of its parts.

Another question is the extent to which exogenous global pressures and endogenous Community reforms (the CTP) have combined to ameliorate differences between member states. Recent analysts (e.g., Wright 1995) suggest a convergence of national strategies and submission to market-driven imperatives of commercial freedom for operators. Even so, there is a tendency to focus on the four major states at the expense of the much more heterogeneous EU15, whereby smaller northern states have been key innovators and others, the Cohesion 4 especially, cannot merely be dismissed as trouble cases. The traditionally sharp analytical distinction between Anglo-Saxon laissez-faire and continental *dirigiste* European approaches, seems less and less descriptive, particularly as Helmut Kohl's Germany has succumbed to pressures to liberalize its long-closed road sector and has sold off Lufthansa.[2] More persistent have been north-south differences, whereby national airlines and state rail systems in France, Italy, and elsewhere in southern Europe contrast sharply with the privatizations and system decentralizations further north. Tentatively planned transport selloffs in the south could easily meet delays and union opposition.

Two other trends are evident. One is states' use of EU major policy initiatives, centering on restrictive EMU criteria, as a kind of "surrogate surgeon" for long-delayed action at the national level. States can fairly claim to be subject to EU rules, which enables profligate governments to use the EU as an ally in reducing red ink, including transport subsidies. Election victories in 1996 by (relatively) strict budgetary disciplinarians in Spain, Italy, and Greece—the latter two nominally of the Left—illustrate the strength of this potential. The second trend is the transposition of national policies, especially by "liberal" states (Netherlands, Britain) onto the broader European level, using the EU as a vehicle through which to advance policies already instituted nationally (Menon and Hayward 1996).

Indeed the smaller and wealthier European states have been trend-setters in industry reform (Sweden in HST systems; Austria and Swizerland in combined transport; Scandinavia in developing transport franchising as a halfway alternative to outright privatizations) (Andersen 1995). The prevailing institutional EU imbalance favoring smaller states (a guaranteed Commissioner; outsized Council weighted voting) has advanced these trends more broadly at EU level with the 1995 expansion and demonstrated the difficulty of separating policy from institutional questions. Even among the reformers, however, it is possible to overstate tendencies; Britain, characterized by Grant (1995) as a neoliberal "spectator state," nonetheless has favored major operators rather than creation of a genuinely competitive market.

PROBLEMS IN OPERATIONALIZING
A COMMON TRANSPORT POLICY

The CTP's rebirth and its targeting as an instrument to achieve broader EU ends raises a number of problems. One is the considerable, perhaps even growing, expectations gap between the many goals and programmatic proliferation of a holistic transport "master plan" and actual accomplishments. The EU's enunciation not only of common policies (both modal and intermodal) but of sustainability goals, citizens networks and the like are bound to raise undue expectations that such lofty and even desirable aims can readily translate into action. Problem-identification remains a considerably easier exercise than working out viable solutions.

A second problem for the EU is enunciation of goals that are inconsistent or even contradictory. It remains difficult to reconcile expansion of transport networks, with its expectations of rising traffic demand, and environmental-based sustainability objectives; the building of new road systems yet lower pollution levels; promoting short-sea shipping yet also new fixed links that will reduce the viability of sea travel; promoting air liberalization and lower air fares yet also modal switching from air to rail; attention to safety concerns while championing deregulation; and attention to Europe's long-term needs while advocating greater market involvement, with its inevitable focus on short-term goals and narrow financial objectives.

A third problem for the EU is an uncomfortable disjunction between stated and actual goals, or rather between a stated menu of balanced aims and a de facto hierarchy of policy priorities. EU policy statements suggest an admirable balancing of three key elements of growth, efficiency, and sustainability objectives across the modes. To this end, it has advocated four holistic policy thrusts: industry liberalization, including lower state aids; infrastructure development; technical innovation and harmonization; and environmental protection. In actual policy terms, however, the post-SEA thrust has prioritized primarily growth objectives; in the 1990s a second wave of technology-inspired efficiency objectives has emerged, with greater DG XII emphasis on traffic management and incorporation of digital information systems. In contrast, sustainability and environmental objectives—involving more sensitive issues of behavioral change by individuals and firms—have lagged. Cuts in energy savings programs, and the quiet abandonment of the earlier pledge to stabilize CO_2 emissions at 1990 levels, are but two recent casualties. It could be that a third, environmentally inspired wave will emerge, but with attention riveted on EMU convergence criteria and budget-cutting, evidence is hard to find so far.

In some respects, this problem results less from deliberate obfuscation of intentions than from genuinely competing aims and goals of different Commission organs, industry/competition and transport/environment being but two sources of built-in institutional tension. The EP's interest in the equity elements of transport conflicts at times with Commission priorities; Jacques Santer's agenda differs from that of his predecessor, Delors; and the Commission and the states clash frequently over the EU's role. Two key strands of the EU's transport thrust—liberalization and structural policy—often appear as divergent and even opposing developments, the former shifting the transport focus from the public to the private sector and fragmenting formerly cohesive markets, the latter suggesting pan-European strategic objectives coordinated at European level. Yet the inconsistency is more apparent than real, and the two approaches converge in two crucial respects. One is that they together aim at creating a stronger, competitive European presence in the international transport sphere, mirroring the broader Single Market thrust of which they form a part. The loosening of state ties to transport industries is not inconsistent with a broader European strategy, since it expands the EU's scope for shaping developments; the U.S. case demonstrates that governments can vigorously and effectively promote their own industries abroad, even with a deregulated domestic environment.[3]

The second, even more crucial linkage between liberalization and structural policies is that both are, in essence, growth policies that do little to foster, and may actually hinder, sustainability objectives. Chapter 1 indicated the tendency for transport use to outstrip overall economic growth; liberalization promises to strengthen these upward patterns. In turn, completion of "missing links" and the creation of standardized motorway and rapid rail connections across borders will expand traffic use internationally. The gradual shift in TENs emphasis noted in Chapter 7, from a broad networks focus to attention to financial viability of individual projects, is further evidence of this prioritization of growth and efficiency aims. Thus the EU's enunciation of sustainability objectives in its 1993 Green Paper (CEC 1993b) via fuel emission reductions, restrictions on car use, and modal switching inducements are justifiably questioned by some (e.g., Whitelegg 1993) who regard them as mere crumbs of comfort in response to environmentalist pressures.

These growth- and efficiency-oriented policies have, naturally, also reflected the patterns and relative strength of European interest representation, in which the weakness and fragmentation of the international environmental movement[4] and declining union membership have contrasted with the success of targeted self-interests (e.g. the car, oil, and air industries) and overarching European industrial interests via the ERT, to shape the EU policy agenda. For all the current fears about a powerful Eurocracy in Brussels, much of the real driving force has been powerful industry interests operating from below. Paradoxically, European industry's competitive decline in the 1970s and early 1980s may actually have contributed to its agenda-setting power, motivated by fear of encroachment by American and Japanese interlopers.

Transport Policymaking and Political Intrusion

Despite the advances of recent years, the EU's targeting of the transport sector has highlighted the political nature of transport issues, and has fragmented and complicated the political debate itself. Three chief reasons can be given for this development. One is the internationalization of transport issues, which creates new pressures on, and tensions within, states over conforming to new rules such as subsidy cuts (French labor strikes in 1995 being one manifestation) and its "spill down" effects at state level. The second reason is the Maastricht-inspired subsidiarity principle, which has brought regional and even local decision makers into the European debate, creating "spill up" pressures as unresolved domestic issues press on the EU agenda.

In certain cases (the Öresund bridge-tunnel; the Spata airport contract) this has created international political tensions out of issues resolvable, but not resolved, at much lower levels; in such instances, governments are not above machinations aimed at influencing EU thinking in their direction and by pressing the Commission to take decisions that were not, properly, its to take at all. Struggles between Brussels and member states over negotiating competency in air services have been symptomatic of the political tensions that accompany the complication of policy networks by the addition of new actors. Even in sectors where an EU negotiating mandate has been established (as in the OECD ban on shipyard subsidies), the effect has been blunted by exceptions and the growth of indirect and hidden subsidies that by nature are even more difficult to locate, much less address.

A third troubling element has been the mixed signals from governments regarding TENs projects. While they have enhanced networks progress with unprecedentedly firm political support for Commission initiatives, transport mega-projects uncomfortably echo old national champion strategies and large but commercially unviable prestige projects that seem neatly to extrapolate Thorstein Veblen's notion of conspicuous consumption onto the wider European plane, as grand symbols of European integration. Denmark's Great Belt works and the associated Öresund bridge-tunnel well illustrate the frequent preference by otherwise rational-minded politicians for the large and visible, as opposed to the efficient. Further, states' advocacy of TENs is also a case of burden-sloughing no less than burden-sharing, since it helps shift the onus of infrastructure financing off pressured national budgets, and onto the EU and the private sector.

Indeed, one element which certainly figures in this analysis has been a reconfirmation—as if one is needed—that economic and political self-interest are alive and well in the transport sector. EU governments remain protective of politically sensitive jobs and industries that form a bedrock of crucial middle class political support. Britain's championing of road (and later air) liberalization reflected directly national interests no less than did France's reluctance to open its airspace or Germany's longtime resistance to road haulage liberalization. Similarly, the prevalence of car manufacturing interests in the large producer countries (France, Spain, Italy, and Germany), often against the will of smaller, nonproducer states has hindered the development of a single European car market by distorting competitive elements and strictly limiting competition from outsiders. It is no surprise that Britain, whose domestic car manufacturing industry has now been subsumed by foreign predators, is also the location of most Japanese "transplant" car production facilities in Europe.

Another dimension, namely intermodal competition, may have diminished in certain respects as the lines of division soften in transport planning (for example, where easy intermodal connections can help both modes attract business, such as airport-based HST links), although it may be increasing in others (e.g., where new infrastructure like the Channel Tunnel threatens to usurp business from channel ferries). But perhaps the most far-reaching political effect has been the emergence of intramodal competition on the heels of market fragmentation. Even rail, ostensibly the focus of an overarching policy community in favor of regeneration, has been undercut in at least four ways: (1) by separating high-speed from regular rail services, the latter often starved of development funds; (2) by the emergence of two separate HST systems, one French/western and one German/eastern, that continue to compete for supremacy both in Europe (threatening east-west economic divisions) and globally (for export markets); (3) by competing HST priorities between conventional and mag-lev systems (resolved in France, but still a problem in Germany); and (4) by lingering interoperability problems between different national HST systems. Intramodal tensions also characterize the air industry, pitting smaller and regional airlines against flag carriers still determined to control markets. Further, perceived differences in national priorities can exacerbate tensions even to the point of sabotaging agreements that appear mutually beneficial (e.g., the Alcazar air project).

Yet another point of division pertains to the Commission itself, which is showing signs of increasingly fractiousness in the post-Delors era. The combination of a larger size (20 members), a looser rein held by President Jacques Santer, and what may be an increasing tendency to politicize high-profile Commission posts has added to the pressures on this collegial, consensus-oriented body. The Commission's visibility and central policy role may be strengthening the tendency for grandstanding of its individual members; it is no accident that two of its outspoken members, Environment Minister Bjerregaard and Transport Minister Kinnock, were both prominent national politicians before their appointments. All this affects, indirectly or directly, the challenge of maintaining a vision of overall EU policy priorities.

UNRESOLVED PROBLEMS FOR EUROPEAN TRANSPORT

The removal of industry barriers and physical obstructions to a seamless European market has required a considerable EU effort which would be churlish to deny. Even so, if sustainability objectives are to be pursued as serious aims rather than mere appendages to predominantly growth-oriented policies, they will require measures to induce behavioral change by individuals and hauliers alike. Such an effort will be fraught with potential pitfalls, political and otherwise, sufficient to warrant skepticism about the short-term possibilities of large-scale modal switching. At the very least, it will require both a readjustment of policy priorities and, most likely, organizational changes as well.

Three crucial yet unresolved issues hang in the balance:

1. The creation of a truly level playing field for operators.
2. The promotion of modal switching to more environment-friendly modes, especially rail and waterborne transport.
3. The coordination of fragmented political interests.

The difficulty of creating a genuine level playing field in European transport markets is complicated by the multiple meanings of the term itself. At least four different elements can be noted: to give all countries roughly equal access to the European network; to create a truly equal competitive standing between the different transport modes; to put all operators within the modes themselves on an equal competitive footing; and to ensure nondiscrimination toward foreign operators in home markets.

The first question, equal national access, remains problematic because of the EU's growing geographical reach, but it is being addressed through active structural policies and application of competition rules. The other three questions involve decisions more directly in the transport sphere. The question of putting all the modes on an equal footing involves, first and foremost, the question of fair and equitable pricing. Road travel has proliferated, it is widely held, because many of the overall costs of travel (energy used, economic costs, pollution expended, time lost) are not fully internalized by the user. Many (Button 1994; Topmann 1994) have argued for application of cost-benefit analysis (CBA) to bring about equitable cross-modal costing, so that road costs can be more fully internalized, via methods such as higher gasoline taxes and peak-use charges. Transport users, as rational actors, will weight the costs and benefits on an equitable basis and, it is said, choose their modes accordingly. The other elements, promoting EU-wide equal market access and doing so for all operators, remain fraught with difficulty because of the inherent competitive advantages and market muscle held by large carriers and manufacturers and lingering protectionist sentiments.

Attempts have been made to create a model for sustainable systems based on equitable pricing between the different modes (Nijkamp and Vluegel 1995a). The EU Commission has responded with an initial attempt, via a detailed Green Paper (1996b) analyzing the problems and potential for adopting fairer costing methods in transport. But even if ways can be found to operationalize CBA, it remains a necessary but not sufficient instrument for limiting road use and fostering modal switching, for these reasons:

1. Widespread attachment to the numerous non-economic benefits of road use (flexibility, mobility, freedom, speed);

2. Current urban living patterns, whereby increasing numbers live beyond reach of convenient public transport, with the car as the only means of motorized transport readily at hand;

3. Established and targeted promoters of growth-oriented EU policies, in contrast to fragmented environmental interests;

4. Relative ease of measuring efficiency and growth gains (GDP, employment figures) versus costing equity and social gains;

5. Frequent non-rationality of transport decision making, due to psychological perceptions, aesthetic considerations, or other factors aside from straightforward costing considerations;

6. High market inelasticity, as demonstrated by the continued sharp rise in auto use in Europe despite very high costs of gasoline compared to other highly mobile societies (especially the U.S.);

7. Liberalization effects, whereby potentially lower overall costs of travel (e.g., air fares) could offset even relative rises in auto costs, and whereby enforced absolute cost rises would be, in turn, economically damaging and politically unfeasible;

8. The established economic thrusts of the Single Market and EMU, and the prioritization of transport policies to promote overall economic growth.

Any attempts to motivate significant modal switching would also require the following:

a. Stronger disincentives for road use ("sticks"), such as peak-use road charges, restricted parking zones, and pedestrian zones;

b. Stronger incentives for alternative use ("carrots"), such as significantly higher spending on public transport systems;

c. Public campaigns to encourage voluntary behavioral changes (e.g., walking or bicycling rather than motoring short distances);

d. Incorporation of information technologies into European lifestyles and work situations to reduce the need for travel, rather than merely improving efficiency of that which does occur;

e. Changing the policy environment to limit the exaggerated influence of road-based interest groups and other industry interests that depend on road use.

European Transport Governance: Reform or Overhaul?

The issue of organization in transport planning remains a crucial concern. For all the emphasis on transport initiatives at EU level, much of the impetus for change has come from below; for example, complex new technologies, developed largely by the private sector and often in cooperative ventures like Eureka, are being rapidly incorporated into transport systems planning. In itself, EU emphasis on liberalization and competition has created a fertile environment in which traditional means of regulation (namely, governments operating through national transport monopolies) have been loosened, but without a corresponding transfer of power to any other body. Thus far, there has been an extraordinary degree of faith in self-regulating mechanisms in industry governance.

The result has been a lack of an identifiable, single agent to establish overall transport priorities (social as well as economic); to push for further technical and administrative harmonization; to put each of the modes on a more even competitive footing; and to sanction recalcitrant governments if necessary, so that "policy" does not degenerate into meaningless and unenforceable guidelines. Even the TENs program stops well short of being a Commission harmonization initiative, since it widens the scope of interested actors, involving them in Commission-sponsored seminars on a consultative rather than a coercive basis, and relies on hopes for enticing private sector involvement—all hardly indicative of the strong top-down organizational guidance many regard as imperative to the realization of a European-wide intermodal strategy capable of dealing with future challenges.

A key issue facing the EU in transport governance is that of balancing the numerous political interests and, flowing from point (e) just above, of redressing modal imbalances that reflect economic rather than social interests. Most broadly, the problem is one of managing diversity—arriving at a set of policies capable of achieving the broad aims already set out. Without considerable organizational reform over the medium term, the modal imbalances are likely to worsen further after 2000, when massive transport dislocations in eastern Europe become direct EU concerns. The expected supplanting of traditionally dominant but woefully inefficient rail systems and growing dominance of road use, as the exigencies of consumer freedom and growing wealth lead to a massive increase in car ownership in the east, will create pressures likely to challenge, perhaps even overwhelm, the careful balancing act attempted thus far.

On current trends, therefore, it is reasonable to expect the efficiencies and network progress in western Europe to be more than offset by growing traffic use and congestion, with all its environmental and safety ramifications, in eastern (and southern) Europe. For this reason, many believe that there is a compelling case for a much stronger EU regulatory body, or set of bodies, in order to establish rules and override attempted system manipulation by more focused and determined modal or national interests. Clearly, arguments for industry self-regulation of information systems (as with the Internet and the World Wide Web) have less relevance for transport, which will always be more heavily based on hardware and immovable physical infrastructure, requiring coordinated decision making over lengthy time periods. For all its efforts and institutional competence, the Commission's transport directorate-general (DG VII) alone may be insufficient for the task, but it is less apparent what if anything should supplement, or even supplant, its efforts.

While in this age of privatization the advocacy of organizational or bureaucratic solutions may seem anomalous, the scale of current unresolved problems, plus the wide range of actors calling for better organizational solutions to them, lends credence to the notion that the transport regulatory regime could be improved by enforcing common standards through new mechanisms. Yet disagreements about the extent of the problems of transport are more than matched by the lack of consensus regarding the solutions to them. In 1990, the advisory "Group Transport 2000 Plus" emphasized three possible elements: (a) improvement of coordination of the existing EU bodies, including Commission-Council relations; (b) upgrading the Commission's DG VII to include personnel better equipped to take a long-term strategic outlook; and (c) closer involvement of the European Parliament in decision making (though this last point has since been addressed by Maastricht co-decision procedures). Others, such as the European Round Table of Industrialists (ERT), have gone further in calling for a single European infrastructure authority to streamline planning and prioritizing, and to promote compatibility of national systems.

Button (1994) has examined a number of possible approaches within the most likely form of authority, a mixed (free market-centralized) system. These include: (1) the strategic/operations divisions approach, in which long-term strategic considerations are separated from their implementation; (2) the spatial-based approach, deriving from principles of subsidiarity, in which transport decisions are made at their most relevant level, whether local, national, or international; (3) the private/public ownership approach, in which central infrastructure remains in public hands while operations are market-oriented, long the case in road transport; and (4) the reactive/pragmatic approach, in which progress is ad hoc and incremental, thus slower but also less threatening to existing interests.

Button advocates greater centralization of infrastructure decision making (including uniform charging policies on a cost-benefit basis) while permitting private companies to take a greater role in provision of operations, which seems to merge the first and third of his points. This is based on the reasonable assumption that the best way forward is to encourage present positive trends, although his emphasis on equitable charging for common infrastructure could be considered tinkering rather than overhauling, since it focuses mainly on economic efficiency rather than on pressing social concerns with safety, congestion, and pollution. The same could be said for the EU costing paper (1996b), which effectively rules out new taxation policies. Heinze and Kill (1994) address another issue, putting more emphasis on use of new technologies to reduce the need for individual trips.

Naturally, there is much opposition to the very idea of creating a stronger EU transport authority, given the inherent conservatism of modal interests and the national DOTs that channel those interests. Others, particularly free marketeers, assert that meddling in the transport sector would merely erect more artificial barriers in an already imperfect market, and would thwart postwar society's clear prioritization of road use. In addition, there is national-level resistance at both ends: market-oriented states, such as Britain, oppose any extension of powers to Brussels, while key states in central Europe, such as France and Germany, tend to be skeptical precisely because transport planning has been generally successful (if costly) at the national level. In such an environment, high hopes for major change seem unwarranted.

Even if such concerns can be overridden in the higher interests of creating a level playing field for all modes and balancing the efficiency and equity elements of transport, there would have to be some agreement on two key questions, namely: (1) What form should such an authority take?, and (2) What should its mandate be?

Some Future Alternatives

A whole range of organizational possibilities presents itself over the longer term, only the outlines of which can be presented here. In ascending order of innovative change (but also descending order of likelihood of near-term implementation), the menu of choices would likely include the following:

1. *Maintenance of the current regulatory regime,* including the Commission structure and the careful balance between states, industry interests, and Brussels. One argument for this option is that reform is already occurring from below, and that the EU is already capable, as recent harmonization and R&D initiatives have demonstrated, of an innovative capacity even in transport.

2. *Gradual reform of the present system as sectoral realities permit.* The benefit of gradualism is its realistic character and the possibility of flexible response as opposed to adherence to an artificially rigid formula. The Commission, for example, could urge states to deepen their mutual cooperation along many fronts, such as in traffic management or in rail interoperability. It could also encourage further progress in areas as they emerge, rather than setting top-down policy criteria.

3. *Bolder EU reform.* This might include strengthening DG VII (Transport) via more professional staff and/or greater authority, or the creation of a reformed and strengthened, Commission-based body with close institutional linkages with sections of other DGs (e.g., Environment, Energy) and with the EP's Transport Committee, but without having powers of override of individual states.

4. *The creation of separate modal authorities.* One example might be the formation of a single European air traffic control network to transcend the currently decentralized Eurocontrol system, or a single railway agency to coordinate rail interoperability.

5. *The creation of a European infrastructure agency.* Deriving from (but also transcending) the TENs initiative, such an agency could override separate modal interests and prioritize overall intermodal transport infrastructure planning, without involving itself in the operational side of transport.

6. *The creation of a single European transport organization with authority to override,* including national DOTs. Perhaps the boldest step of all, this change would be impossible without dramatic steps in the federalist direction for the EU as a whole. While hardly likely under present or even foreseeable future circumstances, there are parallels with the Maastricht EMU provisions, which provide for a European Central Bank with

effective power to overrule national central banks and finance ministries; thus as an idea with operational potential it is not unprecedented.

The question as to the extent of mandate for any such authority is equally vexing, as it deals more directly with questions of decision-making power and encroachments on national sovereignty in a traditionally sensitive domain. Numerous questions crowd the agenda. Should such a body be authorized to override state, regional, and local planning authorities? Should it have the power of the purse, in order to raise needed funds and target spending? Should it aim to manage, contain, or even reduce traffic growth? Should it use cost-benefit analysis (CBA) as a basis for action or some other method better at reflecting social concerns? By what process should such methods be arrived at? Should it have power to negotiate with third parties? What would be its legal mandate?

For several reasons, the second option (gradual reform or "tinkering") seems most likely to be pursued in the near- to medium term, but the fifth option, a single infrastructure agency, may be a desirable longer-term solution. Prevailing circumstances suggest dramatic overhaul to be neither a viable nor desirable aim. On the other hand, a single infrastructure agency would provide a forum for dealing with the question of competing national priorities, and could address the numerous nonpolitical (technical and administrative) problems that hinder the even development of cross-border, especially intermodal projects. Even so, this solution would leave the operational side as a separate question, to be determined by market forces within the bounds of governmental and EU safety and environmental regulations. Furthermore, there is now a solid precedent on which to build cooperation in this area, via the TENs initiative, which has done much already to alleviate the previous climate of confrontation between the EU and member states. A single agency, however, would be better positioned to deal with the critical financing question, and might even revive the possibility of direct EU fundraising (Union bonds) for major infrastructure projects.

In contrast to Button's suggestion that pricing policy be the determinant of setting modal priorities, I would argue that the most effective and well-rounded strategy to be pursued within such an organizational framework would have to be equally responsive to qualitative factors that resist quantification in cost terms. It is increasingly apparent that for modern firms, transport costs are marginal—not decisive—factors, and are coupled with quality of services, including reliability, flexibility, and speed (The Regional 1992). Much the same could be said for passenger travel, which suggests that a reliance on pricing strategies alone would divert attention from other, equally salient choice factors. Further, it would maintain the imbalance of emphasis on individual choice of mode to the detriment of broader societal needs.

Such an agency could concentrate on redressing the present competitive imbalance between the modes by putting much greater emphasis on rail and maritime development, and on public transport solutions that have been sorely neglected. The evidence suggests that most transport research efforts are being directed toward future motor vehicle development, reflecting the traditional predominance of road interests. But such efforts are arguably building on, rather than transcending, past mistakes. R&D in the car sector has several pernicious effects. First, it keeps attention focused on the road sector to the detriment of others (e.g., rail). Second, it maintains an imbalance of investment flows away from mass transit solutions already overdue for attention.

Third, it maintains possibly inflated hopes for "intelligent" road and vehicle management as the solution to ever-growing congestion, since there are limits to technological solutions for problems which are largely organizational or behavioral in nature. Fourth, while it may increase efficiency in wealthier, more heavily trafficked core EU regions, it would further peripheralize other regions less able to afford expensive computer-guided roadbeds or to entice private road management. And fifth, more efficient vehicles do not reduce overall energy consumption or pollution levels if their sheer numbers overwhelm system capacity. Increasingly critical issues of congestion and time-loss are only temporarily resolved by technical innovations, putting off the day of reckoning. Such problems can only be addressed via an alternative focus away from road use, toward modes with underutilized capacity and inbuilt attractions, especially rail and maritime shipping.

Noting one of the major themes of this work, namely the growing politicization of the transport debate, it seems advisable that any such agency be innoculated as much as possible from interest group manipulation and from political intrusion by governments. This would mean two things, first a wide degree of participation of representative and responsible actors, including industry and planners as well as officials; and second, an independent authority to make decisions, including for external relations, and have them implemented in due course. Much use could be made of independent advisory councils, such as the *Comité des Sages* which has initiated tougher steps to liberalize European airlines.

A collegial-style body, involving independent experts with wide experience in the fields of economy, finance, diplomacy and law, yet with no axes to grind or hidden agendas to pursue, could provide the forum for pursuing the difficult, long term decision-making clearly necessary under present circumstances. George Kennan (1993) has argued for the establishment in the U.S. of such a panel, a Council of State, to consider broader national interests and help counterbalance the many short-term, fragmentary political pressures. Although here the context is clearly different, the prevailing logic—namely the need to override narrow and persistent sectoral interests—is perhaps not. Further, such organs themselves can foster a sense of convergence of goals; absolute prior agreement on what such an authority should or should not do is not always necessary or even desirable.

Such an agency could focus on an ambitious but realistic agenda including: greater financial incentives for firms to become involved in infrastructure building on a consistent basis; stronger restrictions on use of private cars, particularly in crowded urban areas and along congested intercity corridors (a particularly politically sensitive question); shifting the policy thrust more decisively toward more environmentally sound modes, particularly rail; and encouraging the active incorporation of new information technologies into public transport systems in addition to individual motorized travel, which would not only increase system efficiency but would also (as with teleworking schemes in Scandinavia) reduce the necessity for individual trips as such.

As indicated, the current, loose TENs system could prove a useful transitional step toward such a collaborative arrangement, although the question of a firmer mandate must be addressed at some stage. As most such "wise men" committees thus far have operated on an advisory basis, such would require a tangible transfer of political clout; but the extent of the problems involved, and the considerable success so far of such bodies on an advisory basis, suggest that such a shift of authority would not necessarily require a leap of faith.

The main counterargument to such an authority is undoubtedly the question of democratic control, rather than the sovereignty-based argument of preventing excessive European centralization; how would it be made accountable for its decisions? One response to this important issue is by reference to the negative example of the decision-making process up to this point. A more substantial Community role in transport planning in past years has been opposed, perhaps above all, by the member governments themselves—all of them elected via the democratic process—in favor of defending national monopoly strategies in which policy has been guided by unaccountable public servants and industry interests, rather than by public debate. At the European level this has produced a cacophony of interests jostling for attention, less pluralistic than chaotic, narrowly interest directed rather than broadly representative. Individual democrats can pursue policies through collectively undemocratic methods.

There is no reason to assume that a panel of enlightened and experienced individuals would be any less responsive to democratic concerns, as voiced in the EP and national parliaments, than the Council of Ministers has been in the past, given its reluctance to heed parliamentary opinion in formulating European legislation or to open its deliberations to public scrutiny. Indeed given all the recent emphasis on narrow economic and financial concerns at the expense of long-term transport planning (e.g., who will pay for infrastructure, rather than what is its strategic value), it is even likely that such an independent authority would be more sensitive to those prevailing (social) issues and interests. Methods could be found for parliamentary input, such as regular briefings or EP representation on authority committees, to ensure that its voice is heard and incorporated. The crucial issue is surely responsiveness to general concerns, not direct accountability for specific actions. A body does not itself have to be democratic to reflect democratic interests. Only with a degree of insulation from direct, short-term political pressures is such responsiveness possible. Such a step would provide a necessary, even if not sufficient, move toward encouraging the types of pan-European transport solutions—those that truly balance growth and efficiency aims with equity-based objectives—most likely to reap the widest benefits for European society as a whole.

NOTES

1. The Ciampi group's 1995 report on European industrial competitiveness indeed stressed the need to promote greater competition in transport services alongside denationalization.

2. Esser (1995) has however argued that German foot-dragging, especially in road haulage, shows the persistence of paternalistic interventionism more representative of a by-gone era than of the international dynamism suggested by German industrial power.

3. Notable here is the post-Dayton, U.S.-led Southeast European Cooperative Initiative aimed at practical (e.g. transport) cooperation to rebuild Balkan infrastructures, with incentives for private sector involvement. Witholding approval of (private) air alliances until (intergovernmental) open-skies air treaties are completed further exemplifies public-private muddling.

4. Environmental activism's partial resurrection is suggested by creation of the "Group of Seven" Europe-based NGOs, consisting of the European Environmental Bureau, Greenpeace, Climate Action Network, World Wide Fund, Friends of the Earth, Transport and Environment, and Birdlife. This umbrella group, created to facilitate more effective lobbying of the Commission, calls for a new "Commission for Sustainable Development" within the EU and for more transparent decision-making procedures.

Selected Bibliography

PRIMARY SOURCES

BEC [*Bulletin of the European Communities*], various monthly issues.

BEU [*Bulletin of the European Union*], various monthly issues.

CE [Council of the European Communities] 1990a. "Council Decision of 21 December 1990 Adopting a Specific Research and Technological Development Program in the Field of Transport (euret) 1990 to 1993." Doc. 91/11/EEC.

CE 1990b. "Council Regulation (EEC) for an Action Program in the Field of Transport Infrastructure with a View to the Completion of an Integrated Transport Market in 1992." Doc. 3559/90.

CE 1991. "Council Directive (EEC) no. 440/91 of 29 July 1991 on the Development of the Communities Railways."

CE 1992a. "Council Regulation (EEC) No. 2408/92 on Access for Community Air Carriers to Intra-Community Air Routes."

CE 1992b. "Council Regulation (EEC) No. 2409/92 on Fares and Rates for Air Services."

CE 1992c. "Council Regulation (EEC) No. 3578/92 of 7 December 1992 Amending Regulation (EEC) No. 1107/70 on the Granting of Aids for Transport by Rail, Road and Inland Waterway."

CE 1994a. "Council Directive of 21 November 1994, on the Approximation of the Laws of the Member States with Regard to the Transport of Dangerous Goods by Road." Doc. 94/55/EC.

CE 1994b. "Council Directive of 22 November 1994, on Common Rules and Standards for Ship Inspection and Survey Organizations and for the Relevant Activities of Maritime Administrations." Doc. 94/57/EC.

CEC [Commission of the European Communities] 1985. "Completing the Internal Market." COM (85) 310 Final.

CEC 1986a. "Medium-Term Transport Infrastructure Program." COM (86) 340.

CEC 1986b. "Towards a High-Speed Rail Network." COM (86) 341.

CEC 1988. "Proposal for a Council Regulation for an Action Program in the Field of Transport Infrastructure with a View to the Completion of an Integrated Transport Market in 1992." COM (88) 340.

CEC 1989a. "Communication from the Commission to the Council Regarding a Transport Infrastructure Policy—Concentration of Efforts and Means." COM (89) 238 Final, 5 June 1989.

CEC 1989b. "A Community Transport Market." ISEC/B20/89, 6 July 1989.

CEC 1990. "Communication on a Community Railway Policy." COM (89) 564 Final, 25 January 1990.

CEC 1991. "Transport in a Fast-Changing Europe." ISEC/B10/91, 22 April 1991.

CEC 1993a. "The Future Development of the Common Transport Policy. A Global Approach to the Construction of a Community Framework for Sustainable Mobility." *Bulletin of the European Communities,* Supplement 3/93. Luxembourg: OOPEC, 1993.

CEC 1993b. *SCAD Bibliographies: Transports.* Luxembourg: OOPEC, 1993.

CEC 1993c. "Trans-European Networks: Towards a Master Plan for the Road Network and Road Traffic," Motorway Working Group Report. Luxembourg: OOPEC, 1993.

CEC 1994a. "Commission Proposal for a Council Directive on Access to the Groundhandling Market at Community Airports." COM (94) 590 Final, 13 December 1994.

CEC 1994b. "Commission Proposal for a Council Directive on the Interoperability of the European High-Speed Train Network." (COM (94) 107 Final, 15 April 1994.

CEC 1994c. "The White Paper—or Reasons for Hope and Action." *Frontier-Free Europe,* 5/94.

CEC 1995a. "Address by Jacques Santer, President of the Commission, to the European Parliament on the Occasion of the Investiture Debate of the New Commission." *Bulletin of the European Union,* Supplement 1/95. Luxembourg: OOPEC, 1995.

CEC 1995b. "The Common Transport Policy Action Program 1995–2000," Communication from the Commission, COM (95) 302 Final, 12 July 1995.

CEC 1995c. "Coordinating Research in Europe." *Frontier-Free Europe,* no. 7/8 1995.

CEC 1995d. "Preliminary Draft General Budget of the European Communities for the Financial Year 1996." Brussels: European Commission, 1995.

CEC 1996a. "The Citizens' Network: Fulfilling the Potential of Public Passenger Transport in Europe." Luxembourg: OOPEC, 1996.

CEC 1996b. "Towards Fair and Efficient Pricing in Transport." BEU Suppl. 2/96. Brussels: OOPEC, 1996.

CER [Community of European Railways] 1989. "Proposal for a European High-Speed Network." Paris: CER, 1989.

EC [European Communities] 1990, Economic and Social Committee, "Own-Initiative Opinion on the Channel Tunnel and Its Transport Policy Implications." Doc. CES 1061/90.

ECMT [European Conference of Ministers of Transport] 1990. "Transport Policy and the Environment." Paris: OECD, 1990.

ECSA [European Community Shipowner's Association], Annual Reports 1992, 1993, 1994. Brussels: ECSA, 1992–1994.

EIB [European Investment Bank] 1994a. "EIB Financing for Trans-European Infra-structure Networks." *EIB Information* 81 (September 1994).

EIB 1994b. "The EIB and Regional Development." *EIB Information* 82 (November 1994).

EIS [European Information Service] 1994. "Trans-European Networks: EU Commission Anticipates an ecu 4–5 billion Financial Shortfall." Brussels: EIS, 29 June 1994.

EP [European Parliament] 1987. "Resolution on a European High- Speed Rail Network." Doc. A2–79/87.

EP 1989. "Problems of the Railways." Doc. A2–119/89.

EP 1995. "Resolution of the European Parliament on the Programme for 1995." BEU, Supplement 1/95. Luxembourg: OOPEC, 1995.

ER [European Report] 1994a. "Finance Council: Problems Persist on Trans-European Network Funding." Brussels: EIS, 9 Nov. 1994.

ER 1994b. "Transport: Guidelines for Trans-European Networks." No. 1938, 29 March 1994.

ER 1994c. "Trans-European Networks: European Union to Pay 2.395 billion ecus." No. 1931, 5 March 1994.

Europe 2000+: Cooperation for European Territorial Development. Luxembourg: OOPEC, 1994.

Eurostat: Basic Statistics of the European Union. 32nd edition. Luxembourg: OOPEC, 1995.

Eurostat: Transport Annual Statistics 1970–1990. Luxembourg: OOPEC, 1993.

Expanding Horizons: A Report by the Comité des Sages for Air Transport to the European Commission. Luxembourg: OOPEC, 1994.

"The Fourth Framework Programme (1994–1998)." Luxembourg: OOPEC, 1994.

"Fourth Framework Programme: Up and Running." *RTD Info,* no. 8 (January 1995).

General Report of the EU, 1995. Luxembourg: OOPEC, 1996.

HSR 1995. "The European High-Speed Train Network." Luxembourg: European Commission, February 1995.

OJ [*Official Journal of the European Communities*], various issues.

The Regional Impact of the Channel Tunnel Throughout the Community. Final Report for the Directorate General XVI of the Commission of the European Communities, February 1992.

Trans-European Networks. Interim Report by the Chairman of the Group of Personal Representatives of the Heads of State or Government to the Corfu European Council (Christophersen group). BEU, Supplement 2/94. Luxembourg: OOPEC, 1994.

Trans-European Networks. Report by the Group of Personal Representatives of Heads of State or Government. Luxembourg: OOPEC, 1995.

Treaties Establishing the European Communities (abridged edition). Luxembourg: OOPEC, 1979.

Treaty on European Union. CONF-UP-UEM 2002/92. Brussels: Office of the European Communities, 1992.

United Nations Annual Bulletin of Transport Statistics. New York: UN, various years.

SECONDARY SOURCES

Books, Monographs, Manuscripts

Abbati, Carlo degli. *Transport and European Integration*. Luxembourg: OOPEC, 1987.

Andersen, Svein S., and Kjell A. Eliassen. *Making Policy in Europe: The Europeification of National Policy-Making*. London: Sage Publications, 1993.

Andrewes, Anthony. *Greek Society*. London: Penguin Books, 1971.

Archer, Clive, and Fiona Butler. *The European Community: Structure and Process*. London: Pinter, 1992.

Ash, Timothy Garton. *In Europe's Name: Germany and the Divided Continent*. New York: Vintage, 1993.

Aspinwall, Mark. *Moveable Feast: Pressure Group Conflict and the European Community Shipping Policy*. Aldershot: Avebury, 1995.

Bainbridge, Timothy, with Anthony Teasdale. *The Penguin Companion to the European Union*. London: Penguin, 1995.

Banister, David, Roberta Capello, and Peter Nijkamp, eds. *European Transport and Communications Networks: Policy Evolution and Change*. Chichester: John Wiley, 1995.

Barnes, Ian, and Pamela M. Barnes. *The Enlarged European Union*. New York: Longman, 1995.

Boorstin, Daniel J. *The Discoverers*. New York: Random House, 1983.

Bredima-Savopoulou, Anna, and John Tzoannos. *The Common Shipping Policy of the EC*. Amsterdam: Elsevier, 1990.

Butler, Michael. *Europe: More than a Continent*. London: Heinemann, 1986.

Button, Kenneth J. *Transport Economics* (2d edition). Aldershot: Edward Elgar, 1993.

———. *Transport Policy—Ways into Europe's Future*. Gutersloh: Bertelsmann Foundation, 1994.

Button, Kenneth J., and David E. Pitfield, eds. *Transport Deregulation: An International Movement*. New York: Macmillan, 1991.

Cipolla, Carlo M., ed. *The Fontana Economic History of Europe*. Glasgow: William Collins, 1976.

Coopers and Lybrand Europe. *Transport* (1994) (on Internet).

De Burgh, W. G. *The Legacy of the Ancient World*. Middlesex: Penguin, 1953.

Delamaide, Darrell. *The New Superregions of Europe*. New York: Plume/Penguin, 1995.

Doganis, Rigis. *Flying Off Course: the Economics of International Airlines*. London: HarperCollins, 1991.

Drost, Harry. *What's What and Who's Who in the European Union*. London: Cassell, 1995.

Edwards, Amelia. *Untrodden Peaks and Unfrequented Valleys*. London: Virago, 1986.

Etzioni, Amitai. *Political Unification*. New York: Holt, Rinehart and Winston, 1965.

Fussell, Paul. *Abroad: British Literary Traveling Between the Wars*. Oxford: Oxford University Press, 1980.

Galbraith, John Kenneth. *The New Industrial State*. New York: Mentor Books, 1964.

George, Stephen. *The Politics of the European Community*. Oxford: Oxford University Press, 1991.

Giannopoulos, G., and A. Gillespie, eds. *Transport and Communications Innovation in Europe*. London: Belhaven, 1993.

Gibbon, Edward. *The Decline and Fall of the Roman Empire* (abridged version), ed. by Dero A. Saunders. Middlesex: Penguin, 1981.

Grant, Michael. *The Ancient Mediterranean*. New York: Meridian, 1969.

Haas, Ernst. *The Uniting of Europe: Political, Economic, and Social Forces, 1950–1957*. Stanford: Stanford University Press, 1958.

Hackett, Clifford. *Cautious Revolution: The European Community Arrives*. New York: Praeger, 1990.

Hayward, Keith. *International Collaboration in Civil Aerospace*. London: Pinter, 1986.

Healey, Denis. *The Time of My Life*. New York: W. W. Norton, 1990.

Heidenheimer, Arnold J., and Donald P. Kommers. *The Governments of Germany*, 4th edition. New York: Thomas Y. Crowell, 1975.

Holliday, Ian, Gerard Marcou, and Roger Vickerman. *The Channel Tunnel: Public Policy, Regional Development and European Integration*. London: Belhaven, 1991.

Horne, Alistair. *Harold Macmillan, Volume II: 1957–86*. New York: Viking-Penguin, 1989.

Jackson, Tim. *Virgin King: Inside Richard Branson's Business Empire*. London: HarperCollins, 1994.

Joll, James. *Europe Since 1870: An International History*. Middlesex: Pelican, 1976.

Kennan, George F. *Around the Cragged Hill: A Personal and Political Philosophy*. New York: W. W. Norton, 1993.

Keohane, Robert O., and Stanley Hoffmann, eds. *The New European Community: Decisionmaking and Institutional Change*. Boulder, CO: Westview, 1991.

Kintner, William R., and Harvey Sicherman. *Technology and International Politics: The Crisis of Wishing*. Lexington, Mass.: D. C. Heath, 1975.

Lindberg, Leon N., and Stuart A. Scheingold. *Europe's Would-Be Polity: Patterns of Change in the European Community*. Englewood Cliffs, N.J.: Prentice-Hall, 1970.

Masser, I., O. Sviden, and M. Wegener. *The Geography of Europe's Futures*. London: Belhaven, 1992.

Missing Links. Paris: ERT, 1984.

Molle, Willem. *The Economics of European Integration: Theory, Practice, Policy*. Aldershot: Dartmouth, 1990.

Moussis, Nicholas. *Access to European Union: Law, Economics, Policies*, 4th and 6th rev. editions. Brussels: Edit-Eur, 1994 and 1996.

Norwich, John Julius. *A Taste for Travel: An Anthology*. New York: Alfred A. Knopf, 1987.

Ogg, David. *Europe of the Ancien Régime, 1715–1783*. London: Collins, 1965.

Owen, Nicholas. *Economies of Scale, Competitiveness, and Trade Patterns within the European Community*. Oxford: Clarendon, 1983.

Owen, Richard, and Michael Dynes. *The Times Guide to 1992.* London: Times Books, 1989.

Pinder, John. *European Community: The Building of a Union.* Oxford: Oxford University Press, 1991.

Pinson, Koppel. *Modern Germany: Its History and Civilization,* 2d edition. New York: Macmillan, 1966.

Ross, John F. L. *Neutrality and International Sanctions: Sweden, Switzerland, and Collective Security.* New York: Praeger, 1989.

Round Table 90: *Privatization of the Railways.* Paris: ECMT, 1993.

Runciman, Stephen. *Byzantine Civilization.* Cleveland and New York: World Publishing Company, 1956.

Sampson, Anthony. *The Changing Anatomy of Britain.* New York: Vintage, 1984a.

———. *Empires of the Sky.* London: Hodder and Stoughton, 1984b.

Schiavone, Giuseppe. *International Organizations: A Dictionary and Directory.* London: Macmillan, 1983.

Strohl, Mitchell. *Europe's High-Speed Trains: A Study in Geo-Economics.* Westport, Conn.: Praeger, 1993.

Swann, Dennis. *The Economics of the Common Market.* London: Penguin, 1995.

Taylor, A. J. P. *English History 1914–1945.* Middlesex: Penguin, 1965.

Thomson, David. *England in the Nineteenth Century.* Middlesex: Penguin, 1950.

———. *England in the Twentieth Century.* Middlesex: Penguin, 1965.

———. *Europe Since Napoleon.* Middlesex: Penguin, 1966.

Transport and the Environment: The Royal Commission on Environment Pollution's Report. Oxford: OUP, 1995.

Transport in a Fast Changing Europe: Vers Un Reseau Européen des Systemes de Transport. Paris: Group Transport 2000 Plus, 1990.

Trevelyan, George M. *A Shortened History of England.* London: Penguin, 1959.

Tsoukalis, Loukas. *The New European Economy: The Politics and Economics of Integration.* Oxford: Oxford University Press, 1993.

Turner, Barry, with Gunilla Nordquist. *The Other European Community: Integration and Co-operation in Nordic Europe.* London: Weidenfeld and Nicolson, 1982.

Tyson, Laura d'Andrea. *Who's Bashing Whom? Trade Conflict in High-Technology Industries.* Washington, D.C.: Institute for International Economics, 1992.

Urwin, Derek. *The Community of Europe: A History of European Integration Since 1945,* 2d edition. Essex: Longman Group, 1995.

Vickerman, Roger W., and A. D. J. Flowerdew. *The Channel Tunnel: The Economic and Regional Impact.* The Economist Intelligence Unit, special report no. 2024. London: 1990.

Vidal, Gore. *At Home: Essays 1982–1988.* New York: Vintage, 1990.

Wallace, William. *Regional Integration: The West European Experience.* Washington, D.C.: Brookings Institution, 1994.

Whitelegg, John. *Transport Policy in the EEC.* Andover: Routledge and Kegan Paul, 1988.

———. *Transport for a Sustainable Future.* London: Belhaven, 1993.

Williams, Philip M. *Crisis and Compromise: Politics in the Fourth Republic.* London: Longman Group, 1972.

Zacher, Mark. *Governing Global Networks: International Regimes for Transportation and Communications*. Cambridge: Cambridge University Press, 1996.

Articles, Chapters, Unpublished Papers

Allen, G. Freeman. "Intermodal Impasse in Europe." *Modern Railways* (September 1995), 564.

Andersen, Bjørn. "Franchising Alternatives for European Transport." In *European Transport and Communications Networks*, ed. by David Banister, Roberta Capello, and Peter Nijkamp, 222–246. Chichester: John Wiley, 1995.

Andersen, Svein S. "Towards a Common EC Energy Policy." In *Making Policy in Europe: The Europeification of National Policy- Making*, ed. by Svein S. Andersen and Kjell A. Eliassen, 133–154. London: Sage, 1993.

Andersen, Svein S., and Kjell A. Eliassen. "Complex Policy-Making: Lobbying the EC." In *Making Policy in Europe: The Europeification of National Policy-Making*, ed. by Svein S. Andersen and Kjell A. Eliassen, 35–54. London: Sage, 1993.

Aspinwall, Mark. "International Integration or Domestic Politics? Anatomy of a Single Market Measure." Unpublished paper, 1994.

Banister, David, Roberta Capello, and Peter Nijkamp. "European Transport and Communications Networks: All Change." In *European Transport and Communications Networks: Policy Evolution and Change*, ed. by David Banister, Roberta Capello and Peter Nijkamp, 3–30. Chichester: John Wiley, 1995.

Banister, David, Bjørn Andersen, and Sean Barrett. "Private Sector Investment in Transport Infrastructure in Europe." In *European Transport and Communications Networks: Policy Evolution and Change*, ed. by David Banister, Roberta Capello, and Peter Nijkamp, 191–220. Chichester: John Wiley, 1995.

Bayliss, B. T. and A. I. Millington. "Deregulation and Logistics Systems in a Single European Market." *Journal of Transport Economics and Policy* 29 (3) (September 1995), 305–316.

Biehl, Dieter. "The Role of Infrastructure in Regional Development." In *Infrastructure and Regional Development*, edited by Roger W. Vickerman, 9–35. London: Pion, 1991.

Blum, Ulrich. "The New East-West Corridor: An Analysis of Passenger Transport Flows Inside and Through Germany in 2010." In *Infrastructure and Regional Development*, ed. by Roger W. Vickerman, 135–149. London: Pion, 1991.

Blum, Ulrich, H. Gercek, and J. Viegas. "High-Speed Railways and the European Peripheries: Opportunities and Challenges." *Transportation Research A*, Vol. 26A, no. 2 (1992), 211–221.

"Broadening the Mind: A Survey of World Travel and Tourism." *The Economist*, 23 March 1991, supplement.

Bruinsma, F., P. Nijkamp, and P. Rietveld, "Infrastructure and Metropolitan Development in an International Perspective: Survey and Methodological Exploration." In *Infrastructure and Regional Development*, ed. by Roger W. Vickerman 189–205. London: Pion, 1991.

Burley, Anne-Marie, and Walter Mattli. Europe Before the Court: A Political Theory of Legal Integration." *International Organization* 47 (1) (Winter 1993), 41–76.

Button, Kenneth, and Dennis Swann. "European Community Airlines: Deregulation and its Problems." *Journal of Common Market Studies* 27 (4) (Fall 1989), 259–82.

"Cash Mountain Dulls the Pain of Change." *Lloyds Ship Manager* 16 (6) (September 1995), 35–41.

Collins, Neil, and Leonidas Louloudis. "Protecting the Protected: the Greek Agricultural Policy Network." *Journal of European Public Policy* 2 (1) (March 1995), 95–114.

Cowles, Maria Green. "Setting the Agenda for a New Europe: The ERT and EC 1992." *Journal of Common Market Studies* 33 (4) (December 1995), 501–526.

"Cruising Towards Higher Volume." *Mediterranean Passenger Shipping* (Autumn 1994), 6–8.

Daalder, Hans. "Building Consociational Nations." In *Building States and Nations,* ed. by S. N. Eisenstadt and Stein Rokkan, vol. 2, 14–31. Beverly Hills: Sage, 1973.

Delors, Jacques. "Guidelines for Economic Renewal in Europe." Commission of the European Communities, monthly newsletter, 7/1993.

Deutsch, Karl, and Hermann Weilenmann. "The Swiss City Canton: A Political Invention." *Comparative Studies in Society and History* 7 (4) (July 1965), 393–408.

Dobbin, Frank. "What Do Markets Have in Common? Toward a Fast Train Policy for the EC." In *Making Policy for Europe: The Europeification of National Policy-Making,* ed. by Svein S. Andersen and Kjell A. Eliassen, 71–92. London: Sage, 1993.

Dunn, James A., Jr., and Anthony Perl. "Policy Networks and Industrial Revitalization: High Speed Rail Initiatives in France and Germany." *Journal of Public Policy* 14 (3) (1994), 311–343.

Esser, Josef. "Germany: Challenges to the Old Policy Style." In *Industrial Enterprise and European Integration: From National to International Champions in Western Europe,* ed. by Jack Hayward, 48–75. Oxford: Oxford University Press 1995.

Field, Frank R., and Joel P. Clark, "A Practical Road to Lightweight Cars?" *Technology Review* (June 1997), 28–36.

French, Trevor. "A Breath of Fresh Air." *Airline Business* 11 (10) (October 1995), 34–37.

Frosig, Poul. "ETCS: Key to Seamless Cross-Border Operation." *International Railway Journal* (September 1995), 21–23.

Grant, Wyn. "Britain: The Spectator State." In *Industrial Enterprise and European Integration: From National to International Champions in Western Europe,* ed. by Jack Hayward, 76–96. Oxford: Oxford University Press, 1995.

Gwilliam, Kenneth M. "The Future of the Common Transport Policy." In *Britain Within the European Community,* ed. by M. el-Agraa, 167–186. London: Macmillan, 1983.

Hall, Peter. "Policy Paradigms, Social Learning, and the State." *Comparative Politics* 25 (3) (April 1993), 275–96.

Hart, Paul. "State Aid and the Shipping Industry: A European Community Analysis." In *Shipping Policy in the European Community,* ed. by Paul Hart, Gillian Ledger, Michael Roe, and Brian Smith, 42–78. Aldershot: Avebury, 1993.

Hayward, Jack. "Introduction: Europe's Endangered Industrial Champions." In *Industrial Enterprise and European Integration: From National to International Champions in Western Europe*, ed. by Jack Hayward, 1–22. Oxford: Oxford University Press, 1995.

Heinze, G. Wolfgang, and Heinrich H. Kill. "Traffic Growth Plus History Plus Geography: Repercussions of a European Transport System on Western and Eastern Europe." In *Transport Policy—Ways into Europe's Future*, ed. by Kenneth Button, 127–165. Gutersloh: Bertelsmann Foundation, 1994.

Holliday, Ian. "The Channel Tunnel: The Problems of Binational Collaboration." In *Industrial Enterprise and European Integration: From National to International Champions in Western Europe*, ed. by Jack Hayward, 215–238. Oxford: Oxford University Press, 1995.

Holzapfel, Helmut, and Karl Otto Schallabock. "The Need for Further Integration in the Integrated European Transport Concept." In *Transport Policy—Ways into Europe's Future*, ed. by Kenneth Button, 199–215. Gutersloh: Bertelsmann Foundation, 1994.

Hooghe, Liesbet, and Michael Keating. "The Politics of European Union Regional Policy." *Journal of European Public Policy* 1 (3) (1994), 367–393.

"IMO Proposals Put Pressure on Ferry Fleets." *Cruise and Ferry* (September-October 1995), 12–15.

Jeziorski, Andrzej. "On with the Show." *Flight International,* 149 (4522) (May 1996), 40–43.

Kammerer, Klaus. "The Integration of Systems and Non-Systems—EC-92 and the West German Transportation Carriers." In *The Technical Challenges and Opportunities of a United Europe*, ed. by Michael S. Steinberg, 28–41. London: Pinter, 1990.

Kassim, Hussein. "Air Transport Champions: Still Flying the Flag." In *Industrial Enterprise and European Integration: From National to International Champions in Western Europe*, ed. by Jack Hayward, 188–214. Oxford: Oxford University Press, 1995.

———. "Air Transport." In *The European Union and National Industrial Policy,* ed. by Hussein Kassim and Anand Menon, 106–131. London: Routledge, 1996.

Larsson, Stig, with Alf Ekström. "The Case of the Swedish Railways." In *Round Table 90: Privatization of the Railways,* 55–79. Paris: ECMT, 1993.

Ledger, Gillian. "Maritime Policy in the European Community and the United Kingdom: Contrasts and Conflicts." In *Shipping Policy in the European Community,* ed. by Paul Hart, Gillian Ledger, Michael Roe, and Brian Smith, 5–34. Aldershot: Avebury, 1993.

Lee, Norman. "Transport Policy." In *The Economics of the European Union: Policy and Analysis,* ed. by M. J. Artis and N. Lee, 238–268. Oxford: Oxford University Press, 1994.

Lemberg, Kai. "Decision-Making for Trans-European Links: The Danish Case." In *European Transport and Communications Networks: Policy Evolution and Change,* ed. by David Banister, Roberta Capello, and Peter Nijkamp, 265–286. Chichester: John Wiley, 1995.

Lodge, Juliet. "Introduction: Internal Perspectives." In *The European Community and the Challenge of the Future,* ed. by Juliet Lodge, 83–93. London: Pinter, 1989.

Maggi, Rico. "Swiss Transport Policy for Europe? Federalism and the Dominance of Local Issues." *Transportation Research-A,* 26A (2) (1992), 193–98.

Mathieu, Gerard. "The Growing High-Speed Net Envelopes France." *Railway Gazette International* 151 (10) (October 1995), 639–646.

McDonald, Robert. "Doldrums and Maelstrom: Currents in Greek Shipping." *Industrial Review,* special survey no. 12 (May 1994), 5–58.

———. "Race for the Future: European Union Funds and the Major Projects in Greece." *Industrial Review,* special survey no. 19 (March 1996), 5–49.

McGowan, Francis. "The European Electricity Industry and EC Regulatory Reform." In *Industrial Enterprise and European Integration: From National to International Champions in Western Europe,* ed. by Jack Hayward, 125–157. Oxford: Oxford University Press, 1995.

McGowan, Francis, and Peter Seabright. "Deregulating European Airlines." *Economic Policy* (October 1989), 283–344.

McGowan, Lee, and Stephen Wilks. "The First Supranational Policy in the European Union: Competition Policy." *European Journal of Political Research* 28 (1995), 141–169.

Menon, Anand, and Jack Hayward. "States, Industrial Policies and the European Union." In *The European Union and National Industrial Policy,* ed. by Hussein Kassim and Anand Menon, 267–290. London: Routledge, 1996.

Molina, G. "An Improved Image for Public Transport: How Are We to Match the Environmental Stakes for Better City Living?" In *Energy Policies and Trends in the European Community,* 63–70. Luxembourg: OOPEC, 1995.

Moravcsik, Andrew. "Negotiating the Single European Act: National Interests and Conventional Statecraft in the European Community." *International Organization* 45 (1) (winter 1991), 19–56.

Muller, Pierre. "Aerospace Companies and the State in Europe." In *Industrial Enterprise and European Integration: From National to International Champions in Western Europe,* ed. by Jack Hayward, 158–187. Oxford: Oxford University Press, 1995.

Munch, Rainer, and Norbert Walter. "Requirements to Be Met by a European Transport Infrastructure." In *Transport Policy—Ways into Europe's Future,* ed. by Kenneth Button, 167–179. Gutersloh: Bertelsmann Foundation, 1994.

"Neil Kinnock, European Commissioner." *Europe* (October 1995), 12–16.

Nijkamp, Peter, and Jaap Vluegel. "In Search of Sustainable Transport Systems." In *European Transport and Communications Networks,* ed. by David Banister, Roberta Capello, and Peter Nijkamp, 287–300. Chichester: John Wiley, 1995a.

———. "Transport Infrastructure and European Union Developments." In *European Transport and Communications Networks,* ed. by David Banister, Roberta Capello, and Peter Nijkamp, 3–30. Chichester: John Wiley, 1995b.

Odell, Mark. "None the Wiser." *Airline Business* 11 (10) (October 1995), 28–33.

O'Toole, Kevin. "Low-Fare Europe?" *Flight International,* 149 (4522) (May 1996), 28.

Peterson, John. "Decision-Making in the European Union: Towards a Framework for Analysis." *Journal of European Public Policy* 2 (1) (1995), 69–94.

"Poor Response to Need for European Networks." *European Freight Management* 5 (21) (April 1995), 12–14.

Richardson, Jeremy. "Actor-Based Models of National and EU Policy-Making." In

The European Union and National Industrial Policy, ed. by Hussein Kassim and Anand Menon, 26–51. London: Routledge, 1996.

Rosen, Robert, and Louis J. Williams. "The Rebirth of Supersonic Transport. *Technology Review* (February-March 1993), 23–29.

Ross, John F. L. "High-Speed Rail: Catalyst for European Integration?" *Journal of Common Market Studies* 32 (2) (June 1994), 191–214.

———. "When Co-operation Divides: Öresund, the Channel Tunnel, and the New Politics of European Transport." *Journal of European Public Policy* 2 (1) (March 1995), 115–46.

Rossera, Fabio. "Freight Traffic Through the Alps—Peculiarities and Impacts of Abnormal Routing." In *European Transport and Communications Networks*, ed. by David Banister, Roberta Capello, and Peter Nijkamp, 141–56. Chichester: John Wiley, 1995.

Schneider, Gerald, and Lars-Erik Cederman. "The Change of Tide in Political Co-operation: A Limited Information Model of European Integration." *International Organization* 48 (4) (Autumn 1994), 633–662.

Smith, Alasdair. "The Market for Cars in the Enlarged European Community." In *Unity with Diversity in the European Economy: The Community's Southern Frontier*, ed. by Christopher Bliss and Jorge Braga de Macedo, 78–99. Cambridge: Cambridge University Press, 1990.

Smith, Brian. "Euros: The European Community Shipping Register." In *Shipping Policy in the European Community*, ed. by Paul Hart, Gillian Ledger, Michael Roe, and Brian Smith, 82–101. Aldershot: Avebury, 1993.

Staniland, Martin. "The United States and the External Aviation Policy of the EU." *Journal of European Public Policy* 2 (1) (March 1995), 19–40.

Stasinopoulos, Dinos. "Common Transport Infrastructure Policy and the Development of Trans-European Networks." *Journal of Transport Economics and Policy* 29 (2) (May 1995), 220–222.

Streeck, Wolfgang, and Philippe C. Schmitter. "From National Corporatism to Transnational Pluralism: Organized Interests in the Single European Market." *Politics and Society* 19 (2) (1991), 133–164.

Sturmey, Stanley G. "The Greek Ferry System." *Mediterranean Passenger Shipping* (Autumn 1994), 19–22.

"Sund & Bro." Information on the Swedish/Danish Öresund Link, no. 5 (June 1994), 1–8.

"Taming the Beast: A Survey on Living with the Car," *The Economist*, survey, 22 (June 1996), Supplement.

Topmann, Gunther. "The Integrated European Transport Concept—Its Political and Social Acceptance." In *Transport Policy—Ways into Europe's Future*, ed. by Kenneth Button, 181–198. Gutersloh: Bertelsmann Foundation, 1994.

Union of Greek Shipowners. *Annual Reports* 1991–1995. Piraeus: UGS, 1991–1995.

Van de Voorde, Eddy, and Jose Viegas. "Trans-European Networks: Short-Sea Shipping." In *European Transport and Communications Networks: Policy Evolution and Change*, ed. by David Banister, Roberta Capello, and Peter Nijkamp, 31–46. Chichester: John Wiley, 1995.

Vickerman, Roger W. "Transport in the European Community: New Developments, Regional Implications and Evaluation." In *Infrastructure and Regional Development*, ed. by Roger W. Vickerman, 36–49. London: Pion, 1991.

———. "Transport Infrastructure and Region Building in the European Community." *Journal of Common Market Studies* 32 (1) (1994a), 1–24.

———. "Transport and Spatial Development in Europe." *Journal of Common Market Studies* 32 (2) (June 1994b), 249–56.

Vogel, David. "The Making of EC Environmental Policy." In *Making Policy in Europe: The Europeification of National Policy- Making*, ed. by Svein S. Anderssen and Kjell A. Eliassen, 115–131. London: Sage, 1993.

Weidenfeld, Werner. "Introduction: Transport Policy in the Europe of Tomorrow." In *Transport Policy—Ways into Europe's Future*, edited by Kenneth Button, 11–26. Gutersloh: Bertelsmann Foundation, 1994.

Wright, Vincent. "Conclusion: The State and Major Enterprises in Western Europe: Enduring Complexities." In *Industrial Enterprise and European Integration: From National to International Champions in Western Europe*, ed. by Jack Hayward, 334–360. Oxford: Oxford University Press, 1995.

Yannopoulos, Dimitris. "Construction and the Delors Challenge." *Greek-American Trade*, 31 (5) (September-October 1994), 30–36.

———. "Greek Ferry Lines: New Routes, More Ships for Adriatic Crossing." *Greek Business Review* no. 1 (October 1995), 6–10.

Newspapers

Athens News (AN)
The Economist
The European
Financial Times (FT)
International Herald Tribune (IHT)
Kathemerini
The New York Times (NYT)
The Times/The Sunday Times
The Wall Street Journal Europe (WSJE)

Name Index

Subject Index

About the Author

JOHN F. L. ROSS currently teaches at the American College of Greece in Athens. He has written and lectured widely in the fields of International Relations and European affairs since taking his Ph.D. at the London School of Economics in 1987. He taught political science at Northeastern University in Boston until 1995. He held a visiting appointment in 1993–94 as Fulbright fellow at the International School of Social Sciences at the University of Tampere in Finland. His book *Neutrality and International Sanctions* was also published by Praeger, in 1989. His numerous publications have appeared in academic journals in Europe and the U.S., and he has also been a frequent contributor to the international press.

ISBN 0-275-95248-7

90000>

EAN

9 780275 952488

HARDCOVER BAR CODE